T0354481

A Life of Hermann Cohen

From Franz Liszt to John of the Cross

Timothy Tierney

BALBOA.
PRESS

A DIVISION OF HAY HOUSE

Balboa Press books may be ordered through booksellers or by contacting:

Balboa Press
A Division of Hay House
1663 Liberty Drive
Bloomington, IN 47403
www.balboapress.com.au
1 (877) 407-4847

Because of the dynamic nature of the Internet, any web addresses or links contained in this book may have changed since publication and may no longer be valid. The views expressed in this work are solely those of the author and do not necessarily reflect the views of the publisher, and the publisher hereby disclaims any responsibility for them.

The author of this book does not dispense medical advice or prescribe the use of any technique as a form of treatment for physical, emotional, or medical problems without the advice of a physician, either directly or indirectly. The intent of the author is only to offer information of a general nature to help you in your quest for emotional and spiritual well-being. In the event you use any of the information in this book for yourself, which is your constitutional right, the author and the publisher assume no responsibility for your actions.

Any people depicted in stock imagery provided by Thinkstock are models, and such images are being used for illustrative purposes only.
Certain stock imagery © Thinkstock.

Print information available on the last page.

ISBN: 978-1-5043-0862-5 (sc)
ISBN: 978-1-5043-0932-5 (e)

Balboa Press rev. date: 07/05/2017

Contents

Part 2 Selections from the Writings of Hermann Cohen

Dedicated to the memory of Antonine Newman OCD,
who encouraged me to take up the Story of Hermann Cohen.

Introduction

*H*ermann Cohen was a renowned international pianist in his day and later a significant Carmelite figure in France in the second half of the 19th century.[1] About nine years ago Cohen was in the news again in Carmelite circles as he once was in France and beyond. Here is a summary of what appeared in an edition of a Carmelite news outlet from Rome, *Communicationes*, on December 15, 2008.[2] With all necessary authorisation received, at 7.00 am on December 2nd last, a small group of people proceeded to open Hermann Cohen's tomb in a cemetery in Berlin just inside the area of the former Berlin Wall. A doctor and a lawyer took note of the remains. The skeleton was well preserved after 137 years in two different burial places. His small wooden crucifix was intact. The zinc urn was handed over to Fr. Damaso (Zuazua) who would later have it transported by plane to Bordeaux. Fr. Herman Cohen's remains will stay in the priory church of Le Broussey, where he had been student-master in 1868. He will be placed beside the tomb of Dominic Arbizu y Munarriz, with whom Herman Cohen was a close collaborator in the restoration of Carmel in France. The

---

[1] Hermann Cohen is not to be confused with the later German philosopher of the same name, 1842 - 1918.

[2] A regular newsletter on Carmelite topics from Rome. This is the successor to 'Sic', the previous newsletter which was initiated by Jorge Luis Gonzalez OCD.

translation was carried out in view of the proximate canonical beatification process.[1]

Starting then in Part 1, Chapter 1, we will follow Hermann Cohen's journey from boyhood in the Northern German port of Hamburg to the wider fields of France, especially Paris, where, by his own admission Cohen lived a frivolous and dissolute life. Subsequent chapters will trace his steps as a Christian convert and Carmelite priest in a busy and varied ministry throughout the length and breath of France. This ministry extended to his native Germany and to Switzerland, expanding also to a period of pioneering ministry in England. He even preached in Waterford, Ireland to a crowd of thousands on one occasion. I will emphasise his apostolate in England which may have greater interest for our readers. The Franco-Prussian war hastened the end of his life and occasioned his heroic and untimely death.

After introducing the person of Hermann Cohen and his artistically successful if misspent youth, a central focus of the book will be the extraordinary experience of conversion which can be attributed to the power of the Eucharist during the month of May. We shall see how this experience will energize Cohen to engage in unprecedented Eucharistic and Marian zeal. He will found a Eucharistic Movement and an Archconfraternity of Thanksgiving whose members, in quite a short time, ran into tens of thousands. Meanwhile his artistic and musical gifts remained to the fore and enhanced his Carmelite ministry. Hermann Cohen has always held an interest, if not fascination for English speaking readers. The first biography of him in English translation appeared in 1925.[2] On a personal level I can say that reading about this attractive

---

[1]   A funeral service took place in Le Broussey chapel on December 4, 2008.

[2]   Abbé Charles Sylvain, *The Life of Father Hermann*, Translated by Mrs. Raymond-Barker, New York, P.J. Kennedy and Sons,1925. This book quotes from a document called 'Confessions' that Cohen wrote at the request of his Superiors while in the novitiate. It is now lost.

personality while on retreat during my first years at a Carmelite High School, made a big impression on me and possibly helped to maintain my own desire to become a Carmelite priest. It is my further wish that reading this modern biography of Hermann Cohen may also attract some young men and women today to follow the call to Carmel. Cohen's life and death are the stuff of drama - the pleasure-loving, passionate artist who turns even more passionately to God!

This book is a companion volume to my biography of St. Raphael Kalinowski, an admirer of Hermann Cohen, also published by Balbao Press, (2016) It is my hope that the book will make a contribution to Cohen's Cause for eventual sainthood and help to hasten it. As a French Carmelite wrote: 'Let us endorse the wish to see Fr. Hermann's beatification introduced. For us his holiness is beyond doubt and his canonisation highly desirable at the present time.'[1]

As a candidate for sainthood, his official title is now "Servant of God" and is also known as Father Augustine-Mary of the Most Blessed Sacrament.

In Part 2, I have collected, edited and translated many of the extant writings of Hermann Cohen in the most extensive collection produced so far in English. All but two of these are from French sources. One long extract is Cohen's sermon at the Profession of Bernard Bauer (who later left the Order and married). I have translated the sermon from an Italian version. Bauer's defection caused Cohen much anguish as did that of Carmelite colleague Hyacinthe Loyson. Loyson's case was made famous by St. Thérèse who offered her last Communion for his conversion. Thérèse talks about him in letters to her sister Céline. Cohen wrote him a moving letter begging him to return to his Carmelite family and this I have also included in the selections from his writings. Both

---

[1] Fr. Joseph a St. Marie OCD, Pensée Catholique 1982.

Bauer and Loyson were famous preachers and celebrities in 19th century France. The second non-French item is Hermann's letter to Cornelia Freeman written (in English) while he was prior of the new Kensington house he had founded.

This book is a revision and enlargement of my biography of Hermann Cohen first produced by Teresian Press in 1991. I would like to thank Fr. Yves-Marie of the French Carmelites in Le Broussey, Vice-Postulator of Cohen's Cause, for permission to quote from "Flamme Ardente au Carmel", the 2009 edition of Sylvain's original French biography of Cohen. Fr. Yves-Marie writes:

> The cause for the beatification of Fr. Hermann, being introduced in the diocese of Bordeaux (France) on 19th of January 2016, manifests the urgency for a better knowledge of the life of this Carmelite friar, which marks an important step in this process. Accordingly, I am grateful to Fr. Timothy Tierney for this book and it is my earnest wish that it will help in bringing many people into contact with this apostle of devotion to the Blessed Sacrament and more importantly, like him, to become worshippers of the Holy Eucharist in spirit and in truth.
>
> Fr. Yves-Marie du Très Saint-Saint Sacrament ocd
> Vice Postulator
> (Toulouse – France, June 25, 2017)

I appreciate the comments of Richard P. Hardy, author of "John of the Cross, Man and Mystic" who wrote to me:

> I was thoroughly engaged as I read about the life and "adventures" of Fr. Hermann Cohen, OCD. Truly he was a special man in Carmel and whose life needs to be known far and wide....I do hope the editors can help to make this work

published and disseminated among the English Speaking world and in other languages as well.

Grateful thanks also to friends who helped in the production of the book:– Bernadette Micallef who offered suggestions and corrections, and David Barry and Beatrix Reuter who translated sections from Walther Victors's German biography of Cohen.

Thanks also to the staff at Balboa Press for their unfailing courtesy.

Timothy Tierney OCD.

Part One

Chapter I

Beginnings

*H*ermann Cohen, the subject of this biography, was born on November 10, 1821, at 189 Ellerntorbrucke, Neustadt, Hamburg, Northern Germany. Hermann's father, David Abraham Cohen, thirty-five years old at this time, was one of the richest people in Hamburg.[1] His mother's name was Rosalie, née Benjamin, an intelligent and elegant woman, though nothing is known about her family background. After her son's conversion to Catholicism, she strongly resisted his efforts to get her to also change her religion. Cohen's parents were quite influential people in the Jewish environment of Hamburg. An ambitious merchant, David had travelled to Paris to set up business deals with the great Jewish banking dynasty of Rothschild. But David Cohen was also a

---

[1] D. A. Cohen appeared in the Hamburg Directory from 1828 to 1831 under the company name 'D. A. Cohen and the Brothers Benjamin, Merchants.' The business partners in question were two older brothers of his wife, Isaac and Daniel Benjamin. As we learn later, the company was also established in Manchester, UK under the name "Cohen & Benjamin." The company went bankrupt in 1831. (Information supplied by email correspondent Vincent)

cultured man.[1] They had four surviving children, Albert, Hermann, Henrietta, and Louis. Two other children died young: Auguste: 1816-1817; Julius Joseph: 1832-1834.

Ever since the sixteenth century the city and port of Hamburg, now Northern Germany, has witnessed the growth of its economic and financial prosperity and the rise of a notable artistic, musical and intellectual culture. Even the Beatles began their rise to fame in Hamburg! It was a city of rich and powerful bankers largely made up of Jews from Spain and Portugal and was the first place in Germany to boast a theatre. This helped to open it up to art and music for the whole of Europe. Hamburg thus became the crossroads for the diverse cultures of Europe. Cohen's parents were in fact quite influential people in the Jewish environment of Hamburg. The name 'Cohen', Hermann explains in his "Confessions", means 'priest' in Hebrew.[2] The name suggested descent from the High Priest Aaron, through the priestly tribe of Levi. In the synagogue the "Cohennim" exercise the office of priesthood. They lay their hands in blessing on the people from the steps of the sanctuary. Cohen remembered seeing his father and his uncles blessing the people in this way.

---

[1] Walther, Victor, *Puzzi*, Verbano-Verlag 1936, p. 9. "He [Hermann's father] bought the latest books for his library, *Poetic Meditations* by Alphonse de Lamartine, the works of Count Chateaubriand who, like Lamartine, was a poet and politician, and a book containing the opinions expressed by Napoleon's enemy Stael, which you could still get in every book store. A man with alert senses and an open mind. A man of his time."

[2] The first biography of Hermann Cohen by Canon Charles Sylvain in French, quotes from a document called the "Confessions", covering the earliest period of his life, which Cohen wrote at the request of his superiors during his novitiate year. It is now lost. The biography was translated into English under the title, "The Life of Father Hermann", and was published by P.J. Kennedy and Sons, New York, 1925. The French original under the title *Flamme Ardente au Carmel* was published by Traditions Monastiques (Flavigny) in 2009. I will quote from this book in my own translation.

The family subscribed to the Jewish Liberal or Reform movement which preferred not to put too much emphasis on the ceremonial and ritual elements in Jewish tradition. But the young Hermann appears to have preferred the mystery which accompanied the more ancient ritual. Indeed later as a Catholic he remained somewhat conservative in his views. He writes in his "Confessions": "When I saw the Rabbi mount the steps of the sanctuary, draw the curtain and open the door, I waited expectantly."[1] He continues: "My expectation was not satisfied when I saw the Levites solemnly take out from a magnificent container a large roll of parchment studded with Hebrew letters and surmounted by a royal crown. The roll of parchment was then carried with great ceremony to a lectern. The cover and crown were removed and the Hebrew scriptures were read aloud. I was full of anxiety during the whole of this ceremony."[2]

Hermann and his sister liked singing German hymns as well as psalms and other prayers which fed their religious feelings. He and his eldest brother Albert were sent to the best college in town which was in fact non-Jewish. On account of being from a Jewish background the two brothers met with a hard time at the school. It was a big shock to the pampered boy, but Cohen reacted with some courage and tried to prove himself in study. So even at the tender age of nine he made rapid progress. Cohen writes: "With regard to Latin, French and the other subjects that they taught us, it was the same with all of them, like another Jacob I stole the birthright from my brother and drew to myself all the rewards and praise and I knew so well how to dominate, that my poor brother must have suffered very much because of me."[3] In fact at nine years old, he was capable of following the fourth form in High School.

[1] Sylvain, Flamme Ardente au Carmel, p. 26.
[2] Ibid., p.26.
[3] Ibid., p.28.

Cohen's scholastic ability however was overshadowed by his musical talent, and at the age of four and a half he wished to learn to play the piano like his elder brother. He soon surpassed Louis and at six years of age he could play the tunes of all the operas then in vogue! Furthermore, Cohen began to improvise, an astonishing achievement in a child and one which impressed experienced musicians. In view of Cohen's unusual musical talent, the family harpsichord was replaced by a grand piano. And so it was that, still a child, he was launched on a long musical career, in which compositions were merged with faultless execution to produce brilliant concerts.

There were two distinct periods in Cohen's musical work. Before his conversion, his piano pieces were brilliant, worldly, and often of great virtuosity. One of the best pieces was a long waltz entitled, "The Banks of the Elbe." Another piece, published by the "Messaggiero Musicale" was called, "A Shining Fantasie," and was reminiscent of Verdi's "Lombardi." Other more expressive pieces were tinged with a religious atmosphere: a nocturne entitled "Venetian Night" and "Lullaby" composed in 1841. In spite of his gifts, in this first period Cohen did not make a name for himself in the musical world. After his conversion a second period of musical output took place.

At an early age a doctor advised a period of rest from school because of Hermann's tendency to overdo things. During this time he was somewhat spoiled by his family. Cohen lived in a world where money ruled. He makes this amusing remark: "Our house was like a nest of ants where people came and went. Merchandise was everywhere, people counting money all over the place, and the only distinction accorded to businessmen was that of the size of their fortune to which every honour was given."[1] In addition to this, his parents family confided the young pianist to a professor of music of great talent but not a shining example for an impressionable youngster. He was thought to be a genius. Cohen writes:

---

[1] Sylvain, p. 5

4

And that was sufficient to justify in the eyes of the ordinary person all his caprices, and his foolish and scandalous behaviour. As I saw him admired by everybody, I soon wanted to imitate him, and I began to ape his behaviour. He loved gambling, so I too took to it very early on. He loved horses and pleasure, and as he always found admirers ready to supply him with money for his exploits. I began to conceive the notion that there was no life happier than that of an artist. My master often said to my mother, 'Hermann is a genius.' That encouraged me still more.[1]

Until that time his father had opposed the choice of a musical career for his second son. Rosalie, on her side, seems to have kept silent on the subject. But, besides the repeated affirmation of the professor that her son was a genius, it was due to an initiative on the part of the child himself which persuaded her to let him follow his ambition. In spite of the opposition and displeasure of his teacher, Hermann studied and performed a piece of music composed by his tutor, which required skill of an exceptionally high degree. The professor was won over and showed his satisfaction by taking his pupil with him to the cabaret and did the round of his friends to show him off. David Cohen fell into financial difficulties at this time and dropped his opposition. Hermann was delighted and the world was at his feet. He wrote: "Success, honours, celebrity - the pleasures in which artists spent a great part of their time, journeys, adventures. I saw everything through rose coloured spectacles in my imagination which was highly developed for my age."[2]

Hermann's tutor took him on a trip to Frankfurt and after an absence of several weeks the young virtuoso returned to Hamburg full of dreams of artistic glory, and still more firmly set in his determination to become a great pianist. Looking back from a

---

[1] Ibid., p. 6
[2] Ibid., p 7

contrite state as a Carmelite he commented: "Latin, Greek and Hebrew were forgotten but in exchange, at twelve years old, I learnt many things harmful to me."[1]

The young pianist made such rapid progress that his tutor decided on his debut in the musical world. A first concert in nearby Altona had an immediate success. Then he gave a second concert at Hamburg itself, before a more difficult and sophisticated audience. All whom the town considered distinguished turned out to hear the gifted youngster. The room was packed and his success surpassed that of Altona. The next day, everyone talked about Hermann's talents.

In 1830 his father suffered the financial ruin which had been threatening him. So with the two-fold intention of furthering her son's musical career, and escaping the place where the memory of the wealthy life she had led was a constant irritant, mother Rosalie considered leaving Hamburg and living in Paris. With this in mind, she took her son to the court of the Grand Duke of Mechlenburg-Strelitz. The Grand Duke was so impressed by the talented youth that he gave him a letter of introduction to his ambassador in Paris. The Grand Duke of Scherwin, did likewise. Both men made much of him and loaded him with presents. Cohen commented: "We returned to Hamburg in triumph."

At this time a domestic incident almost jeopardised his career. While helping himself to a pot of jam, Cohen nearly compromised his musical future. The jar broke and cut his finger badly. He was more frightened than hurt but the wound quickly healed. In the middle of the preparations for the departure to Paris, and in spite of his impatience to be off, Hermann wrote a cantata for his mother's birthday. Surprisingly enough - but this was a feature which repeated itself in his musical works - this cantata had a religious inspiration. This intimate piece was given a public airing in the newspapers of the region. A local newspaper had

---

[1]   Ibid., p. 8.

this to say: "Furthermore, the pianist Herrmann Cosen (sic) from Hamburg, is a burgeoning *artiste* aged twelve. The young newcomer demonstrated a major talent which hopefully will thrive in Paris, where he proceeds for higher education."[1] What began as a child's work, fresh and spontaneous in thought, degenerated into an exercise in self-promotion. Hermann became haughty and over-confident and judged that in future, it would be superfluous for him to prepare any pieces he was going to play in public! His mother became anxious this time and reproached him gently but in vain: Hermann commented: "I had already lost all respect, and disobeyed openly. I believed myself to be independent."[2]

The time of departure for Paris arrived and while Hermann's father remained at home with his eldest son, Albert, Rosalie Cohen took Hermann and his younger brother and sister with her and they left for Paris. At the beginning of the 19th century Paris was indeed the centre of things. Some people might say it still is! Famous musicians from every country met there and some took up residence. There was Cherubini who directed the Converatoire, Chopin, Zimmermann, Mendlesohn, Paganini and Richard Wagner a little later. Finally Franz Lizst arrived on the scene, then just twenty years old. The presence of such 'stars' explained the irresistible attraction the great city had for talented young people eager for fame. The success which the young pianist gained for himself at the Courts of Hanover, Cassel and Frankfurt, where he was feted by famous musicians, served to increase Cohen's arrogance still more even towards his mother, whose wise observations and corrections he totally ignored. During the last stage of their journey, the weather was very hot and the coach very uncomfortable, but that did not matter to Cohen, he was so excited about reaching Paris. He was just thirteen years of age.

---

[1] No Reference. The journalist got the spelling of Cohen's surname wrong!
[2] Sylvain, p.10.

A Star Is Born (1833).

In later life, Hermann Cohen would remark how, in his impatience to reach Paris, he kept asking his travelling companions, "Can you see Paris yet?" Finally on July 5, 1834, when the conductor shouted "Paris" to the travellers, Cohen couldn't contain his excitement. It seems that the Cohens took up residence on what is now Rue de la Batelière in the city.[1] When the new, young pianist arrived in Paris from Hamburg, as we said earlier, the city was at a high politically, philosophically, and artistically. Getting ensconced there, however, was no easy matter, in spite of the letters of recommendation to persons of note in Rosalie Cohen's possession. For a start, only French citizens were allowed to study at the Conservatoire. Moreover, no one could decide on a tutor for the boy. One friend said such a boy should not be entrusted to the "melancholy Chopin";[2] others suggested the "classical Zimmermann" or the "fiery Liszt." The young Cohen had one lesson each from Chopin, Zimmermann, and Liszt but said he preferred Franz Liszt. On a certain autumn day in Paris, Cohen had managed to get introduced to Liszt through the good offices of the great German poet Heinrich Heine. Heine proceeded to direct Cohen to the ranks of high society in Paris, such as the "salon" of the noble family of Belgiojoso. In his biography of Hermann Cohen, Walther Victor wrote: "A brilliant 'salon' opened before Hermann Cohen. One person, who immediately caught his eye, sat at the piano in rigid, austere beauty like a god producing divine harmonies. 'That's Liszt,' said Heine. 'And that's Putzig,' said Liszt.

---

[1] A later dinner invitation was addressed to Hermann at No. 18, Grange-Batalière on this street. It is now an elegant apartment building with restaurant and small art gallery at street level. It is situated near Rue Rossini.

[2] Chopin's first musical position was as organist in the Carmelite church in Warsaw.

Princess Belgiojoso smiled. A boy had thus received his nickname. And Puzzi stepped over to the piano."[1]

In his own youth, Liszt had been given the nickname "Putzig" by his tutor, Austrian count Karl Czerny, who in turn had Beethoven himself for his tutor. The name was soon softened to the less Germanic sounding "Puzzi." The novelist and celebrity George Sand found this nickname charming and amusing, and she gave it wide currency in her writings. This first audition was enough to make Liszt decide to tutor this precocious talent, even though as a busy and popular star he didn't wish to take on more pupils. Young Cohen soon became the favorite pupil of Liszt and accompanied his master to the distinguished salons of the capital where he got to know several contemporary celebrities.

Meanwhile, Liszt and his pupil were inseparable. Liszt was indeed extremely popular. He has been described as the first "pop star," with fans hunting for souvenirs after his concerts as they do with his modern counterparts. A film appeared many years ago describing this as "Lisztomania." Liszt had been quite religious in his youth but became lax later on. He then threw in his lot with the likes of Lamartine, Lamennais, Victor Hugo, Sainte-Beuve, Heine, and their friends. Liszt was also a noted philanderer. This must have had some influence on Cohen, and certainly he seems to have been caught up in the whirlwind. Later, writing to George Sand, Liszt remarked, "It is our old friend, young Hermann Cohen from Hamburg, painted by you at the age of fifteen, who accompanied Prince Belgiojoso under the name of "Puzzi," his pale, sad face, dark hair, and frail figure contrasting with the fair hair and open features of the prince. The dear child has again given proof of his precocious mind and his deep artistic feeling, which makes me forecast for him a brilliant and eventful future." These last lines are evidence of the wholehearted attachment of master to pupil and indeed of Liszt's unselfish nature.

---

[1] Victor, Walther, *Puzzi*, p. 55.

Through association with Liszt, Cohen would meet many celebrities. There was the French priest, philosopher, and political writer Félicité Lamennais, "the fallen eagle," whose ideas eventually brought him into conflict with the church and who was famous throughout France and beyond. Concerning Lamennais, Cohen writes, "He took me on his lap and placed his hands on my head. He took a book from the drawer in his table and inscribed it: 'A souvenir offered to my dear little friend, Puzzi, from F. Lamennais.' It was a book called *Paroles d'un Croyant* or *Words of a Believer*."[1] This book was Lamennais's reaction when his ideas were rejected in Rome by Pope Gregory XVI. Cohen eagerly read this book. "I dreamt of nothing else than of battles, prisons, liberty, and equality . . . in my eyes the creations of these two great geniuses seemed destined to become the beginning of an new era for suffering humanity; they would bring about the golden age, this unqualified happiness for which I longed so passionately."[2]Walther Victor is intrigued by the impression made by this precocious youngster from Hamburg on the ascetic "Saint of Bretony." He writes:

> The ideas of Lamennais fell on receptive soil in a youth who held this new prophet in high esteem. Perhaps nothing is more indicative of the effect that, beguiling even to himself, emanated from Puzzi in those years than the interest that such a man of the most profound spirituality took in him, a man whom some call the most significant mind that Catholicism possessed at the beginning of the last century. . . . But what did someone like Lamennais find in this bemused looking, effeminate young man who purported to be a boy wonder? We don't know. A romantic magic must have emanated from this figure. It came from that which lay dormant in Hermann Cohen, from the hidden treasure of his soul

---

[1] Ibid., p. 32

[2] Ibid., p. 32.

that shone all the more brightly the less it was discovered, which worked its magnetism all the more strongly the less it produced. Seeing Hermann in the arms of George Sand, who didn't love him and before whom he surely felt only fearful admiration, childish reserve, and that boyish shame, in which the first pride is mixed, we sense that it was the lack of genuine feeling and deep thoughts, the absence of a true love, of a real love, that condemned Puzzi to remain a 'gong booming or a cymbal clashing.' (1 Cor13: 6)[1]

"A romantic magic must have emanated from this figure"— that's a perceptive comment from Victor, and it goes a long way to explaining the magnetism Cohen exerted over people in his youth and in a different way after conversion. This was true in spite of the faults of character that may be urged against him. Sand wrote as follows in her typical flamboyant style to her friend Liszt:

> In the light of the candles, through the radiance of admiration that crowns and envelops you, while your fingers are creating miracles, I love to meet your tender glances that seem to tell me: brother, you understand me. I am talking to your soul! Yes, young friend, I understand this divine language, but I don't speak it. Why am I not a painter, that I might capture in your portrait that celestial radiance that sets it ablaze at that moment where God descends upon you and the most chaste of all muses bows smilingly before you! . . . Do you remember Puzzi, seated at the feet of the saint of Brittany, who said such marvelous things to him with the directness of an apostle. Behind you stood the child, pale, touched, as motionless as marble, and yet shaking like a flower shedding its leaves and seemed to imbibe the harmony with every pore and to open his pure lips to drink the honey that you

---

[1] Victor, *Puzzi*, p. 66. (This section trans. David T. Barry).

were pouring into him. It's said that art has lost its poetry: in truth, I noticed nothing of the sort. Have the fine days of Italy ever called forth a more sacred, pious artistic existence than yours, Franz? Did heaven create a more beautiful soul, a more excellent intellect, a more interesting face than that of our Hermann, or rather of our Puzzi? For he must continue to bear this name for a long time, which you sanctified in your childhood and which brought you luck.[1]

This was typical Sandian adulation indeed. Cohen could only be spoiled by friends like these who insisted on putting him on a pedestal. The cleric Lamennais became a flashpoint for the French church of his time. A rigid conservative early on in his career, cast in the Ultramontane mould, he seemed destined for higher things. His early disciples were brilliant young men like Count Charles de Montalembert and Henri Lacordaire, later the famous preacher of Notre Dame and restorer of the Dominican Order to France. There was also Prosper Guéranger who would restore the Benedictine Order to France. Lamennais moved swiftly across the spectrum to adopt a determined liberal approach after the crisis caused by the July revolution of 1830, and he prophetically urged the separation of church and state. He had started a newspaper called *L'Avenir* (The Future) to propagate his ideas, with Lacordaire and Montalembert doing a major share of the journalism. However, Lamennais and his followers moved too quickly for the climate of the times, and they were condemned by Pope Gregory XV1. After initial outward submission, Lamennais continued to diverge from the accepted line; and when he heard indirectly that the pope was grieved with him, he reacted in a very angry manner. He enlisted his friend Sainte-Beuve to publish without delay his manifesto referred to above, *Paroles d'un Croyant*. This signalled Lamennais's final break with the church.[2]

---

[1] Sand, *Lettres d'un Voyageur*, p. 211.

[2] Many of Lamennais' aphorisms were memorable: "Life is a secret to which only faith has the key." *Or again*, "Conscience is a sacred sanctuary which

Cohen's biographer, Victor, remarked that "he later pinned his cap on the Jacobin cross."[1] The first time Cohen met Sand, he appears to have fallen under her spell. He tells us:

> I did not know exactly in what her fame consisted, though I heard people refer to her as the greatest genius of the time. It enhanced my own reputation that I was known to be a friend of the author of "Lélia." It even provoked jealousy that I had access to such a person. I was constantly quizzed about her and the contents of her house, which were quaint and unusual. People suggested I looked like her with my fine, long hair and pale complexion. My name was constantly linked with hers, imagination supplying the answer as to what took place in her attic. But I can say this. She was extremely good to me. She sometimes entertained me for days on end and, as she wrote, I used to prepare cigarettes for her which stimulated her literary efforts. Occasionally she would ask me to play the piano, and as I played, she continued to write. I had not in fact read any of her books, but I was certainly impressed from what I heard about them. They were eagerly awaited by the publishers and devoured by the public. I wish now I had never read them and remained satisfied with her acquaintance. Otherwise I might have retained the few principles I had.[2]

The young man's devotion must have meant a lot to George Sand. She certainly publicized "Puzzi" in the various articles and letters she wrote. In a letter to Liszt, she wrote, "I should not like to forget the charming 'Puzzi,' your star pupil. Raphael and his friend Tebaldeo could not have appeared more graceful before gods and

God alone may enter as judge," sentiments that would have been echoed by Cardinal Newman in England in those days.
[1] Victor, *Puzzi,* p. 48.
[2] Sylvain, p.15.

men as you two appeared to me recently in the orchestra when all were hushed listening to you and the youngster standing behind you, pale and intense, not moving a muscle."[1] It was thanks to Sand that Cohen gained access to other salons, not only in Paris but also around Europe. Such was the atmosphere in which he moved. Like Liszt in his childhood, Cohen was idolized by many young women in Paris. But unlike Liszt in his youth, there was no father in Cohen's case who would insist on work and discipline. He neglected piano practice and usually had one of Sand's latest novels open on the piano stool beside him. When Cohen's friend, French artist Horace Vernet, arranged a meeting between Sand and Cohen in later life, Cohen, now a Carmelite friar, said she just looked at him in his brown habit and said, "So you have become a Capuchin."[2] She then turned on her heel and walked away. "She hadn't changed," remarked Victor; "she had remained faithful to herself."[3] A nice backhanded compliment!

---

[1]   Sand, p. 210.

[2]   In her autobiography, Sand refers to Cohen as a Carmelite. "Story of My Life": Autobiography of George Sand. State University of New York, 1991.

[3]   Victor, Puzzi, p.48.

15

Chapter Two

Who was Puzzi?

In his biography of Hermann Cohen, Walther Victor remarks in the context of the publicity the young pianist received in Paris: "Thus there was more said of his appearance than of his playing, and the high society ladies, the *flaneurs* from the suburbs, the intellectual camp-followers of the literary salons, had their food for conversation: the mysterious melancholy of Puzzi, George Sand and Liszt's love for the beautiful lady of the Hôtel Orleans, the Countess d'Agoult."[1] Melancholy was indeed a well-worn theme of the romantics. The English poet John Keats wrote his "Ode to Melancholy," and Kierkegaard examined this topic at length in his book *Sickness Unto Death*. At its best, melancholy represents a state of soulfulness that is unfortunately all too often absent in modern life. In its place, we find an undue emphasis on ephemeral qualities. There was something about the young Cohen that observers noted, a kind of openness to the spiritual dimension of life. As we shall see in the next chapter, many of his friends and a girl with whom there appeared to be a mutual attraction witnessed to his innate goodness.

---

[1]   Victor, *Puzzi* (this section trans. David T. Barry). A "flaneur" is an aimless wanderer—usually through the streets of Paris.

The melancholy mood seeped into the music, poetry, and fine arts of the period, bathing all it touched in a romantic glow. Later on in the century, Cohen's spiritual sister Thérèse of Lisieux would also reflect this mood: "The day after my first Communion was still beautiful, but it was tinged with a certain melancholy."[1] Here, however, we have an overemphasis on the other world, the heavenly homeland, typical of French piety of the time, sometimes to the neglect of the legitimate demands of life here and now.

Liszt really recognized in his pupil a mirror image of his own early life. From then on, he liked to have young Cohen accompany him like a shadow. There is an extant portrait of the adolescent Cohen, sketched on a medallion, showing him with an intense expression. He holds his head straight and proud. Cohen was only thirteen, but his small stature made him look even younger. In this face, however, as we see in another drawing, willpower was dominant, touched by an expression of basic goodness. Cohen's fame spread rapidly, the newspapers took notice of him, and invitations to give recitals poured in. He was out until all hours and began to disregard his mother's anxiety about his welfare. He tells us that he became the tyrant of his family. Everything was geared around him; brother and sister were at his beck and call. He admits later that his young brother often had to go out in heavy rain to hail a carriage for him. Writing later on to Marie-Alphonse Ratisbonne, Cohen says:

> I was spoilt in the salons with its secular society. Soon they were determined to make me the scapegoat of all their reprehensible ideas—atheism, pantheism, Fourierism,[2]

---

[1] Thérèse of Lisieux, *Story of a Soul: The Autobiography of Saint Thérèse of Lisieux*, trans. John Clarke (Washington, DC: ICS Publications, 1996).

[2] Fourierism is the socialism of Charles Fourier; together with Charles Babeuf, they sowed the seeds of communism. According to Andrew Hussey (*Paris: The Secret History* [New York: Penguin, 2006]), communism really originated in Paris.

Saint-Simonism,[1] anarchy, terrorism and abolition of marriage, Communism, and hedonism. There was soon room for all this in the head of a fourteen year old. I then became a zealous propagandist of these groups and, consequently, the Benjamin of more than one of the modern prophets of so-called civilization.[2]

This is quite a list of "isms" in one paragraph. Here we catch glimpses of the somewhat reactionary Cohen of later years who apparently did not have the time or energy to sort out the many contradictory trends in the French politics, religion, and culture of his day. Some of the change that was taking place was positive and should not have been dismissed out of hand.

Meanwhile Hermann did in fact assimilate his tutor's technique at the piano. Liszt was anxious to demonstrate the prowess of his protégé and arranged for him to give a concert. His age was even understated, twelve rather than fourteen, in order to enhance his reputation. A large audience attended, and all were impressed by the young pianist from Hamburg. On the threshold of great success, Cohen suffered a blow with the news that Liszt was about to elope with Marie, Countess d'Agoult. She was trapped in a loveless marriage with Count Charles d'Agoult, twenty years her senior. Beautiful and clever, she was a wife and mother, but even the fashionable life of Paris failed to hold her, and she dreamt of a life of escapism with Franz Liszt. It was indeed a great blow to Cohen who felt it was the end of everything. But he vowed to follow Liszt, even if he had to beg his bread! At first Liszt refused but after a lot of persistence capitulated, and agreed Cohen could join him in Switzerland three months from then. Rosalie Cohen had no option but to pack up and go with her son. She placed Albert in boarding-school and took Henrietta and Louis with her and they left for Geneva. It was hardly an ideal situation for Cohen, but deep down he had nothing but admiration for the

---

[1] Saint-Simonism is another form of socialism founded by Count Saint-Simon.

[2] Beaurin, p. 29

young Countess who had left everything to follow her dream. The admiration was not reciprocated however; she was jealous of Cohen and not unnaturally thought of him as an embarrassing extra and in the end managed to oust him. At the time however Cohen suspected nothing. The Mayor of Geneva asked Liszt to establish a School of Music there. Cohen was appointed a Professor of Music. Then with his customary kindness Liszt was able to obtain students for the young professor who was only fifteen! Thus Cohen earned quite a lot of money but he also squandered it. It was perhaps irresponsible of Liszt and Cohen's mother to allow the boy the use of so much money.

Moreover at this time Cohen fell under the influence of the ideas of Voltaire and Rousseau who were both highly regarded in Geneva. The Church was in fact flourishing at this time with, for example, the rise of new religious orders. Some reference will be made to individual members of these congregations in the course of our story. The Teresian Carmelites, as we shall see, were restored to France in 1839. But at this time, Cohen was unaware of this new upsurge of new life in the Catholic Church—and he certainly would not have learned about that in the writings of Voltaire and Rousseau! Cohen seems to have read attentively Rousseau's *Confessions*, which set a benchmark for autobiographical writing. In regard to his veneration of Voltaire, Cohen even went on pilgrimage to the château of Ferney on the Swiss border where Voltaire resided for a time. It has been renamed Ferney-Voltaire in his honour. Following the escapades of Liszt and his entourage, there was one memorable occasion on which George Sand joined up with Liszt and his friends in Geneva. This was meant to be an Alpine pleasure excursion. They checked into the Hôtel de La Union. In true romantic fashion, they entered the following in the hotel register:

Franz Liszt
Place of Birth: Parnassus
Occupation: Musician-philosopher
Provenance: Doubt
Destination: Truth

And George Sand logged in as follows:

Place of Birth: Europe
Residence: Nature
Provenance: God
Destination: Heaven[1]

This also demonstrates the romantic world-embracing vision of Liszt and Sand. Historian Norman Davies adds, "Their comments in the hotel register said as much about their good humor and about the outlook of their romantic generation . . . in 1835, the idea of Europe was hardly less fantastic than that of Parnassus."[2]

Sand and Liszt would have done justice to any contemporary new age travellers of our time. George Sand, in her *Lettres d'un Voyageur*, has left an amusing account of this rendezvous with Liszt, Marie d'Agoult, and Cohen at Chamonix. Liszt and his group left on a walking expedition in the Valley of Chamonix. They were dressed in outlandish Bohemian fashion. Cohen was done up as a page wearing a brown medieval tunic and sported a ribbon bow on his long, curling hair. No wonder the landlord took him for a girl in this costume. Sand caught up with them there, and she describes the scene:

> The first object I stumbled upon was what the innkeeper called a young girl. It was Puzzi, sitting astride a suitcase and so changed, so grown; his head was covered with brown curls, a feminine blouse around his waist that, my goodness, I was so bewildered I didn't recognize the young Hermann, so I doffed off my hat to him and said, "Fair page, tell me where is Lara," whereupon from the depths of an English

---

[1] Norman Davies, *Europe: A History*. Pimplico, London, 1997 p. 784.[One of the illustrations in his book is "Musical Evening," by J. Danhauser (Liszt am Flugel, 1840).

[2] Ibid., Davies, p. 784.

hood popped up the fair-haired Arabella.[1] As I rush toward her, Franz throws his arms around my neck; and Puzzi utters an exclamation of surprise. We certainly made up an incredible group.[2]

This kind of publicity from the popular Sand gave Hermann Cohen widespread coverage in her extensive circle of readers. Later, the group of tourists converged on the cathedral church of St. Nicholas in Fribourg where a Mooser organ had recently been installed. Sand referred to it as "the finest organ that had ever been built." Sand was possessed of an acerbic tongue and pen that she demonstrates to full effect in her observations of Marie d'Agoult. The countess had looked haughty and bored in the cathedral, and Sand rasped, "You're hard to please, the glacier wasn't white enough for your taste the other day in the mountains! Its great summit that might have been hewn from the flanks of Paros, its sharp needles, beside which we look like pigmies, you didn't find worthy of your proud gaze . . . so what planet have you come from, you who despise the world in which we live?"[3] Phew!

The organ builder Mooser himself was there to give a demonstration, and Liszt took the keyboard of the great instrument. Sand wrote, "It was only when Franz Liszt let his hands run freely over the keyboard and played us a fragment of Mozart's 'Dies Irae' [requiem] that we realized the extent to which the Fribourg organ surpasses anything we know of its kind."[4] The majestic sound "haunted her like a passion," and the Latin words of the old Latin requiem Mass "Sequence" sprang to her mind:

---

[1]   Lara was Sand's nickname for Liszt, based on the hero of a poem by Byron. Arabella was Sand's pet name for Marie d'Agoult, probably based on the pianist Arabelle Goddard, who was known to Sand. Bestowal of pet names was a 19th century fashion, especially in France.

[2]   Sand, *Lettres d'un Voyageur*, p. 269.

[3]   Ibid., p. 271.

[4]   Ibid., p. 272.

Quantus tremor est futurus,

Quando judex est venturus, etc.[1]

(How terrifying the future when the judge shall come)

She refers to these as "terrible syllables."

Observing Marie d'Agoult's calmer reaction to her lover's virtuoso playing, she thought perhaps "she had been moved by a sweeter, more touching passage," something like "Recordare Jesu pie" (Dear Jesus remember). And she continues, "In the meantime, the organ thundered like the voice of Almighty God and the composer's inspiration caused all Dante's hell and purgatory to soar upwards under narrow arches with their ribs painted pink and grey."[2] She then refers to a figure of King David painted nearby that may have prompted Cohen's reaction. He, too, was profoundly moved by what was a new experience for him, and years later, he described the scene:

> Liszt touched the great keys of this colossal harp of David, whose majestic sounds gave me a vague idea of your grandeur, O my God. I was filled with a foretaste of holiness. Did you not cause to stir in my soul an intimation of religious faith? What then was that deep feeling, which I always experienced since my youth when I myself touched or heard someone else play the notes of an organ? It would affect me so much that I became unwell and was advised to avoid the

---

[1]   Sequence for the Latin requiem Mass, attributed to Thomas of Celano.

[2]   Sand, *Lettres d'un Voyageur*, p. 272. George Sand, *Lettres d'un Voyageur*, trans. Sacha Rabinivitch and Patricia Thomson (New York: Penguin, 1987.) Sand was an extraordinary figure. Born Amantine-Aurore-Lucie Dupin in 1804, she came to Paris after, having left her husband, and wrote successful novels under the pseudonym George Sand. The best known of these was *Lélia*, to which Cohen refers. Later she lived with Frédéric Chopin at her chateau in Nohant. Her published letters run to many volumes, and she mentions Hermann Cohen several times. In keeping with her male pseudonym and persona, Sand smoked cigars and dressed as a man.

instrument. O Jesus, my beloved, you were at the door of my heart; and I would not open to you.[1]

Meanwhile Liszt, who was running low on funds, started on a round of concert tours, and Cohen acted as his secretary and earned his keep. Marie d'Agoult had borne Liszt two children at this stage, so her antagonism to Cohen increased as she felt he would usurp the place and resources due to her children. At this time, Liszt had good reason to fear that his long absence from Paris would cause his fame there to wane in favour of the up-and-coming Sigismond Thalberg, so he decided to return to Paris.[2]

Liszt was uncharacteristically jealous of Thalberg's success and refused to play his music or allow his students to study him. Cohen was determined to follow him to Paris, although it meant giving up his recently acquired lucrative position. Liszt himself tried to persuade him to stay but to no avail. Cohen was still only fifteen. The long-suffering Rosalie Cohen had no option but to leave everything once more and follow her wayward son. Back in Paris, he fell into bad habits, one of which was gambling. Liszt was a relative of Italian-born Prince Emilio Belgiojoso who had a fine tenor voice, and he and his wife hosted concerts in which the prince sang accompanied by Cohen.[3]At one of these concerts, Cohen noticed gaming tables, and later his friends invited him to watch. Later on, Cohen would recall, "I think it was the first time I had never seen this sort of game, and I eagerly followed the fortunes of the players. Large sums of money were lost and won. I asked if I might try something myself. It

---

[1] Sylvain, p. 26.

[2] Sigismond Thalberg, composer and pianist, was praised by many of the most prominent artists and declared as being "sensational." This caused a rivalry between Liszt and Thalberg; however, they always remained cordial with one another.

[3] He was descended from a Milanese noble family, Count of the Holy Roman Empire and Marques of Grumello. Only `Emilio` is known, seems he had only one forename.

was there that the vice that ruled the best years of my life originated. It didn't give me a moment's rest and often drove me to the verge of suicide because of the enormous losses I sustained."[1]

Here he echoes the teaching of St. John of the Cross in his classic book *The Ascent of Mount Carmel*, where he describes how such behavior can enslave a person. St. John indeed devotes several chapters of *The Ascent* to describing the various ways in which one's energies are diverted from God by uncontrolled desire. He maintains that the damage done is twofold: (1) uncontrolled desire deprives us of the Spirit of God, and (2) it wearies, torments, darkens, defiles, and weakens us.[2] And Cohen himself gave a self-description of a gambler in these words: "He had become a slave to an implacable tyrant, which gave him no rest by day or night. If he did happen to snatch a few moments sleep, he was disturbed by bad dreams, incessant hopes of gain, or the horror of loss. He woke up with a start, memory recalling a picture of his desperate plight. During these long sleepless nights, he planned to take his life but wanted to try his luck just one more time before carrying out his plan."[3] Here we seem to be dealing with a real addiction, and it reminds us of contemporary addictions such as drugs, alcohol, smoking, caffeine, and sexual abuse.[4] In overcoming his addiction so quickly

---

[1]   Beaurin, p. 39.

[2]   St. John of the Cross, "Ascent of Mount Carmel," in *The Collected Works of St. John of the Cross* (Washington, DC: ICS Publications, 1979). In *The Bhagavad Gita*, it is interesting to notice what the Hindu author has to say about desire. He thinks in exactly the same terms as John: "Wisdom is clouded by desire, the ever-present enemy of the wise, desire in its innumerable forms which like a fire, cannot find satisfaction." *The Bhagavad Gita*, trans. Juan Mascaro (London: Penguin, 1980, p. 59).

[3]   Sylvain, p. 24. As we shall note later, writers like Alexander Dumas and Cohen's friend Céleste Mogador also described the effect of becoming a slave to gambling. See "A Selection from the Writings of Hermann Cohen" for the complete text of his essay on gambling.

[4]   Cohen was accustomed to taking snuff and cigarettes as well as being an inveterate coffee drinker.

and so thoroughly after his conversion, Cohen provides inspiration for modern victims of such abuses.

In the meantime, Marie d'Agoult and Liszt began to drift apart, while Cohen himself drifted more deeply into a life of gambling and attendant disorders. He abandoned his mother and set up in an apartment of his own. He had thrown away an opportunity that promised a bright future, but his adulation of Liszt prevented him from maximizing his opportunities as one of the youngest music professors ever. Now ensconced in his own home, his life really began to unravel—from an artistic, human, and spiritual viewpoint. He writes: "Music lessons provided me with ready money, and money provided me with the pleasures I craved. At that time, my life was given over to indulging every desire. But did this make me any the happier? Not at all. My God, the thirst for happiness could never be quenched in that way."[1] An increasing weakness for gambling left him no peace, and he longed for the "kick" a lucky stroke afforded. Cohen neglected the piano practice essential for a good performer. His nights were spent in the gaming casinos, and his days were spent in bed. He sometimes took refuge in solitude to get away from his friends, but afterward he felt oppressed by that very solitude: Again: "I began to suffer from that disease that devours the world of idlers, even in their places of indulgence and takes a grip of everyone."[2] But eventually Cohen tired of this lifestyle and returned to his mother's house. He developed a friendship with Princess Belgiojoso who was herself a very musical person. Cohen states: "In the salon which the Princess opened in Paris, some of the most distinguished writers and musicians met—Rossini, Meyerbeer, Bellini, and Liszt. Wednesday was 'concert day' and the remarkable singing voice of Prince Emilio Belgiojoso, the Princess' husband, contributed to their success."[3]

---

[1] Beaurin, p. 45.
[2] Ibid., p. 41.
[3] Ibid., p. 41.

At about this time, the events narrated in his *Confessions* come to an end. He had undertaken to write an account of God's mercies to him during his year of formation as a Carmelite, but when this period expired, he no longer had the leisure to continue writing his life's story. There is an interlude of about ten years between now and the date of his conversion, but we have no detailed knowledge of these years. But it seems there was no diminution either in his habit of gambling or his love of travel—England, Germany, another visit to Italy, and finally home to Paris. Through Princess Belgiojoso, Cohen gained access to all the fashionable places in the Faubourg Saint-Germain.[1] Indeed her patronage did much to rehabilitate him; she put him in charge of her household arrangements, concerts, and so on. When Liszt returned to Paris from Geneva, he kept in touch with the princess, and Cohen was a kind of go-between. Later when a distinct coolness developed between Liszt and Cohen, the princess intervened: "I gave your message to Hermann, who told me he had written to you without receiving an answer. He concluded that he was writing to you too often."[2] Later she helped Cohen organize a concert to assist with his finances, but this turned out a failure. He was neglecting music practice and discipline. As a result, feeling frustrated, he decided to go back to Hamburg to visit his father, but the old man sent him packing. This was hardly surprising in the circumstances; apparently the two had become estranged. However, Hermann undertook a successful concert tour while home in Hamburg, and Liszt himself shared one of those concerts with him. Back in Paris, Cohen met an Italian singer named Mario. He was an aristocrat whose real name was Giovanni Matteo Mario, Cavalière di Candia. They became friends, and Cohen accompanied Mario on his concert tours. Mario was the Pavarotti of his day, acclaimed throughout Europe and indeed the world. Mario and

---

[1] Princess Christina Belgiojoso-Trivulzio, whom we met in the last chapter, was a beautiful woman of twenty-six at this time.

[2] Beaurin, p. 42.

beautiful soprano Giulia Grisi, whom he married in 1856, divided their time between Paris and London. Cohen also spent some time tutoring Mario into a deeper appreciation of his musical art.[1]

They stayed some time in London, and Cohen gave piano lessons, though he continued to gamble. He ended the season in London with a highly acclaimed concert. With some resources in his pocket, Cohen left for Italy, hoping to meet up with Liszt. He was still only eighteen years of age. At this period, he began to compose some new melodies with a view to writing operatic works. He met up with Liszt, and they spent some time in Rome sightseeing, visiting all the churches and also the Colosseum, the arena of gladiatorial and other Roman games, as well as the probable martyrdom site for some early Christians. One day they were at the Villa Hadrian from which they could see St. Peter's Basilica. Sainte-Beuve composed a poetic record of the occasion, which he dedicated to Liszt.

> The rays of the setting sun fall gently on the arena.
> Soon it will flood it with the full force of its mighty power.
> The horizon is now no more than a boundless ocean.
> In the distance, the sharp outline of St. Peter's cuts across it.
> Near us, your Hermann, so obviously proud of you,
> Puzzi of former days, happy and excited,
> Eagerly questioning you about flowers and medals and relics.[2]

Cohen indeed must have been intrigued observing people in Rome wearing religious medals publicly and by the flower displays surrounding altars and statues and images of Our Lady in the churches. The days passed quickly, and Cohen used up his resources. He had enjoyed Italy, but now he had to leave it—and Liszt. He again

---

[1] Giulia Grisi was a sister of Giudetta Pasta for whom Bellini composed the title role of Norma in his opera of that name.

[2] Sainte-Beuve, *Poésies complètes*, Charpentier et Cie, Paris, 1869, p. 447. Charles Augustin Sainte-Beuve was a French literary critic and a major figure in literary history. My translation.

set out for London. Soon afterward, Princess Christina Belgiojoso, who was also in England, visiting friends in Kenilworth, wrote to Liszt, and in a letter written in 1839, she complains about Cohen: "Thick-Thorn House. August 6, 1839. As for Hermann, I think he is a good boy; and I have nothing against him. He is really still a child, but he has done something which hinders me from helping him as I would like. It's like this: I quite honestly thought I was helping him, but according to him it seems that it's the other way round and that I have offended him."[1]

Hermann was now nineteen and had become obstinate, almost embittered, toward his mentor, even though she had really been a mother to him and had tried to better him. Naturally the princess was very hurt. In the above letter she wrote: "I know that he will now say that he never meant what he said, and that he only complained in a fit of depression. But for me the fact that he entertained the thought for one moment has changed everything. I hope you will not reproach me for this, my conscience is clear—I never did him any harm."[2] Obviously the princess was very sensitive herself, and it was the end for Cohen as far as she was concerned. She had done a lot for him, and now he would feel the consequences of his foolish remarks. Liszt, who remained rather distant, didn't answer her letter until October. "I don't know how I can put in a good word for Puzzi with you since I will need one myself."

But the princess did reply to Liszt:

> Kenilworth House
> October 14, 1839
>
> In regard to Hermann, I can assure you that I have not been hard. The poor boy, however, does not know how to maintain friendships. You are right in saying that he is to be pitied, being left to fend for himself so young. His situation

---

[1]   Ibid., p. 22.

[2]   Ibid. p. 23.

becomes more and more difficult. I think he supports his family, and his professional life puts him in contact with some undesirables, which is sad. Theatrical life is not good for a young man. He is right to accompany the singer Candida, and he is well paid. He would be better off, however, if he confined himself to accompany her on the piano and not behind the scenes as well! I can't believe that he is not wasting a lot of time and money in that way. Hermann needs moral protection and example. I'm not in a position to provide him with this—you should do it, Hermann respects you and you would be doing him a great service.[1]

But perhaps Liszt himself was in no position to direct others. The princess bore Cohen no ill will and concluded, "For my part, I have nothing against the poor boy; and if I can be of any help to him, I will."[2] In the following spring, Cohen returned to Milan, Italy. He wrote a short operatic work that he tried to stage in Verona but without success. The work had some merit, but its very failure seemed due to the religious content of his compositions. During this time, Cohen's mother continued to support him, but the Countess d'Agoult stepped up her intrigues. On November 30, 1839, she wrote to Liszt as follows: "Puzzi is in love with the wife of a doctor, and the young woman's parents have thrown him out." She failed to see the similarity to her own case. On December 6, she returned to the attack: "Hermann shows me respect and is anxious to be of service to me, but he is the vainest person I know. He doesn't know how to behave, has no real ability, and demeans himself. I think when you return you should give him the brush-off. It's high time you cut [him] adrift and gave him up as a bad job."[3]

Liszt was on a tour of Europe, giving concerts and earning some money. Cohen was meanwhile sinking into debt, and this annoyed

---

[1]   Ibid., p. 23.

[2]   Beaurin, pp. 47 - 49

[3]   Ibid., p. 47.

Countess d'Agoult. Liszt, however, was not immediately influenced by her. He welcomed Cohen on a visit to Prague where they met up, and he showed him around. The countess was furious: "What you tell me about Hermann really surprises me. It amazes me that you can treat so royally someone I have thrown out." Liszt did not take her too seriously, and no doubt he preferred the opinion of the princess who had urged him to help the boy. Indeed, Liszt crosses the Rhine bridge at Mainz (where he was performing) in the early hours to rescue Cohen "after he did something stupid," as Liszt wrote to Princess Sayn-Wittgenstein, with whom he would later live. He didn't even reply to the countess's attacks, but he wrote the following from Metz, where he was then residing, to Franz Schubert: "One of my old pupils, Monsieur Hermann, has agreed to organize my concerts. This has been a great help to me."

So here we find the two, reunited and working together. This did not at all please the countess, and she again wrote to Liszt on May 17: "Your mother came this morning to give me further news of Hermann, which she heard from Ferco. If what she says is true, this boy is utterly depraved." So it was really gossip. Liszt was still not perturbed and took Cohen with him to Baden in Germany. From there, they went to Hamburg where they met his older brother Louis. The countess was still furious at her failure to have Cohen debunked, and she wrote from Coblenz to a friend, Henri Lehmann, in July 1840: "You know that Franz wants to have Hermann again organize his concerts. Hermann has not even succeeded in making a good job of this. He continues to gamble and has lost a thousand francs in a fortnight. His behavior is as bad as ever. So he has been dismissed, and I am going to send someone else from Paris to Franz."[1]

No doubt she thought she had been successful this time, but it didn't happen; Cohen remained with Liszt until the end of 1840.

---

[1] Tierney, Tadgh, *The Story of Hermann Cohen*, Teresian Press, Oxford, 1991, p. 25. Henri Lehmann was an artist, and there are two separate portraits by him of Liszt and Marie d'Agoult in the Musée Carnavalet in Paris.

He then left for Venice. Liszt replied to the countess, with whom he never lived again, "Hermann is making a name for himself in Venice. He is involved with Miri, an impresario, who wrote to me on the last page of Hermann's letter. They go around together." Liszt realized that the countess knew Miri, and he was afraid she might use her acquaintance to damage Cohen's reputation again. So he urged her, "When you write to Miri, please refrain from saying spiteful things about him." But the countess returned to the assault on January 18, 1841, writing: "Shake down from the tree the Puzzi-caterpillars, which are eating up the leaves." She was referring to Liszt's earnings from his concerts. This time it worked. Much later in a long letter to Alphonse Ratisbonne relating his conversion, Cohen referred to a "hellish conspiracy" that succeeded in separating him from Liszt and sowing seeds of hostility between the two. Eventually, Liszt allowed himself to be won over. He began to take the countess's accusations seriously and suspected Hermann of diverting some of his earnings for his own use. Cohen got in touch with his mother and gave her a copy of the accounts he kept of Liszt's concert earnings. His mother examined them and then gave them to Liszt pointing out that the countess's accusations were at the very least greatly exaggerated. But Liszt refused to look at them and instead accepted the countess's allegations. He wrote to the countess on December 7: "Hermann has stolen more than fifteen hundred francs from me, which were the proceeds of the first concert in Dresden, and nearly as much from my second concert. I do not wish to hear any more about him."[1] So where does the truth lie? To what extent was the conspiracy Cohen mentioned bound up with accusations of theft?

But there is no doubt that the repeated attacks by Marie d'Agoult, trying to get rid of Cohen, as well as the intemperate and aggressive tone of her words, renders these attacks suspect. We also have to weigh the fact that when Cohen became a Catholic,

---

[1] Ibid., p. 26.

he confided in Ratisbonne and in fact sincerely related all his lapses without hiding anything. The idea of a conspiracy seems to be obvious in Marie d'Agoult's letters to her lover, subjective and spiteful as they were, by contrast with the kindly letters of Princess Belgiojoso. So there is no real proof that Cohen robbed his master, although he was capable of doing so, and certainly a gambling addiction would have both encouraged him to do so and diminished his responsibility. What is certain is that Liszt underwent a profound change in regard to Cohen, and it was a really severe blow to him.[1] He attempted a reconciliation in February 1843, but Liszt remained unmoved.

Then there was a new twist to the story when Marie d'Agoult accused Cohen of being about to publicize some of Liszt's letters involving his women friends. Again Liszt believed her and was naturally furious. Marie d'Agoult had won out in this tussle, but she was not to savour her triumph for long as Liszt eventually left her. As we shall see, however, Liszt and Cohen were later reconciled, but circumstances had vastly changed. At this point, Cohen rejoined his mother and sister in Venice where they seem to have been on an extended holiday. His mother provided great support for him, and he passed a peaceful period with her composing piano pieces and gaining popularity. In the spring, we find him off again, first to Paris, then to London, and back again to Venice. In Venice, he struck up a friendship with a well-known artist named Adalbert de Beaumont; later on they would spend some time together sharing the same house in Paris just before his conversion. Cohen was really running away from himself at this time. At a future date, when he became a Discalced Carmelite, he would describe in a sermon to a Paris congregation what this period of his life was like. He had become the complete dandy in the best traditions of his famous

---

[1]   Liszt was long-suffering in regard to lapses by his students. One young lady had been helping herself to some of Liszt's belongings for some time. One morning, he placed the score of *The Thieving Magpie* before her and asked her to play. It had the desired effect.

contemporaries Count Alfred d'Orsay or Beau Brummell, the "Regency buck" who was also a notorious gambler. In his sermon, Cohen used the image of a great storm in which "my great loss appeared certain to me."[1] But in meantime, his tortured soul could not gain any relief, and he remained a prisoner of himself and of his passions and desires.

[1] See "Sermon in Church of St. Sulpice," in "Selections from the Writings of Hermann Cohen" in Part

Celeste Mogador

Chapter 3

Former Courtesan and Future Carmelite

Hermann Cohen achieved some success on his concert round, though he was extremely disappointed over the split with Liszt. From the first time he met him, he had idolized the Hungarian composer and arranged his life and his future around him. But now Cohen was on his own. He continued to waste his money on the gaming tables and waste his time in idle pursuits. Later Cohen would write to his friend and fellow convert Marie-Alphonse Ratisbonne: "When I say all the young people I knew lived like me, I don't exaggerate. They looked for pleasure everywhere and wanted the resources to buy it. They never thought of God, only of themselves, and their desire to accumulate material things; and their only moral guidelines were human respect and a desire to keep on the right side of the law."[1]

That is probably an accurate description of some young people in the Paris of that time. With its casinos and theatres, Paris provided immense opportunities for living a Bohemian lifestyle. One particular rendezvous was at the Café Mommus situated near the

---

[1] Sylvain, p. 35.

church of Sainte Germaine-L'Auxerrois, "the Church of the Louvre."[1] Renoir would later meet his friends here and create there the famous painting of his lover Lise. Cohen, the dandy, carried on with his life in this soulless way. The term *playboy* had not yet been invented, but it would fit. However, the French term *flaneur*, indicating aimless wandering, was in use, and it fitted perfectly. His mood swung up and down, and his heart always ruled his head if in fact he made any decision at all. He had a deep distrust of the Catholic Church and of clergy in particular, although the only Catholic clergyman he had ever spoken to was the ex-priest Félicité Lamennais. At twenty-seven, he hardly retained any of his youthful religious leanings. I have mentioned how profoundly sacred organ music moved him, which perhaps reflected the sensitivity of the artist. The positive aspects of his melancholy temperament—and there is a positive side—were slowly coming to the surface. He treasured a Bible given him by Liszt during their escapade in Geneva. It carried the inscription "Blessed are the pure of heart." It was his first acquaintance with the words of Jesus. But any good influence seems to have been short lived. Later on in his *Confessions*, Cohen protested his sinfulness. Certainly he was a compulsive gambler. His dress was the height of fashion as befitted a young man who moved in high society. And on the romantic level, he seems at one point to have cultivated the affections of the famous pianist Marie Pleyel, also a pupil of Liszt and wife of the famous piano maker. Her artistry was acclaimed by Chopin, Liszt, and Berlioz, to whom she was briefly engaged.

The experience to be described in the present chapter may have been the catalyst for what followed later. At least all the signs point in that direction. Hermann Cohen seems to have had only one genuine love affair in his life; however, it appears to have fizzled out before it even began, due to a number of reasons. It might even have been a defining experience for him, firming up a decision to find his happiness in God alone. We have a tantalizing and, in many ways,

---

[1] Cohen's friend Père Legrand was curé here.

A Life of Hermann Cohen

touching account of the sequence of events, or better, nonevents, from the young lady involved. To understand the story from her angle, we need to fill in more of the background. In Paris, then as now, there was no shortage of the good-time set—young people from privileged families with money to burn plus all the trappings of wealth and celebrity.

Céleste Mogador

This background introduces us to a famous young lady who would become the object of young Hermann Cohen's unrequited affections. These two had some traits in common. Elizabeth-Céleste Venard, better known as "Mogador" was born in Paris in 1824.[1] In her *Memoirs*, Mogador tends to embroider the truth, and although she stated that her father died when she was only six, it appears he joined the army before she was born and never returned.[2] Soon after an encounter with famous poet Alfred de Musset, Mogador caught smallpox and after hospitalization was rescued by a rich friend. Her face would subsequently be slightly marked by traces of this disease. Mogador next turned her energies to the stage and joined the Bal Mabille or Mabille Ballroom, which was on the site of a café called Le Petit Moulin Rouge near Montmartre.[3] Her dance partner and teacher, Brididi, nicknamed her "Mogador."[4] She was instrumental

---

[1] She has been thought to have inspired Bizet's *Carmen* as they were near neighbours at one stage. Mogador also knew Henri Murger whose work was the source of Puccini's, La Bohème. In the same way tragic courtesan Marie Duplessis who died at the age of 23, is said to have inspired Dumas, *fils Lady of the Camelias* and Marguerite in Verdi's La Traviata.

[2] Céleste Mogador, *Memoirs of a Courtesan in Nineteenth-Century Paris*, trans. Monique Fleury Nagem (Lincoln: University of Nebraska Press, 2002).

[3] Founded by a man named Mabille, it was a forerunner of the Folies Bergère and the Moulin Rouge in the Montmartre area later on in the century.

[4] At this time, the Algerian town of Mogador had fallen to the French, and Brididi remarked that it would be easier for him to defend Mogador than fight off Mogador's suitors.

37

in the early development of the dances known as the cancan and the polka, which became all the rage, as well as scandalizing polite society. During her time there, she befriended a lonely, tragic figure who was equally famous, namely Lise Sergent.[1] Mogador was soon offered an opportunity to ride horses at the Paris Hippodrome and she took up this challenge with her usual enthusiasm, prepared to start from scratch. She became successful and popular at this also, enjoying the name of equestrienne, until a serious accident in a chariot race almost led to her losing her leg.

Meanwhile, the party scene remained a constant for these young people, often daily. One night in the Spring of 1847, at the Café Anglais, it was mentioned that one of their number, Alphonse R, was quite despondent and had not been attending their parties. It was decided that they all descend on him next day in an effort to cheer him up. Alphonse was asked to invite some of his friends along. One of these was Hermann Cohen. Mogador and her friend Sergent attended. Sergent sang with great exuberance and got things moving. Mogador takes up the story:

> There was music. A short young man went to the piano. At the first notes I recognized a master. His hair was blond and his eyes were blue with somewhat prominent lips and white teeth; he was more good than bad, but his appearance lacked expression. His hands ran lightly across the keyboard with incredible agility. When he finished there was unanimous applause. It wasn't just music but a harmony that enveloped the heart. I took the opportunity of the lull to ask M. Gustave who this young man was. 'He is H(ermann) the composer, H the young prodigy! I shall introduce him to you.' He walked over to him, took his hand and brought him to me. I imagined I saw M. H blush. 'I am thankful to

---

[1] She was known as "La Reine Pomaré," after the contemporary Tahitian queen. They and others, such as Clara Fontaine, were the dancing queens of Paris.

38

my friend,' he said, in a slight German accent that was not at all unpleasant, 'for introducing me to you. Since the day I first saw you, quite some time back, I wanted to get to know you.' I asked him with some anxiety where he had seen me. 'Oh, I saw you on horseback, and my heart has been racing with you since that day. He bowed to me and left.'"[1]

Not a bad opening gambit! When she was told he was Jewish, however, she was very taken aback. Apparently she had childhood prejudices about some Jewish neighbors. Mogador continues: "Poor H[ermann] invited everyone to spend the evening at his house, Rue de Provence. Everyone accepted." To tease him, Mogador told him she had an engagement. "'In that case, let us do it another day,' he said so loudly and so quickly that I regretted refusing." She responded, "'No, I shall cancel my dinner, and I shall go to your house.' He implored me, 'Do not miss it; that would hurt me greatly.'" Mogador said, "There was one child of Israel in this group, and he was falling in love with me." She continued, "We kept our promise to M. H[ermann], and we went along to spend the evening with him." They played cards. "H[ermann] was seated next to me, and he was giving me advice. He was more interested in me than in my cards." She had to fight him off by saying she cared deeply for him but could never love a Jewish man.

Cohen's response to this is interesting in view of his subsequent life. "I swear, Céleste," he replied with a gravity that did not lack wit, "that it is not my fault that I am of Jacob's race. If we could be born as adults, and if we could choose our religion, I would become a Catholic to please you." While this was going on, someone entered the room and came up to shake Cohen's hand. Her heart skipped a beat; it was Alfred de Musset. She leaned on Hermann's shoulder as if for protection—her one fear being that he would recognize her

---

[1] Mémoires de Celeste Mogador, Paris Nouvelle, 1858, pp. 70, foll.(My translation.)

and remember where they had met. Fortunately, he moved away. But she kept observing him just in case. Cohen quickly sensed the situation and asked her if she knew him. She denied that she did. But to make matters worse, he went over to speak to de Musset. In the meantime, a young man approached Mogador and said, "You are not very nice. Poor H is madly in love with you." To this, Mogador contributed a little of her own hard-won feminist wisdom. "Oh, you are all alike! In your opinion, to be nice means you have to give yourself to whoever wants you." The young man counters, providing an insight into what others thought of the not-yet-reformed dandy: "But with him it is different, his heart is wounded. He is so kind! He has a tender nature." Writing about meeting Cohen in her memoirs, Mogador reflects: "My love affair with H is a sad example of the dangers of passion. Thinking I was satisfying a whim, I might have altered his life instead."[1] When it was time for everyone to go, to the surprise of Mogador's friend Lise, she stayed behind. Mogador continues, "I believe H was overjoyed." To facilitate the swift departure of his guests, he helped them on with their cloaks. Mogador assures us that nothing untoward happened. She explains:

> I placed the stool near the grand piano. I was leaning against it and it was covered with sheets of music notations. I looked at H when he came back inside. He wanted to kiss me, but I stopped him. "If you were sensible you would take me home . . . if you love me, I am going to make you miserable." "I do not care, [he said] "I shall give my life to have you to myself, even if it is just for one day." I pointed to the piano bench. He sat down and kissed my hand. "I am," he said, "between the two great passions of my life." ....Then he played from the depths of his soul and improvised with such delight that my heart melted. His music possessed such sweet harmony that it resembled the chants of the church,

---

[1]   Memoirs, p. 123.

but as he became completely taken up with his playing, he seemed to have forgotten me, and I fell asleep in the armchair! When I awoke, I noticed that he had composed some music during the night. . . . H(ermann)'s love increased every day, it tormented him so much that it made him ill. He was so sad that I avoided him as much as I could.[1]

Mogador tells us that from then on when he played music it was melancholy and his piano sounded like a church organ. Then a note of desperation crept in. He seemed infatuated with Celeste, and was behaving in true romantic fashion, complete with threats of killing himself. "If I were not Jewish, you would love me, is that right? If I knew that, I would deny my God for love of you." It was obvious that Cohen was becoming obsessed with the equestrienne. Mogador continued in her *Memoirs*, "One day I saw him enter the church of the Madeleine where he stayed for two hours."[2] Here indeed is an interesting development; the unrequited lover turning to the God he seemed ready to deny. Mogador's friends advised her to forget about him, because "it was better to cause a great grief than let him die slowly." Her friend Sergent decided to deliver the coup de grâce. Mogador continues, "Soon after, I had a letter from him in which he said that his life was not his own and he was putting his trust in in God. The letter was so lofty that I wanted to see him, to ask his forgiveness! He would not see me... I thought he had a mistress, and I felt foolish for being naïve."[3]

After this, of course, they went their separate ways. Cohen continued his search for God, visiting Paris churches for prolonged periods of reflection and prayer.

---

[1] Ibid., pp123-124.

[2] The church of the Madeleine dominates the business sector of Paris. It is a huge structure surrounded by Corinthian columns on the outside and inside resembles a Roman basilica. It contains notable works of art. Mogador lived at 19 Place de la Madeleine at the time.

[3] Mémoires de Celeste Mogador, pp. 223-224.(My translation.)

Mogador next took up with a rich duke and was also courted by an opera singer. This French femme fatale seemed to have had an irresistible attraction for men and held them in thrall. It appears that many were mesmerized by her on a first acquaintance, including Hermann Cohen. The pattern would be repeated many times in her life. Some of these men convinced themselves that they could not live without her and, when frustrated, made attempts on their lives. One of these was a kindly and charming Englishman named Richard. On one occasion when Mogador arrived at his apartment, he pulled out a pistol and aimed it at his head. Mogador threw herself upon him, and the bullet hit a portrait of her that hung on his wall! She quipped that she had been shot in effigy. In her *Memoirs*, describing these events, Mogador opens a later chapter with an item of news that had reached her:

> Then I received some strange news that affected me greatly because it related to the ideas, sentiments and doubts that echoed sadly within me since Lise Sergent's death. This news concerned the poor pianist whom I had accused of infidelity and considered myself weak and credulous. Someone told that after our separation, H had been depressed and had taken ill and doctors couldn't explain the cause of the illness. He was advised to take a change of scene, left for Italy, visited Rome, became a Catholic, and entered a religious community. I found it hard to believe that this decision was made as a result of our separation. In any case, I jokingly replied to the person who told me this news that if I had cursed all my friends like that, the Church would owe me a reward.[1] In my inmost heart, however I was more moved than I cared to admit. I took a dislike to my apartment and

---

[1] She obviously means that in that case more of her suitors would have undergone a conversion experience and become monks!

was unhappy there. I couldn't rest and spent my nights away from home.[1]

Mogador wrote several volumes of *Memoirs*. She tried unsuccessfully to block their publication after her marriage to Count Lionel Moreton de Chabrillan, a union that gave her the respectability she craved. (The *Memoirs* were originally intended to raise funds for a lawsuit against her future in-laws and not intended for publication. There was uproar in Paris when they were first published). De Chabrillan decided to join the gold rush to Australia where his reckless and extravagant lifestyle reduced him to penury. He had a long, miserable, second-class trip to Sydney with a ship full of Irish and English emigrants, many also in search of gold. He eventually made his way to Ballarat and got kitted out as a digger in Sofalo, NSW. Conditions were incredibly difficult for a down-and-out aristocrat. Although the strong Irish navvies were accustomed to handling a spade, the soft hands of the spoiled nobleman were soon badly blistered. In the end, he had only garnered a few crumbs of gold, and he decided to return to Paris. He had hoped to help Mogador fight several lawsuits brought against her by his relatives for what was in fact her own property. With her usual spirit, she took them all on, studying law herself to fight her corner and was mostly successful.

This was the circle in which Mogador moved. From being an illiterate young woman, she became a prolific writer, novelist, and playwright. Her *Memoirs* give us a poignant account of her childhood and the struggles already referred to. Her innate intelligence and independence shine through on every page. You also occasionally come across some nuggets of wisdom scattered throughout her story. The celebrated writer Dumas (Sr) was impressed and spoke of them to many people. In reference to girls caught up in vice, her remarks are just as relevant today as they were 150 years ago. "Superior

---

[1] Memoirs of a Courtesan, p.125.

minds and hearts that have protested in the name of humanity against the black slave trade should also do something about the white slave trade." When he met her, Hermann Cohen was, by her own self-description, of a similar cast of mind to her own. Like him she tended to try her hand at gambling but unlike him, she resisted the temptation to become addicted. She wrote: "It is not like me to feel in moderation—joy, sadness, affection, resentment, laziness, activity. I have magnified them all. My life has been one long excess."[1]

As we reflect on Mogador's life and of other women in similar circumstances, I think of her younger contemporary, St. Thérèse of Lisieux, as a study in contrasts. Thérèse of Lisieux was born and died during the course of Mogador's life. We know Thérèse was much taken with the figure of Mary Magdalene. She felt she herself had been forgiven just as much—because she had been prevented from sinning by God's grace. She writes: "I know that without Him, I could have fallen as low as Saint Mary Magdalene, and the profound words of Our Lord to Simon resound with a great sweetness in my soul. I know that "he to whom less is forgiven, LOVES less," but I also know that Jesus has forgiven me more than Saint Mary Magdalene since He forgave me in advance by preventing me from falling. Ah! I wish I could explain what I feel."[2]

Thérèse shows no awareness of the lifestyle of many young women in Paris in the nineteenth century, and yet we cannot be sure that she was entirely oblivious of it. Her father had lived in Paris for a short time as a young man, and when happily married to his wife Zélie, he confided to her the temptations that came his way. Did he ever communicate to his family of attractive girls the perils of life in Paris? We don't know. Had she heard perhaps that performers on the Paris stage were wont to throw a shower of roses over the heads of the audience? There is no indication that Hermann Cohen ever

---

[1] Memoirs, p.75
[2] Story of a Soul, pp. 83-84.

read Mogador's *Memoirs* or that he was aware of any details of her subsequent life. In her account of their brief relationship, we need to keep in mind the fact that Mogador later became a gifted writer, displaying a vivid imagination.[1]

---

[1] During the Franco-Prussian War, Mogador founded a society called "Sisters of France" to care for soldiers and orphans. She wrote and sang patriotic songs at this time. When she returned to her home after the war, she found that it had been ransacked by the Prussian soldiers. She died in a home run by the Sisters of Charity on February 18, 1909, having survived her husband by fifty-one years.

Chapter 4

Converted by the Eucharist (1847)

In the previous chapter, we left Hermann Cohen floundering around in the aftermath of a broken love affair. We have Celeste Mogador's testimony that Cohen was making the rounds of various Catholic churches and at last beginning to take a serious look at his future. And we can be assured that as he entered and prayed in different churches, including the historic twin-towered Saint-Sulpice,[1] the Lord was drawing Hermann to himself in hidden ways. He didn't consciously want to become a Christian or a Catholic yet; that came more dramatically later.

From here on, we note a paradigm shift in Cohen's lifestyle. Or perhaps it was simply the unchanged romantic now finding a true focus for his affections in God. We have an account of the transition from Cohen's Spanish tutor, Chevalier Charles Asnarez, a Spanish diplomat in Paris.[2] Asnarez has left a description of the elegantly dressed young man who had been taking some Spanish lessons from him but suddenly stopped. Cohen approached him

---

[1] In the wake of Dan Brown's novel *The Da Vinci Code* and resultant film featuring Tom Hanks, this church was in the limelight witnessed a huge surge in tourists.

[2] There is no indication why Cohen was learning Spanish.

with some trepidation, at the corner of Rue Saint Dominique and Rue de Borgogne, as he owed him money for unpaid lessons. The once-elegant young man with polished boots was now very simply dressed. He invited Asnarez to his apartment, which was an austere one indeed. Asnarez observed that it contained only an iron bedstead, a trunk, a piano, a crucifix, a little statue of Our Lady, and two pictures, one of St. Teresa of Avila and one of St. Augustine. "The room was certainly austere as was his dress."[1] Asnarez was to become one of Cohen's first groups of adorers of the Blessed Sacrament. Cohen later wrote to Asnarez about the change that had come over him:

> It happened in the month of May last year in 1847. Mary's month was celebrated with great pomp at the church of St. Valère.[2] Various choirs were playing music and singing, which drew people in. The Prince of Moscow,[3] who organized the music, was known to me; and he asked me if I would stand in for him and direct the choirs. I agreed and went to take my place purely from my interest in music and a desire to do the job well. During the ceremony, nothing affected me much; but at the moment of Benediction, though I was not kneeling like the congregation, I felt something deep within me as if I had found myself. It was like the

---

[1] Beaurin, p. 57.

[2] This church, on the Rue Burgogne, was the site of the "Forty Hours" devotion to the Blessed Sacrament pioneered by Mlle Maurois. The church has since been demolished. The basilica of Sainte-Clothilde now stands on the site.

[3] Joseph Napoleon Ney was the "Prince of Moscow." He was a son of Marchal Ney, one of Napoleon's generals, who fought at Waterloo but was executed by the new regime. It is interesting that Cohen's friend, Joseph Ney, was president of the Jockey Club from 1836-1849; this may be where Cohen got to know him. The Jockey Club was Anglo-French, frequented by Paris celebrities. 'Jockey' could be of Gaelic derivation - *eachaidhe* means *jockey* and is pronounced similarly.

prodigal son facing himself. I was automatically bowing my head. When I returned the following Friday, the same thing happened; and I thought of becoming a Catholic. A few days later, I was passing the same church of St Valère while the bell was ringing for Mass. I went in and attended Mass with devotion and stayed on for several more Masses, not understanding what was holding me there. Even when I came home that evening, I was drawn to return. Again the church bell was ringing and the Blessed Sacrament was exposed for veneration. As soon as I saw it, I felt drawn to the altar rail and knelt down. I bowed my head at the moment of Benediction, and afterwards I felt a new peace in my heart. I came home and went to bed and felt the same thing in my dreams. From then on, I was anxious to attend Mass often, which I did at St. Valère and always with an inner joy.[1]

As I try to make sense of what Cohen describes here, I am reminded of a more recent example of spiritual lightning striking twice and almost in the same place. André Frossard was an eminent atheistic writer who was elected to the Académie Française. Here is his testimonial: "Having entered a chapel in the Latin Quarter of Paris at 5:10 in the morning to look for a friend, I left at 5:15 in the company of a friendship that was not of this earth." Fittingly, Frossard was baptized in the chapel of the Sisters of Adoration on July 8, 1935. Cohen had many dealings as we shall see with Marie-Thérèse Dubouché, the founder of this congregation.

So what exactly was happening in these two cases separated by over a century? In a sense, our story revolves around an effort to find an answer to this question. In Cohen's case, in another letter to Marie-Alphonse Ratisbonne, himself a Jewish convert with whom he had become friendly, he continues the story of his conversion up

---

[1] Beaurin, pp. 58-59.

to the time he was baptized: "At the moment of Benediction, I felt a very real emotion though I cannot describe it, as if I had no right to be taking part in the ceremony. The following Friday, the same thing happened."[1] Cohen was naturally somewhat disturbed, and he consulted his friend the Duchess of Rauzan,[2] who later became his godmother, with a view to her introducing him to a priest. Again he writes to Ratisbonne:

> I told her I wished to see a priest to talk things over. This was amazing seeing I distrusted them. However, I didn't meet one immediately, but eventually I was introduced to a priest named Legrand. He listened with interest, calmed me, and told me to continue as I was doing. He told me to trust in Divine Providence who would show me what to do. At the end, he gave me the book, *An Account of Christian Teaching.* I found this churchman good and kind and he certainly changed my opinion of priests, having only known them in the pages of novels where they threatened excommunication and hell-fire. Now I had met a learned man, humble, kind, and open-minded, looking to God— not himself. So in this frame of mind, I left for Ems in Germany to give a concert. As soon as I arrived there, I sought out the parish priest of the little Catholic church, as I had a letter of introduction from Père Legrand. The day after I arrived was a Sunday, but braving the ridicule of my friends, I went to Mass. Everything affected me—the hymns and prayers and God's invisible presence. I was very moved and felt the Lord was touching me. When the priest raised the host, my tears began to flow. It was a consoling

---

[1]   Ibid., p.59.
[2]   Her husband, the Duke of Rauzan, ambassador to France and Turin (1830), was Minister Plenipotentiary to Portugal (1825). The Duchess conducted a salon in Paris frequented by Chopin, Liszt, Cohen, and others. She had also been a pupil of Liszt.

and unforgettable moment. . . . Lord you were there with me filling me with your divine gifts. I really prayed to you, all-powerful and all-merciful God, and this memory of your beauty would be impressed on my inner being, proof against all attack, together with lasting gratitude for your favours. . . . I felt then what Augustine must have felt in the garden of Cassiacum when he heard the famous words, "Take and read" . . . or what you yourself must have felt in St. Andrew's church in Rome on January 20, 1843, when Our Lady appeared to you.[1] I remembered having cried as a child, but I certainly never experienced tears like these. And while the tears flowed, a deep sorrow for my past welled up. I immediately wanted to confess everything to the Lord, all the sins of my life. There they were all before me, countless and despicable and deserving God's punishment. But at the same time, I felt a deep peace that really healed me; and I was convinced that the merciful Lord would forgive me and overlook my sins and accept my sorrow. I knew he would forgive me recognizing my resolve to love him above all things from now on. By the time I left the church at Ems, I already felt I was a Christian, or at least as much a Christian as it is possible to be before being baptized.[2]

Cohen attributed the grace of conversion to Our Lady. Here we have a good introduction to what the late Donald Cave, in a study of the Eucharistic movements of Julian Eymard, Hermann Cohen, and their friends, calls "the emotive piety" of Cohen. He writes, "Hermann Cohen was a passionate man refusing all half-measures."[3]

---

[1] Cohen is alluding to the extraordinary circumstances of Ratisbonne's own conversion while visiting the church of St. Andrea dell Fratte in Rome on January 19, 1842.

[2] Beaurin, pp. 59-61.

[3] Donald Cave, *L'Oeuvre encharistique pour les Hommes* (Rome: Religieux de Saint-Sacrament, 985), p. 1-12.(My translation).

The fact that he wished to pursue this matter while temporarily out of the country speaks for itself. Again Cave goes on to say that "he lived the Christian life with the same intensity, and on some occasions, with the same exaggeration, as characterized the years of his youth." Cave is highly critical of Cohen's spirituality while acknowledging his better points. In fact, when Cohen came out of the church in Ems, he met a friend who noticed the change in him and inquired about it. Cohen told her what had happened, and this friend urged him to thank the Blessed Virgin Mary for this grace and be devoted to her. Then she gave him a picture of Mary's assumption. Cohen himself needed no encouragement to attribute favors to Mary, to whom he became increasingly devoted.

Meanwhile, everyone noticed the change, and Cohen himself was anxious to get back to Paris and see Legrand, the first priest to whom he had been introduced. Perhaps at their first encounter, Legrand was somewhat suspicious of his resolve, considering his past life. Now he was more impressed and felt that the Lord was at work. Legrand asked Cohen to take a course of instruction in Christian doctrine, and he came to see Legrand every evening. Cohen enjoyed Catholic worship and liturgy, and he felt he had shed a great burden. He longed for full communion with the church and especially to receive the Eucharist. Cohen's fervent preparation reminds us how intensely the English poet Gerard Manley Hopkins wanted to become a Catholic some years later. It was Legrand who had introduced Cohen to Marie-Alphonse Ratisbonne, who shared a similar Jewish background to himself. At this time, the Ratisbonne brothers had begun a movement for converted Jewish girls that was growing into the Institute of Our Lady of Sion. Together with his brother, Theodore, he would also found societies for men and women dedicated to Our Lady of Sion. By coincidence, they would develop their congregation in England around the same time as Cohen was restoring the Carmelite Order there. Hermann Cohen, of course, was not exceptional in being Jewish and converting to Christianity. There were many other examples. The two Ratisbonne brothers mentioned above, Theodore and Marie-Alphonse, preceded him into the church and were actively involved in promoting the conversion of Jews, who were numerous in Paris. Naturally, members of the Jewish community resisted this vehemently, and the Ratisbonnes met with stiff opposition.

Venerable Francis Libermann was another famous Jewish convert early in the century with a career that, to some extent, paralleled that of Cohen. As young men, they both read anticlerical authors like Voltaire and Rousseau, which led to long periods of darkness and agnosticism. Both looked forward with great eagerness to baptism, and both record something of a mystical experience at the moment when the waters of baptism flowed over them. And like Cohen, too, soon after baptism, Libermann wished to train for the priesthood. When Libermann moved to Paris, he attended the College Stanislaus,[1] where Cohen would later become professor of music. He also attended St. Sulpice, and this church figures prominently in Cohen's life. Imbibing a missionary spirit from his friends, Libermann founded the Congregation of the Immaculate Heart of Mary in 1842; and in 1848, he joined the Holy Ghost congregation, and the two merged into one. In recent years, the congregations have become known as Spiritans.[2] Another notable convert at the time was Eugénie Foa, a woman writer under the name of Maria Fitz-Clarence.[3]

Cohen attended the reception of some Jewish converts at the Paris chapel of the Sisters of Sion, which had been founded by

---

[1] College Stanislaus was a college of the University of France and numbered many famous names as professors. In addition to Cohen, we find Maurice Blondel, Henri Lacordaire, Frédéric Ozanam, and Jean Baruzi (the latter wrote a controversial study of St. John of the Cross).

[2] It would be entirely appropriate if the holiness of the lives of Cohen and Libermann was eventually recognized and both were beatified.

[3] Foa was an early feminist who, like George Sand, struggled for recognition because of the prejudice of her times. She edited the first periodical aimed at a children's readership. It should be borne in mind too that universal suffrage had been only a recent development.

the Ratisbonnes. He also wanted his own reception to take place there. The date was fixed for August 28, 1847, which was the feast of St. Augustine, whom he would take for his patron. It was a natural choice. On his first visit to the church of Our Lady of Victories, the priest there, Father Charles Desgenettes, spoke on St. Augustine; and Cohen's godmother, the Duchess of Rauzan, chose this name for him. Cohen recalled that he was first touched by grace in Mary's month of May. He would later refer to her as "Mother of the Eucharist," since he felt it was she who revealed Christ to him. Just before his reception, Cohen experienced a sharp struggle, taking the form of a dream, which indeed reminds us of the struggle of his patron.[1] In the Carmelite Order, he would be known as Father Augustine-Mary of the Most Blessed Sacrament.

Another venue for his reception was discussed, so they considered having it at Legrand's church, which was on the site of the old Carmelite church, the scene of the martyrdom of so many friars during the French Revolution. Later it was decided that Ratisbonne's church would be more appropriate. Of the day of his reception into the church, Cohen writes:

> On Saturday, August 28, at three o'clock, the chapel of Our Lady of Sion was brightly lit by candles and the altar adorned with fresh flowers. The chapel bells were ringing, there was a full congregation, and the choir consisted of young girls wearing white veils singing beautifully, and accompanied by the organ. Both Father Legrand and Father Ratisbonne led me into the church. I was feeling nervous but calm, accompanied by my godfather (Dr. Gouraud)[2] and godmother (Duchess of Rauzan). I really felt the support of my brothers and sisters at my spiritual birth. God be forever blessed.[3]

---

[1] See *Confessions of St. Augustine.*

[2] Henri Gouraud cooperated with the famous Paris clinician Armand Trousseau to test homeopathic techniques, two of the first doctors to do so.

[3] Beaurin, pp. 64-65.

In a letter to Ratisbonne, he related how the ritual proceeded:

> "Do you wish to be baptized?"
> "Yes, I do wish it."
> (Yes, you know, Lord, how much I want it. I want to belong to you.)

> Everything was transformed, I was hardly aware of the priest with the holy water shell in his hand. The Lord had promised to possess me at this moment. The priest was pouring the holy water with triple gesture over my forehead and proclaimed solemnly that he baptized me in the name of the Father and of the Son and of the Holy Spirit. . . . At that moment, I was deeply moved; and I can only describe it like an electric shock. My eyes were closed, but I had an inner vision as if the Holy Spirit, as though to seal his promise, took me by the hand and revealed to my gaze, rapt in ecstasy, while directed above, that which no finite being can ever understand—the infinite. Yes I saw (the eyes of my body were closed but those of my soul were awake with joy) a great and unlimited brightness, space without end, or rather not space, for my gaze soared, plunged always further, further . . . and met no obstacle.

Cohen continues to describe in rather glowing terms what he saw and felt.

> A gentle warmth penetrated me and, in spite of the brilliant light which radiated from all sides, my gaze never tired of plunging into the rays of light . . . for deep within there was an even brighter light . . . and there stood a glorious throne and seated on the throne was Our Lord Jesus Christ, beautiful with eternal youth, with his beloved mother on his right, and around his feet a host of saints clothed in the brightest colors of the rainbow. . . . The

saints were prostrated at the foot of the throne in adoration and yet at the same time they looked toward me and smiled kindly. . . . Heaven and its inhabitants seemed to rejoice at my baptism as though the poor soul of a redeemed sinner weighed in the balance of eternity. Well, dear father, how can I be so foolish as to try to describe what I saw. Indeed I should tear up this paper on which I have written, because it doesn't contain a single image remotely approaching what I have seen! Yes, I have seen the abode of the Church Triumphant. . . . No, it was not a vision; it was an apparition. God permitted that I, though unworthy, be given by a grace that is nameless, to conceive, to see in an instant what I hardly dare remember.[1]

Clearly, Cohen's conversion marked a transition phase in his life. We see how his soul-searching yielded unforeseen results. Pivotal to the story are the twin theological themes of Eucharist and Mary (the month of May), but for Cohen there was just one— Mary, Mother of the Eucharist. As we scan these events, it appears that a thunderbolt of grace can indeed strike people unawares. Cohen referred to Augustine of Hippo, but we could also point further back to Paul of Tarsus on the Damascus road. Cohen himself, Charles de Foucauld, and André Frossard are all examples of newfound faith that are extremely hard to explain away or dismiss out of hand.

The phenomenon we have witnessed in Cohen's dramatic conversion experience, then, cries out for further investigation. Like other such stories, it didn't take place in a vacuum but emerges from a web of human relationships. The main characters in the cast with Cohen are Marie-Thérèse (Theodelinde Dubouché), now Blessed, who founded the Sisters of Adoration; Theodore

---

[1] Ibid., p. 34. Sylvain, p.39. This experience and other similar ones seem like those described by St. Teresa and St. John of the Cross in their writings.

and Marie-Alphonse Ratisbonne; Raymond de Cuers; and Peter Julian Eymard. There were others also. Certainly the story doesn't quite break the mould of nineteenth-century French Eucharistic spirituality, but there are hints that the whole religious movement was opening to the future.

French spirituality exerted, you could say, a disproportionate influence on the wider church. This can be partially explained by the widespread dissemination of French spirituality throughout the world by its missionary outreach. There is something about the French character that seems at home with the mystical. Thérèse of Lisieux is one example. Thérèse's mysticism goes further and deeper than the norm. Her spirituality was remarkably devoid of the unusual or sensational. The more noticeably extraordinary mystics were legion in France at this time. As we shall see, Dubouché had several visions regarding the Eucharist. The Carmelite Sister Marie of St. Pierre had very similar visions in Tours, focusing on the Holy Face of Jesus. Marie-Eustelle Harpain of La Rachelle was another lay mystic who had a great influence on Eymard and Cohen. She spoke of Jesus as "a prisoner of the tabernacle," a theme we will meet in both Cohen and Thérèse of Lisieux. Eymard as well as Cohen also became taken up with the child visionaries of La Salette. This event, which occurred in 1846, created a great stir in France at the time. One day, while working in the fields, two children beheld a seated lady weeping dejectedly as she called for prayer and reparation. It presaged the more lasting phenomenon of Lourdes twelve years later. In regard to unusual phenomena, St. John Vianney, and to a lesser extent Eymard, appear to have often encountered the darker side of the supernatural, and the holy curé seems to have diced daily with the devil. In later life, Eymard, like the Curé d'Ars, complained about being occasionally buffeted by Satan. What are we to make of all this? We can, of course, rush to consult good spiritual guides, and none are clearer than St. John of the Cross and St. Teresa of Avila. Almost three hundred years earlier, they dealt with these questions on an almost daily basis.

Was there something in the nineteenth-century atmosphere that, to misquote Blake, could "see a world in a grain of sand and eternity in an hour"?

In the following chapter, we will see how dedication to the Eucharist opens up new horizons for Cohen and brings him into contact with a huge upsurge of Eucharistic piety in Paris and beyond. We will take a closer look at the people already mentioned who were intimately involved in these events.

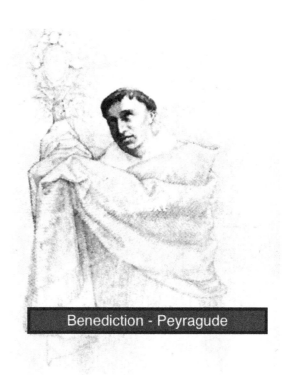

Benediction - Peyragude

Chapter 5

Movement for Eucharistic Adoration (1848)

My well-beloved when all do sleep
And seem to overlook your love;
Allow me at least a vigil keep
Alone with you in this abode.[1]

It is now time to become further acquainted with some of the people referred to already in this book: Bl. Marie-Thérèse (Theodelinde) Dubouché and St. Peter Julian Eymard. Both were significant people in the life and apostolate of Hermann Cohen in the early stages. First we need to take a look at the historical context. The year 1848 was one of dramatic change throughout Europe, a year of international revolution. This became known as the "Springtime of the Nations," just as the revolutions in Arab countries are referred to as the "Arab Spring." and in Prague, in

---

[1] Psalm 118:35, "Memor fui Nocte." This canticle is appropriately called "NocturnalAdoration," put to music by Hermann Cohen for organ or piano, from a collection called "Love of Jesus Christ." Cohen's friend, Sister Marie-Pauline, who composed the verses, lived in the Visitation Convent situated on the Rue d'Enfer.

1968, the "Prague Spring."[1] In 1848, there were uprisings against the established conservative order by motley groups of revolutionaries in many European cities: Vienna, Venice, Milan, Prague, Budapest, Krakow, Berlin, and of course, Paris itself, with the notable exception of London.[2] This was the year in which Marx and Engels published "The Communist Manifesto." In the Paris revolution that broke out in February, Louis-Philippe, the Citizen King, was deposed, and the second empire was ushered in. Louis-Philippe and his wife Queen Amelie fled to England in disguise.[3] Turmoil on this scale had not been seen since the French Revolution and there was much anarchy and bloodshed on the streets of Paris with thousands of people killed.

Cohen's thoughts however, seem to have been elsewhere. Gone were the strong political leanings shared in his youth with

---

[1] Sadly the 'Arab Spring' has now turned into a worldwide winter.

[2] A Chartist movement had begun in England ten years before. There were mass demonstrations in London, but the movement was crushed by the government in 1848 precisely because the establishment feared a revolution. In Ireland resistance to British rule persisted for centuries. In 1848 an unsuccessful revolution was confined to rural areas, especially Tipperary. (Battle of the Widow McCormack's cabbage patch'!) Here Thomas Francis Meagher took a leading role. He was later sentenced to Transportation to Tasmania but escaped to America. He fought in the American Civil War as a Brigadier General of the Union side. He later became Governor of Montana. Of a pattern with these revolutions was the revolution in Dresden, Germany, in which Richard Wagner and Cohen's friend Mikhail Bakunin were involved, but it took place in May of the following year. There is no record of Cohen meeting up with Marx, but it is quite possible he did.

[3] In later years, as the widowed and exiled queen, Amelie would ask Hermann Cohen to act as her chaplain in London when the royal couple escaped to England. Their son Ferdinand married Duchess Helena of Mechlenberg-Schlerin, daughter of the Grand Duke who had provided Cohen with letters of introduction to his ambassador in Paris. Ferdinand was killed in a tragic carriage accident.

revolutionary friends.[1] Cohen's prayer life grew in intensity, and he spent long hours in church. It might be more correct to say that he was still politically aware but now looked to prayer for a solution to France's problems, as did many others.

Hermann Cohen played a leading part in promoting a movement for Nocturnal Adoration of the Blessed Sacrament in France, which was later to become very popular. Another traditional devotion had been renewed in 1843 by Mademoiselle Maroy (or de Marois) known as the Quarant' Ore, or Forty Hours adoration, which began at St. Valère, the church that sparked off Cohen's conversion. This practice acted as a spur for the nocturnal adoration movement.

Moreover, diurnal or daily adoration was already commonplace in Paris. Cohen's friend, Leon Dupont, "the Holy Man of Tours,"[2] describes how the movement started in Paris in November 1848:

> One afternoon the pious convert who loved to visit those sanctuaries where the Blessed Sacrament was exposed, entered the chapel of the Carmelite nuns,[3] and knelt in adoration before Our Lord in the Sacred Host exposed in a monstrance for veneration, without counting the hours or perceiving that night was coming on. It was in the month of November. A portress-sister came in and gave the signal to retire. After waiting some time she had to repeat the signal. Then Hermann said to her: `I will leave at the same time as the persons I see

[1] Although in his sermon at the profession of Bernard Bauer, he gives the impression they both fought under the same flag in 1848 (see "Selections from the Writings of Hermann Cohen" at the end of this book).

[2] Dupont was responsible for the second group of Nocturnal Adorers outside Paris.

[3] The convent was situated on the Rue d'Enfer in Paris, now Rue Denfert-Rochereau near the Orleans road. Later the Marists would also set up here in a house that formerly belonged to Chateaubriand. Under the influence of Berulle, Eucharistic Adoration was practiced here from the beginning. Because of the number of religious houses here, including the Visitation already mentioned, someone referred to it as "heaven on the street of hell!"

at the far end of the chapel.` But *(the sister said,)* these persons will not go out all night.` This answer of the sister was more than enough ; and planted a precious germ in a heart well disposed not to let it vanish in smoke. He who was afterwards to be called the Angel of the Tabernacle hastened at once from the chapel to M. de la Bouillerie.`I have just been turned out,` he exclaimed, `from a chapel where women remain before the Blessed Sacrament the whole night long?`[1]

Theodelinde Dubouché.

She had painted an image of the Holy Face displayed in the Carmelite chapel. She was a fervent person and much devoted to the passion of Christ. In 1846, during Holy Week, some relics of the passion were on display in Notre Dame Cathedral, and Dubouché attended mass there. After Communion she was haunted by the thought *"The Blessed Sacrament is more than all."* She became more drawn to the Eucharist and felt "bound to the tabernacle." Around this time she discovered Carmel and wished to join. On July 8, 1848, a Carmelite nun, Sister Mary of St. Pierre died with a saintly reputation in the convent at Tours. The work of reparation played a big part in her spirituality.[2] St. Thérèse and her sisters acknowledged that they inherited their devotion to the Holy Face from Mary de St. Pierre as transmitted by their founder Sister Genevieve.[3] Thérèse's sister Céline created a beautiful painting of the Holy Face after Thérèse's death. Her uncle Isidore Guerin had sent her the first

---

[1] Sylvain, pp 56-57.
[2] An account of Dubouché's life published in English in 1938 carries the subtitle *A Forerunner of Saint Thérèse of Lisieux.* The Carmel of Tours was first founded by St. Teresa's friend Blessed Anne of Saint Bartholomew.
[3] Leon Dupont, the "Holy Man of Tours," was influenced by Sister Mary and promoted the devotion. A strong component of reparation was built into both the Holy Face devotion and that of Eucharistic Adoration.

photo of the Shroud of Turin, taken by the Italian photographer Secondo Pia in 1898, on which she based her painting.

A year later, Dubouché gathered a group of like-minded young women around her and they began to meet for prayer in the chapel of the Carmel early in 1848. Dubouché organized a forty-day period of penance in the Carmel, and after the Octave of Corpus Christi she arranged a novena of adoration leading up to the feast of the Sacred Heart. In June, a bloody revolution raged on the streets of Paris. We have to admire the courage of these young women who met to pray in spite of cannon fire all around them. On the night of June 29/30, Dubouché had a mystical experience. In her own words, "The Eucharistic veils disappeared; I saw Our Lord on the altar as on a throne; he set a tube of gold against his heart, with its other extremity on mine; then he set flowing into my being a life-force which would have killed me were it not for a miracle. I found myself lost in a superabundance of light and love!" Then Jesus told her he wished her to originate a group that would have similar experience and would "placate" his Father. Then Dubouché realized clearly that she was to begin this "work."[1]

She set to work immediately, and by August 6, the feast of the Transfiguration, Dubouché had inaugurated a "Third Order" of reparation integrally linked to Carmel and consisting of the young women she had already gathered together. The prioress was enthusiastic about the project, given the adoration tradition in the convent. This would later grow into the present congregation now known as the "Family of Adoration," with houses in twenty-three countries. Dubouché would later change her name to Marie-Thérèse.

This digression was necessary to explain Cohen's "lock-out" experience at the Carmel—it was a women-only group. Furthermore, Dubouché's role is important in the ensuing events that form part

---

[1] The French term is *Oeuvre*, and this word would be used widely in this context by Dubouché and her associates including Hermann Cohen.

of our story. Cohen consulted his confessor, vicar general of Paris, Francois de la Bouillerie, who told him, "You find the men and we will allow you to do the same."[1] De La Bouillerie himself was a frequent adorer of the Eucharist at the chapel of Carmel. He was the originator of perpetual adoration in the home, whereby people undertook to observe an hour's adoration in their homes from eight in the evening until eight in the morning. So Cohen set himself the task of finding companions for this work. He thought of going to the church of Our Lady of Victories, which he loved and where he knew that Cyrille de Mont de Benque might be interested. It was in this church that he had been introduced to this devout young man named de Benque by Abbe Desgenettes. Cohen approached de Benque and in fact he was interested in taking part, and together they recruited up to seventeen more men. They saw their prayer vigils as an answer to the problems of the times in the light of the recent violent events. They met together in Cohen's room at 102 Rue de L'Université on November 22, and thus the Association of Nocturnal Adorers was born. The first official meeting for adoration took place on December 6, 1848, in the Basilica of Our Lady of Victories.[2] This first meeting was also a response to the recent news that the pope had been forced to leave Rome in disguise and set up his Curia in Gaeta, near Naples. In the basilica (attached to the pillar near the altar of St. Augustine), there is a marble plaque recalling the first meeting for night adoration and its founder.[3]

---

[1] Sylvain, p.57.

[2] St. Peter Julian Eymard would later refer to this event: "The furies of '93 and its impiety are let loose . . . and no hope of salvation looming on the horizon. But a timely thought inspires a few pious souls: they would save France by perpetual adoration", (André Guitton, *Peter Julian Eymard: Apostle of the Eucharist* [Ponteranica, Italy: Centro Eucharistico, 1996)

[3] The inscriptions reads, "The movement for Exposition and Night Adoration of the Blessed Sacrament in Paris was inaugurated in this church on December 6, 1848, through the efforts of Father Hermann and Monsignor de la Bouillerie, then Vicar General of the Diocese of Paris."

The church of Our Lady of Victories was Louis Martin's favorite refuge for prayer during his time in Paris and on subsequent visits.[1] He introduced his family to this church also. Thérèse herself passed over the glories of Paris and Notre Dame to sing the praises of this little church that for her was the jewel in the crown of Paris. In recent years, a new central altar, octagonal in shape, has been installed in the basilica. It contains eight panels illustrating the stories of those connected with the church. One of these is dedicated to St. Thérèse of Lisieux to commemorate her link with the church. On May 13, 1883, she was cured during the course of a novena of Masses being offered there. Thérèse tells us in her autobiography that the Blessed Virgin smiled at her and cured her. On November 4, 1887, she visited there with her father and sister Céline on her way to Rome in order to thank Our Lady for her intercession. It was because of the connection with St. Thérèse that Pope Pius XI raised the church to the rank of basilica in 1927. Another panel of the altar is devoted to Hermann Cohen, her Carmelite brother. It depicts him holding a chalice and host accompanied by a colleague and with a pipe organ in the background, suggesting his musical accomplishments. It is indeed a fitting tribute to two Carmelites whose memories are enshrined in this place of prayer. This unprepossessing church is the most frequented shrine of Our Lady in the whole of Paris. There are supposed to be around 30,000 plaques covering the walls as expressions of thanks from grateful members of the faithful.

Later, as Bishop of Carcassonne, Cohen would preach the panegyric here at the funeral of Henri Lacordaire.

[1]   On his first visit to this church, Cohen heard the priest Charles Desgenettes preach on St. Augustine. Notably it impacted greatly on English conversion since the Passionist priest Ignatius Spencer, now beatified and a relative of Princess Diana, visited the church around this time and prayed there for the conversion of England. This was followed up by a visit of Bishop Wiseman to Desgenettes the same year. By the following year, Blessed John Henry Newman with Frederick Faber and others joined the Catholic Church. Newman called to the church later on his way to Rome.

Meanwhile, de La Bouillerie was anxious that the movement should grow and become a good influence for Paris and indeed the whole of France. He wanted to make the Carmel the center of the overall endeavor, with Dubouché as the directress of the Third Order, coordinating the whole association. Unfortunately, things didn't work out quite like that.

As Cohen's Nocturnal Adoration group expanded, they had to look for other premises to avoid disrupting parish activities at Our Lady of Victories. At the end of January 1849, Cohen, Count Raymond de Cuers, and Charles Fage approached the Marists on Rue Montparnasse. De Cuers was a leading navy captain on sick leave in Paris. Fage was a military attaché who died soon after Cohen entered the Carmelites. Cuers was born in Cadiz, Spain, of French parents. He was later ordained as a member of Julian Eymard's newly founded Blessed Sacrament congregation and became its second superior general. Spiritually, his temperament was very close to that of Cohen's. It was here Cohen also met Peter Julian Eymard, now canonized, who was on a visit to Paris for the first time. Eymard was a Marist priest at the time and vicar general of the congregation. Cohen asked permission from him to continue their prayer vigils there; Eymard willingly granted this permission. Furthermore, he allowed Cohen and his assistant Cuers and Fage to reside in the Marist community. Eymard was greatly impressed by Cohen and his two followers, and they seemed to have inspired him to pursue the idea of a religious congregation devoted to the Eucharist. Damien Cash writes, "As Cave and others have argued, Eymard's Eucharistic spirituality had been evolving, but this contact with the Paris group was the catalyst that reaffirmed his 'early attraction for Communion' and his rejection of Jansenism's emphasis on infrequent reception of the Sacrament."[1] Here they lived on subsistence diet, and their devout lifestyle showed all the exuberance of first fervor. For instance, they

---

[1] Damien Cash, *The Road to Emmaus.* (Kew East, Australia: Congregation of the Blessed Sacrament Fathers and David Lovell Publishing, 2007, p.11).

would not turn their backs on the Blessed Sacrament exposed but would backtrack from their places in the chapel, sustaining bruised elbows and knees in the process.

When the new home of the Blessed Sacrament Fathers was set up in the Villa Chateaubriand on the Rue d'Enfer, Cohen's friends, the Lemann brothers, also Jewish converts, provided them with furniture. When they had to move to a new property on the Rue de Faubourg Saint Jacques, Cohen obtained a generous donation from a Carmelite convent for the purchase of the house. Later tensions developed between Eymard and Cohen. Eymard and Dubouché are major figures in the evolution of Eucharistic devotion in France in the 19th century, and there was a veritable explosion of such devotion at this period. Both were founders of religious institutes still flourishing in the church. Eymard's own Eucharistic understanding was evolving around the time of his first visit to Paris. He was pleased to encounter perpetual adoration groups there.

However in spite of the bright ideals of Eucharistic devotion shown by all involved, dark clouds were gathering on the horizon. The storm centered on the tension between Monsignor de la Bouillerie and Monsignor Jean-Joseph Gaume, and it involved the Carmel itself. In February 1849, the question arose of reappointing a superior for the Paris Carmels. Dubouché explained that though the incumbent Gaume had held the position for a long time, De La Bouillerie would be hurt if he were not chosen in view of his commitment to Eucharistic adoration. The nuns were caught in a dilemma. They opted to stay with Gaume, and the decision had immediate deleterious consequences for them. Dubouché tells us that both

De La Bouillerie and Marois opposed them strongly.[1] As vicar general, Gaume tried to prevent her from getting her new religious

[1] Donald Cave describes this good lady who caused so much trouble for Dubouché as "this ardent, energetic, and it would seem, tyrannical apostle of devotion the Holy Eucharist!"

institute off the ground. Despite these obstacles, Dubouché prevailed: in May 1849, she made religious profession, and on June 15, feast of the Sacred Heart, she and her companions received the religious habit. A further factor emerged at this time when Dubouché became convinced that her movement for reparatory adoration should not be confined to women but also be extended to men—and specifically to the Marist Fathers. Consulting her Marist director, she was pleasantly surprised to be told that the founder, Jean-Claude Colin, was at that moment considering setting up Marist contemplative branch or, as Dubouché understood it, "Brothers and Fathers of the Blessed Sacrament." (This would eventually happen under the ex-Marist Julian Eymard.)

Marie-Thérèse Dubouché had a very complete Eucharistic understanding, in many ways anticipating developments in the next century and leading up to our own times. Though herself a visionary, she never allowed her mystical experience to deprive her of a down-to-earth and practical approach. She had certainly imbibed the Carmelite spirit, and some of her reflections were echoed in later years by St. Thérèse and Bl. Elizabeth of the Trinity. She enlisted her visions to serve her apostolate of prayer, involving the people around her. In this she greatly resembles St. Teresa of Avila. Like Teresa, she too encountered more than her share of opposition. By the end of the year, she found herself on the horns of another dilemma. Her religious family would naturally tend to expand but where to? As we saw, it was already linked to her local Carmel as a third order regular. Though the prioress was supportive, other Carmels were not. One horn of the dilemma prevented her from linking up with additional Carmels, and the other prevented her from separating from Carmel. The spurned vicar general appeared to be behind this. He made it clear that he would not favor further expansion. It must have come as a great relief to her when Bouillerie was appointed bishop of Carcassonne in the south of France.[1] After confiding in the Marist

---

[1] Later still de La Bouillerie was appointed coadjutor archbishop of Bordeaux. He composed some popular hymns such as "L'Ame et l'Ange" that were set

Antoine Bertholon, Dubouché was searching for a way out of this impasse. She decided she would write to the Marist founder Colin, asking that her "family" be adopted into that of the Marists. We do not have Colin's answer, but as it happened she received an invitation to open a house of her "family" in Lyons, the Marist headquarters. She departed Paris for Lyons in December 1850. The invitation came from Eymard. She rented a house on the Place Saint-Jean, and Eymard blessed the new convent on January 28, 1851. Dubouché failed in her objective to associate her new congregation with that of a Marist group, the Third Order of Mary. Leaving her community in place she returned to Paris on February 10.

Endnote

In recent years, the spirit of Foucauld has been popularized in the writings of one of his followers in the Little Brothers of Jesus, Carlo Caretto. Foucauld tells us in his journals that his preferred spiritual reading came from St. Teresa of Avila, St. John Chrysostom, and St. John of the Cross. From his letters, we hear that he copied out many passages from St. Teresa's writings in his notebooks. It is interesting to note also that de Foucauld was influenced by Cohen in his Eucharistic spirituality. He admired Cohen's hymns and often sang them. In his spiritual notes written in the Holy Land (1897–1900), he copied out the following stanza of one of Cohen's motets on the Eucharist entitled "Unum petii a Domino" (One Thing I Ask of the Lord; Ps 26).

As this flickering flame,
Lit by faith unswerving,
Which burns by day and night
Before your altar throne,
So may my heart, my God,
Before you self-consuming,
Become at last all yours,
Become at last all yours.

---

to music by Cohen (*Nouveau Recueil de Cantiques* [1875] p. 255.).

(Charles de Foucauld, *Voyageur dans la nuit* (Paris: Nouvelle Cité, 1979, pp. 13 and 16 and Tierney, p. 40).

Charles de Foucauld was an ardent devotee of the Eucharist, and he used to worship in the Basilica of Sacré-Coeur on Montmartre in Paris. Eucharistic adoration began on this site in a provisional wooden chapel on September 6, 1878. It was organized by Cyril Mont de Benque, one of Cohen's first companions at nocturnal adoration in 1848, thirty years earlier. In the very month and year of Cohen's death (January 1871), Alexander Legentil and a companion made a vow to work for the building of a national church dedicated to the Sacred Heart. Two years later, the National Assembly passed a resolution to build a church on the hill of Montmartre. Surely there is a direct link here with the Eucharistic zeal of Cohen. From the very beginning, exposition of the Blessed Sacrament has been maintained in this basilica day and night. Here we have a conscious effort to counteract the boast of Paris nightclubs that their doors never closed.

Franz Liszt

Chapter 6

From Franz Liszt to John of the Cross

*A*t this stage in his story, Hermann Cohen, the recent convert, now intended to clear the debts he had incurred in his gambling days, and these were quite considerable. To achieve this aim, he resumed giving piano lessons. At the same time, Cohen continued to join his friends in weekly nocturnal adoration before the Blessed Sacrament. Since his conversion and even before his baptism, Cohen had expressed to friends the desire to dedicate his life wholly to God as soon as he was free to do so. It would take him two years to reach that point. It was a difficult period for him.

At this time he lived with his artist friend Adalbert de Beaumont and Beaumont's elderly cousin, Baroness de Saint-Vigor, both non practising Catholics.[1] At the very least, they found he talked about religion a bit too much. Beaumont thought he was crazy and mockingly touched his head in his presence to indicate as much. Perhaps Cohen didn't take offense. He tried to influence some of his friends in favour of the Catholic faith, sometimes with an understandable, if exaggerated, zeal due to the newfound faith of the convert. He admitted he could become quite aggressive

---

[1] De Beaumont was a successful artist and designer and promoted interest in Islamic art in Paris. He died in 1869.

defending his religious positions against his former worldly friends. The baroness slowly began to take her faith seriously, and despite her repugnance to making a general confession, eventually did so. Cohen was relieved he had not needed a general confession himself, since all his sins were forgiven by the sacrament of baptism. Later, he parted company with Beaumont.

Cohen certainly moved in high society. He mentions how on one occasion he felt embarrassed by his mud-splashed appearance while visiting the Austrian ambassador Count Rudoph Apponyi and his wife.[1] Though they were gracious to the dishevelled visitor, he made his getaway as soon as possible. Another of his acquaintances was the famous Russian anarchist Mikhail Bakunin, then living in Paris.[2] When the two met up in the street, Bakunin mocked Cohen's newfound sanctity.

It is interesting to note that Cohen, even after his "miraculous" conversion, still felt vulnerable to his old demons at times. He acknowledged as much on one occasion when he had a game of cards with his friend Abbé Goeschler, also a Jewish convert and the principal of the College Stanislaus where Cohen taught music.

---

[1] Their house was in the fashionable Faubourg Saint-Germain. As if to demonstrate the mobility of the aristocracy in those days, we find the countess's name cropping up among the attendance at church functions in London in the 1860s when Cohen was there to establish the Carmelite Order in England. Friend of Liszt also, she would have frequented the Paris salons.

[2] Bakunin was a revolutionary figure and, in 1849, was one of the leaders in the insurrection at Dresden. Bakunin bungled both the insurrection and his escape attempt. The composer Richard Wagner was also involved but managed to escape separately, not being with the main perpetrators when they were arrested in their beds. Later on Bakunin became acquainted with Marx and Engels and translated *Das Kapital* into French. "Bakunin was a fantasist and an anti-Semite. He hated Marx and Marxists because he considered Marx, being German (it was bad enough that he was Jewish) a naturally obedient slave of the state who would bring about a totalitarian slave state if he ever got his way." (Note from my nephew Kieran O'Meara.)

The stakes were low, only two sous (about forty-eight cents), but he experienced a resurgence of the old scary excitement of his gambling days, and his conscience troubled him as a result.

Cohen became involved with helping the poor through the Society of St. Vincent de Paul founded by his contemporary Frédéric Ozanam.[1] Cohen found this work a great source of inspiration while he prepared to enter a religious order. He subsequently supported the society by making appeals for them and using his musical talents to give fund-raising concerts for the poor. Cohen's mother Rosalie had been kept in the dark about his conversion. His brother Louis was anxious for her to know, but his sister Henrietta didn't wish to tell her. Since Cohen visited his mother every week, this must have created a tense atmosphere. She seems to have guessed that there was something unusual, but Cohen remained evasive. Eventually his friend Baroness de Saint-Vigor decided to break the news. At first, she probably didn't take it seriously and thought it was just one more eccentricity in her favorite son.

At this point in his life, Cohen began to compose music for a collection of hymns that were written by a friend of his. These were called, "Praise of Mary," and turned out to be a successful venture as the hymns proved very popular. Cohen needed to give a final concert to pay off all his debts. It was a resounding success. Some of his earlier concerts had not been well prepared. A Marist friend, Father Reculon, who accompanied him to this last concert, tells us that there was thunderous applause at the final curtain. He added that if the audience had known this was the last time they would hear Cohen's glorious interpretations of Beethoven, Mozart, Liszt, and Chopin, their enthusiasm would have broken all bounds.[2] As for Cohen, he rejoined his friend in the dressing room of St. Cecilia's Hall and threw out his arms in the dramatic gesture of the romantic.

---

[1] Frédéric Ozanam, now Blessed, was an influential Catholic lay person and the youngest-ever professor at the Sorbonne.

[2] Sylvain, p. 64.

"Ah," he exclaimed, "I have finished with the world forever; with what joy, after my final note, I took my bow and bade it adieu."[1]

So now Cohen was free to look for a religious way of life and searched widely for the right one for him. It seems he was attracted to the Carmelites and wished to be enrolled in the brown scapular of Our Lady of Mount Carmel, in the convent chapel of Carmelite nuns with which he was already familiar. The first priests he consulted discouraged him from joining the Carmelites, so he turned his attention to the Benedictines, who had been recently established at Solesmes by Dom Prosper Guéranger. But a vocation to the Benedictines didn't materialize. He consulted the great orator, Henri Lacordaire, who with great difficulty restored the Dominican Order to France. When Cohen inquired of Lacordaire if he thought he had the necessary qualities to become a religious, Lacordaire asked, "Have you the courage to allow someone to strike you on the cheek and say nothing?" "I have," was the reply. "In that case," said Lacordaire, "become a monk."[2]

Cohen wrote to his friend Count Raymond de Cuers, "I have consulted people with the greatest insight in spiritual matters," and mentions Abbé Charles Desgenettes of Our Lady of Victories; the Jesuit Gustave de Ravignan, like Lacordaire a great preacher at Notre Dame Cathedral; and the Marist priest Antoine Bertholon, with whom he worked in the adoration movement. The work of Guéranger and Lacordaire paved the way for the return of Carmelites and other religious Orders to France in the nineteenth century. In particular, Guéranger's work for the liturgical movement as evidenced in his monumental work *The Liturgical Year* is of the first importance.

---

[1]   Ibid.

[2]   Flamme Ardente, p. 89. At an earlier period, Prosper Guéranger and Henri Lacordaire were close collaborators and disciples of Félicité Lamennais, who was the leader of a group of disciples. They largely wrote the articles for his newspaper *L'Avenir*. All three eventually split up, Guéranger "heaping abuse" on Lacordaire, as would Cohen's friend, the journalist Louis Veuillot.

Timothy Tierney

Teresian Carmelites Return to France

As early as 1812 efforts were made to restore Teresian Carmelite Friars to France in the aftermath of the French Revolution. Bruno Dumesnil opened a house in Paris but the community dispersed through political circumstances only three years later. There were of course scattered Carmelite friars in France, as were members of other suppressed Orders, who were no longer in community, but these never came together to make a new beginning. Bathilde de St. Exupery, became prioress of the Carmel of Bordeaux in 1826. She was a member of a noble family that originated in the Perigord in southern France.[1] Mother Bathilde had written to the Carmelites in Spain about the possibility of making a foundation of Carmelite friars in France, but at first was met with a refusal. In 1827 some friars arrived in Bordeaux from Spain and set up a community there, but again this project came to nothing. Bathilde, showing great persistence, then tried the papal nuncio in Paris and the Carmelite headquarters in Rome, but nothing happened. Then almost ten years later, in 1839, a Spanish Carmelite priest, Father Dominic (Arbizu y Munarriz), came on the scene. Dominic was born in Puente de la Reyna in Navarre on May 7, 1799. In due course, he joined the Carmelites and became a well-known preacher. He was invited to deliver the panegyric at the funeral of King Ferdinand VII. Father Dominic chose the occasion of the sermon to denounce the liberalism that became rampant after the French Revolution and offer a glowing account of the deceased monarch. In the process he made many enemies. In the complicated succession struggle, Queen Maria-Christina put forward her daughter Isabel, a minor, as successor. Dominic, however, supported the rival claimant, Don Carlos, brother of Ferdinand. Dominic became a chaplain in the army of Don Carlos, and when the Carlists were defeated, he had no

---

[1]   Antoine de St. Exupery, author of the classic *The Little Prince*, belonged to this family.

option but to leave Spain. Dominic simply fled over the Pyrenees—just in the nick of time—and arrived in Bordeaux without passport or resources of any kind, lucky to be alive. Dominic's plan was to take the next ship to Mexico and join his Spanish confrères as a missionary. The local priest Abbé Lafargue, suggested that he visit the Carmelite convent. However, he got off to quite an inauspicious start. For some reason, St. Exupery refused to see the visitor—perhaps she thought he was a vagrant cleric. He had to return three times before he gained admission. She was naturally very embarrassed by this in future years. Eventually when they did meet, St. Exupery made known to him her wish to have a foundation of Carmelite friars in France. He asked for eight days to consider the matter. When he had ascertained that Cardinal Ferdinand Donnet of Bordeaux was in agreement, he made up his mind to stay on in Bordeaux and work for the restoration of the male branch of the order there.

On October 14, 1840, Father Dominic inaugurated the first house of Carmelite friars (although he himself was the only one) in an empty property that belonged to the Carmel. It was situated at numbers 44 and 46 rue Parmentade, Bordeaux. The place evoked the beginnings of St. Teresa's reform of the friars at Duruelo in Spain. On the eve of the first Sunday of Advent, Father Louis Mary Puyo y Ugarte and a choir brother/deacon, Manuel y Albizu, arrived in Bordeaux to join the new venture. At the end of November a lay brother, Francis Goicoecheandia, joined them from Spain. As so often happens when people entrust themselves to providence, local people rallied round with everything the friars needed.[1]

However, the political situation in France was volatile as always, this time due to the July Revolution of 1830, which saw Louis-Philippe ascend the throne. The church was under siege again, and the new members of the community were arrested. When it was

---

[1] See De Mendiola, Domingo A. Fdez., *El Carmelo Teresiano en la Historia*, Roma 2015, p. 35.

noted that their passports stated they were 'Carlist priests' they were ordered to report to Amiens.[1] The friars were worn out from their journey trying to beg their way to Amiens; when they got as far as Tours – literally footsore and weary – they sought the help of the local Carmelite prioress. She managed to secure the good offices of a high-ranking official, banker and later government minister named Gouin and soon the friars were allowed to return to Bordeaux. Before long, they received some French novices into the community. That same year, the curé of Le Broussey, Etienne-Pierre Guesnau, and his assistant Stanislaus Chenart, happened to have a suitable house and site at their disposal that was earmarked for a religious order. They first offered it to the Capuchins who declined it, and then to the Cistercians who did likewise. When it was offered to Dominic, he came to visit the area and instinctively knew this would be the motherhouse of the restoration in France. All three key foundation members are now buried there – Dominic, Louis and Guesnau (not a Carmelite); in 2008, the remains of Hermann Cohen were interred in the community chapel.[2] Le Broussey, which is about thirty kilometers from Bordeaux, eventually became the novitiate house for the Discalced Carmelite friars in France. Additional houses of friars were soon opened at Montigny and Agen.

Thus the infrastructure of the renewed Carmel in France began to grow under the wise and strong leadership of Father Dominic. We might think it a providential occurrence for Hermann Cohen and for the Order in France, that this took place in the same decade in which he was searching for a religious way of life. Cohen would soon make a significant contribution to the development that was taking place.

Cohen decided to make a retreat, and it would seem that it was at this time that he discovered the writings of St. John of the Cross,

---

[1] De Mendiola states that another source says 'Carlist soldiers' was noted on their passports! P.36.

[2] Cohen himself preached the funeral panegyric for Fr. Dominic on August 11, 1870 in Le Broussey.

co-reformer of Carmel with St. Teresa of Avila. The ideal of the Carmelite reformer appealed to him. Cohen delighted in reading about the "living flame of love," which longs to communicate itself to the contemplative soul, to inflame it, to transform it into itself, making it a living flame as well. This is the sublime theology of love sung about by John of the Cross in his poems "The Living Flame of Love" and "The Spiritual Canticle." Hermann Cohen would certainly feel at one with John's theology. Here Christ is the mediator and savior in the story of salvation. Christ, dead but risen again; Christ our lover, sacrificed but alive in the Eucharist. The new convert would also have resonated with the song John wrote from his prison cell in Toledo:

> Song of the Soul that rejoices in knowing God through faith.
>
> *For I know well the spring that flows and runs,*
> *although it is night.*
>
> 1. That eternal spring is hidden,
>   for I know well where it has its rise,
>   although it is night.
> ....
> 9. This eternal spring is hidden,
>   In this living bread for our life's sake,
>   although it is night.[1]

Hermann Cohen duly made his way to the Carmelite house in Agen to meet the pioneering Dominic. The house was situated high on a wooded hill above the Garonne and overlooking the town. It was an impressive building called "The Hermitage," and it had formerly been a diocesan seminary. Next it passed to the Marist Order for a period of four years until they moved to the

---

[1]   St. John of the Cross, "Poetry," in *Collected Works*, p. 724.

delightfully named Bon-Encontre (Happy Encounter) not far away. The Hermitage was the traditional site of a martyred hermit, and several saints were also associated with the area. Dominic Arbizu y Munarriz formally took possession of the property known as St. Vincent of Pompejac in the suburb of that name, on May 13, 1846.

It appears that in April 1849, Cohen made up his mind to enter the Carmelite Order. In doing so, he was aware that his friend de Cuers would feel let down by this development; Hermann was leaving him to shoulder responsibility for the nocturnal adoration group on his own. He tried to reassure de Cuers on this point. And it appears from letters Cohen wrote to his friends that he wished to become a priest precisely to support that movement. After all, Marie-Thérèse Dubouché's group of adorers of the Blessed Sacrament was affiliated to Carmel, and Cohen had the same idea for a men's group. From the beginning, he had the needs of the adoration group very much at heart and wanted to ensure its success.[1]

Cohen arrived in Agen at 2:30 p.m. on July 19, the day on which Carmelites keep the vigil of a feast in honour of the prophet Elijah, who has special significance for the order. They were at that moment reciting vespers for the feast. Dominic, the superior, interviewed him, and Cohen asked to make an eight-day retreat. He wrote to his friend de Cuers, "St. Teresa will be my mother, the scapular my habit, a room eight feet square my universe. Yes I am so happy for I feel I'm doing God's will."[2]

At the end of the retreat, rather than pack up and leave, he approached Dominic.

"I ask a great favour, Father."

"What is it, my son?" asked Dominic.

"I wish to stay here in Carmel and be clothed in the holy habit."

---

[1] See "Selections from the Writings of Hermann Cohen" in Part 2 for his letter to de Cuers at this time.

[2] Henri Blanc, *Un Grand Religieux*, p. 122.

"Unfortunately, my son," replied Dominic, "that is beyond my powers to grant. Our Constitutions and the apostolic decrees formally forbid admittance to the novitiate of someone recently converted from Judaism."[1]

Not to be put off, Cohen interjected, "Oh, Father, try to get that requirement dispensed; for I know well that God wishes me to be in Carmel."

"Very well," said Dominic. "Just go to Le Broussey, and I'll do what I can."[2]

This exchange tells us a bit about both men: Cohen's impetuosity and the understanding and openness of the future superior general of the Order. Dominic immediately wrote to Rome requesting a dispensation, but this was refused. Cohen, however, was undaunted and decided he would keep trying even if he had to go to Rome to seek permission from Pope Pius IX. He had not really changed from the youth who had impetuously followed Liszt to Geneva. It was exactly what his future Carmelite sister Thérèse of Lisieux would do some decades later—go directly to the pope. From Bordeaux, Cohen wrote to his family telling them all about the Carmelite Order he was applying to join and emphasizing the fact that it had historic connections with the land of Israel. It was a sensitive letter, showing great understanding, compassion, and tact for his bewildered loved ones.[3]

On the day he received news of the Carmelite general's refusal to allow him to enter immediately, Cohen set out for Rome to the headquarters of the order. He sailed from Marseilles on the way to Rome. Cohen was recognized by some of the wealthy patrons on

---

[1] The Carmelite Constitutions required a certain period of time to elapse before a Jewish convert could be allowed to join the order.

[2] Henri Blanc, *Un Grand Religieux: le R.P. Dominique de Saint-Joseph, restaurateur des Carmes en France en 1830* (Carpentras, France: Chez les Soeurs Carmélites, 1922, p. 122).

[3] See "Selections from the Writings of Hermann Cohen" at the end of this book for the full text of this letter.

board, and they insisted he give a concert. They also insisted he take some remuneration. As it turned out, it provided the funds he needed for the trip to Rome. When he arrived there, the General Chapter of the Carmelites was just about to meet. Cohen presented his petition to the chapter. After considering it, they gave him the necessary permission on September 14, the feast of the Triumph of the Cross, a special day in the Carmelite calendar.[1] Impishly, Cohen wrote again to de Cuers, "I have just carried my position by assault, without having recourse to the Pope."[2] In any case, the pope was then exiled in Gaeta near Naples.

Hermann wasn't idle while in Rome. He contacted the headquarters of the Archconfraternity of the Blessed Sacrament and spent a night of adoration in their church in Rome. He obtained a copy of the available indulgences for the members of his own adoration group and worked on a plan to affiliate the Paris group with the one in Rome. He entrusted a letter containing information about these with the vicar general of Marseilles, Felix Brunello, to be collected in due time by de Cuers. After twelve days in Rome, Cohen returned to Bordeaux to begin his training in the Carmelite novitiate. On October 6, 1849, Hermann Cohen was clothed in the Carmelite habit at Le Broussey. He was given the name Brother Augustine-Mary of the Most Blessed Sacrament.

Novitiate life was certainly a strict regime for him, and there were long hours of prayer and various other exercises to go through.

---

[1] "Since Mr. Augustine Hermann Cohen from Hamburg, born of Jewish parents, but converted to the faith two years ago, baptized and confirmed, without doubt has shown signs of piety and of a vocation, has requested admission to our Order, at the request of the vicar provincial of Bordeaux who has put a proposal before the fathers whether he should be dispensed from the impediment of Judaism in order to be clothed in the habit of a choir brother and be professed in the province of Bordeaux or Aquitaine, after the canonical novitate year has expired." Carmelite Archives, Rome. This proposal was approved by the fathers after a secret ballot.

[2] Sylvain, p. 74-75

During his earlier life, he had been in the habit of taking snuff, which was then very much in vogue, as well as smoking tobacco, and being an avid coffee drinker. He would certainly have been required to give these up in the novitiate. His new life was as far removed as one could possibly imagine from his former lifestyle. The new novice was given the usual reading material used in formation at that time. So he would have made acquaintance with the *Book of the First Monks*, a Carmelite document that at the time was thought to date back to the early beginnings of the order.[1] Chapter 4 contained some forthright ascetical advice on renouncing self and restraining desires of the flesh: "Just as he who is crucified can no longer move his limbs at will, or turn around but must remain still where the executioner has nailed him, so must you attach yourself to the cross, renounce yourself and never turn your will for one moment toward selfishness or day-dreaming, but apply it totally where My will has nailed you, so as to spend the time of life which remains to you not following selfish desires but the will of God."[2]

At Christmas Hermann wrote a little carol that he set to music and that in later years became very popular:

> O solitaries of Carmel
> Interrupt your penance
> Intone a joyful Noël
> To the Infant Jesus of Carmel.[3]

In a letter, Cohen refers to the traditional practice in Carmelite novitiates at that time for each novice to keep a statue of the infant Jesus in his cell for twenty-four hours. In encouraging devotion to the infant Jesus, Cohen evoked what would be, a few decades later,

---

[1] This gave it an authority that was not in fact justified. Among other statements we find the following: "Elijah the prophet of God was the first monk."

[2] Book of the First Monks, Teresian Press, Oxford, 1969, p. 9.

[3] Sylvain., p. 82.

synonymous with his sister in Carmel, St. Thérèse of the Child Jesus. Writing to his friend Mother Marie-Thérèse Dubouché, the founder of the Reparatrice Congregation, now known as the Sisters of the Adoration, Cohen reveals effusive aspects of his personal devotion:

> In the world during my life as an artist, I never had a childhood because I was introduced to the life of the salons at the age of twelve. God, in his great goodness, has amply made up to me for that during my novitiate, where I rejoice in the joys of spiritual childhood. I am bathed in the milk of consolation and want nothing else but to see God's will done in me and in everyone. Holy Communion occupies me totally—either in thanksgiving or in preparation. I prolong these in such a way that my life is a continual Communion. This I think is like the joy of heaven. Here we are always in the Real Presence of the Eucharist. This quiet life appeals to me.[1]

Commentator Donald Cave, perhaps pertinently, quotes this passage as an example of Cohen's "emotive piety."[2]

During this time of novitiate, Cohen's friend Sister Marie-Pauline du Fougerais, in Paris, sent him a hymn from a collection she had written and titled "For the Love of Jesus Christ," which she hoped he would set to music. As a novice, Cohen was not allowed to spend time in musical composition, and he replied, "The Lord does not want me to compose music for the lovely hymn you sent me. But yesterday after reading it once, I seemed to hear within me the melody for the hymn. As I read on, the desire to compose the music grew; and I believe that if I could have read it a second time, I would have known it by heart and would have been able to write down the notes."[3]

---

[1]   Cave, p.1 -11

[2]   Ibid p. 1-11

[3]   Tierney, p. 48.

But then he repeated the fact that he was not permitted to write music during his novitiate. During this novitiate year, he had a long visit from his mother, who was understandably very perturbed to witness the kind of life he had chosen. It was naturally very traumatic for her as a Jewish woman to see him robed in what would be for her an unusual garb, complete with sandals and tonsure. It seems that she exerted every pressure on him to leave the Carmelite Order but to no avail. On the contrary, Cohen wrote a note to de Cuers later, saying how he had hoped his mother might become a Christian as a result of her visit.

Even during his formation year, Cohen had his recently established adoration movement very much at heart. He wrote to congratulate Cyrille de Mont de Benque on his election as leader of the movement in Paris, with the additional motive of providing encouragement to the group there, which had begun to experience difficulties. Among other things he wrote, "Make an appeal to generous hearts. There will again be friends of Jesus in Paris, and I count on your zeal to save this lovely enterprise from shipwreck."[1] In a second longer letter, in addition to demonstrating his usual devout and fervent style, he showed a real gift for organization. He expressed the hope that the movement would grow greatly in France. "Spare no effort in setting up this way of life and expanding the circle of action. I like to think that in a few years it will experience a great development throughout the whole of France."[2] These grandiose ideas had no appeal for Dubouché, who favored a hidden and humble apostolate. Cohen then suggested that all the adoration groups should be coordinated in different towns in the country and be placed under the guidance of a central committee in Paris.

Cohen also followed up on his interest in the development of Dubouché's plans for a reparation society, even to the extent of being thought to interfere in what was none of his business by

---

[1]   Cave, p. 11-26

[2]   Ibid., p. 11-27

the Marist founder Jean-Claude Colin. But Cohen was not aware that Dubouché had made overtures to the Marists with a view to them sponsoring her new movement. Peter Julian Eymard agreed to incorporate her group into the Marists. To be fair to Cohen, however, it might be regarded as his business because it was understood initially that the Eucharistic apostolate would remain linked to Carmel. As it happened, Cohen was left in the dark in regard to ongoing developments. Dubouché felt the same in regard to Cohen as did Colin, and this eventually led to her complete estrangement with him.

Cohen's involvement in these proceedings does not sit easily with what should have been a year of complete withdrawal from external distraction, even of a religious kind. At the very end of his novitiate, he was informed by his superiors that the work of reparatory adoration would have to separate from the Carmelites, and he wrote to Dubouché, "Cruel Carmel! After having given birth to this beautiful work, she drives her daughter away from her."[1] In spite of everything, his novitiate year passed peacefully enough, and Hermann Cohen—now Brother Augustine of the Blessed Sacrament—made his first profession on the feast of the Holy Rosary, October 7, 1850.

---

[1]   Ibid., p. 1V- 61

Chapter 7

"You are a Priest Forever."

After his first profession as a Carmelite in October 1850, Hermann Cohen left Bordeaux to begin his preparations for the priesthood. Studies were scheduled to take place at the Carmelite college that had been established for that purpose. This was a former Marist house known as the Hermitage in Agen where Cohen first sought admission to the Order. Starting a course of study, Cohen seems to have lamented the loss of greater leisure for prayer that he had enjoyed in the novitiate. He was by now thirty years of age. Later as a priest, he remarked in a sermon, "I remember how, when I decided to put my faith in Jesus Christ, all that I read, saw, and heard when I took this decision appeared to me in a new light, a luminous dazzling light which helped me progress so satisfactorily that, in proportion to my convictions, I saw unfolding before me the great perspective of the Scriptures—the Messiah promised in the Old Testament."[1]

During his time of study, Cohen's superiors allowed him to resume composing music for various motets on Eucharistic themes using lyrics composed by his friend Sister Pauline. Cohen's course of studies was not altogether adequate, and it seems to have been rushed through because of what was for those times, his mature age,

---

[1]   Sylvain, p. 89.

and perhaps also because of his celebrity status. In this connection, Marie-Thérèse Dubouché pointedly wrote to her friend Sister Agnes: "I ought to give you some prudential advice in regard to a Carmelite father whom I believe you know. . . . This young father has been caught up in an unfortunate affair in Montpellier, and this is a cause of serious disputes so well known that the bishop has dismissed him from the diocese, and he is now in Italy. . . . The same person has told me that the teaching of these young fathers is very feeble and often doubtful . . . It is certain that, for this reason, Père Hermann has been prohibited from preaching in the diocese of Paris."[1]

When he had almost completed his studies, such as they were, and had been ordained a deacon, the Provincial, Fr. Dominic, decided to take Cohen to Carcassonne to help in the restoration of an ancient Carmelite house that, like so many others, had been closed after the French Revolution of 1789. He wrote to Sister Pauline, "We arrived at last after a hard journey. We encountered a lot of problems which the Lord in his goodness allowed. We were able to take over a lovely gothic church—still a stable—and also the old Carmelite priory. The habit has been welcomed here again. We don't know what providence has in store for the Order. It wouldn't surprise me if in a few years the whole of the south of France were part of a network of St. Teresa's vineyard."[2]

In this, Cohen was indeed proved right for it was really the beginning of a second spring for Carmel in France. Cohen himself couldn't foresee that he would play a significant part in this revival, not only in southern France but in England, too, and indirectly in Poland. There was an amusing aside to the takeover of the church in Carcassonne where, he tells another friend, one of the horses refused to vacate his home, and they had to use some additional persuasion with the help of a stick.

---

[1] Cave, *L'Oeuvre encharistique*, 1-1V, p. 62.
[2] Beaurin, p. 156. The house belonged to the Carmelite Order prior to St. Teresa's Reform

Cohen went on to complete his studies for the priesthood, and his ordination was fixed for Easter Sunday 1851. He looked forward to that day with great anticipation. He expressed as much in letters to friends, particularly to Sister Pauline. On Easter Monday, the day after his first Mass, Cohen wrote to another nun in Paris: "I hope to have more leisure later to tell you about the grace-filled events in which I have been involved these days. I'm still not myself, nor do I wish to be." The first sermon Cohen preached was on frequent Communion, thus keeping a promise he had made.

However, Cohen had worn himself out in the aftermath of his ordination, and he was ordered to take a rest. His state of exhaustion continued into the summer, and he also found that he could not pray as easily as before, which was an additional trial. The newly ordained priest was transferred to the new Carmelite foundation in Bordeaux, which made a welcome change for him. He engaged in ministry to local hospitals and won over people who initially appeared hostile or indifferent, simply by the warmth of his pastoral approach. An account of Cohen's conversion written by a friend of his, a magistrate named Jean-Baptiste Gergères, described Cohen's warmth and sensitivity to people he met.[1] Gergères described how Cohen went out of his way to offer him support and consolation when he was grieving for his sister who had recently died. Even a critic like Donald Cave would admit that Cohen was a person of warm human feeling but needed the affirmation of friends. Cohen also continued to take an active interest in the work of Eucharistic adoration, especially in Paris, which he himself had initiated and which at this time was undergoing a crisis.

---

[1] Jean-Baptiste Gergères, *Conversion du Pianiste Hermann*, 5th ed. (Paris: Ambroise Bray, 1861). Gergères was an admirer of Cohen. Writing to him from Baden, Germany, on March 5, 1868, Cohen states, "I have done nothing but what obedience directed me to do." Sylvain, p. 230.

Timothy Tierney

The Wandering Carmelite

Quite soon after his ordination, Cohen was being entrusted with a busy apostolate of travelling and preaching. Indeed he sometimes jokingly referred to himself as the "Wandering Jew."[1] When someone asked him where he lived, he replied, "In a railway carriage," making full use of the recently established rail lines throughout France. In the course of 1853, he preached in nearly all the towns of southern France such as Béziers, Montpellier, Toulon, Avignon, and Marseilles, and invariably a movement for the practice of nocturnal adoration followed. His preaching never failed to make an impact. There are several references to such preaching engagements in the newspapers of the time. For example, after preaching at the clothing ceremony of a Carmelite in Pamiers, Sylvain tells us: "During three quarters of an hour", said the *Gazette du Languedoc,* he held captive the attention of his hearers, and showed that faith, grace, and piety make the Christian orator – the veritable Apostle of Jesus Christ."[2]

At Lyon on one occasion, he had a congregation of 3,000 people. It was an event sponsored by the St. Vincent de Paul Society to raise money for the poor of the city. The subsequent appeal realized 6,000 francs, an enormous sum at that time. It was planned that Cohen should preach in Geneva, Switzerland, during May, the month of Mary, and though he looked forward to preaching the Gospel in a place where he had lived as a concert pianist, he was forced to cancel this engagement. His health, never robust, had given increasing cause for concern. On his way back to Carcassonne, Cohen made a point of meeting Maximin Giraud and Melanie Calvat, the visionaries of La Salette at Grenoble. Cohen showed a keen interest in these places that gave rise to Marian

---

[1] This was the name of a contemporary play in a Paris theatre. The theme was a fixture in Christian mythology, taken over by the romantics. Cohen's former girlfriend, Céleste Mogador, made her debut in this play.

[2] Sylvain, pp. 109-110.

devotion, as he would later take an interest in Lourdes. Indeed, the happenings at La Salette are sometimes seen as a kind of curtain raiser for those at Lourdes.

The phenomenon of La Salette occurred in the Alpine region of France in September 1846. His friend, Julian Eymard, was even more attracted to these unusual happenings and knew the visionaries personally.[1] St. John Vianney was hesitant at first in regard to this apparition, apparently because of some misunderstanding, and he was not impressed by Giraud. However, the humble curé later showed himself in favor of the apparition. Giraud's visionary companion, Calvat, at fourteen years was of a similar age to Bernadette Soubirous when she experienced her visions at Lourdes in 1858. Calvat later lived for two years in the Carmelite convent in Darlington in England.[2] There she wrote an expanded version of the "secret" of La Salette, as well as a rule for members of a congregation that might derive from the La Salette apparition. Such a congregation, the Missionaries of La Salette, was founded at a later time.[3]

Cohen spent the next couple of months recuperating from physical and nervous exhaustion. In a letter to an unidentified friend, he admitted that he was going through a difficult time, but he maintained that he wished to suffer for the Lord. Up to now, he felt he had been given a lot of consolation, "life on Tabor," but he had not been given the chalice of suffering to drink. As well as exhaustion, Cohen suffered from a painful condition of the leg that became an open wound from foot to knee. His surroundings at Castelbello near Hyères were very beautiful, and he describes the countryside in these words:

---

[1] Dempsey, *Champion of the Blessed Sacrament*. Eymard visited the shrine of Our Lady of La Salette often and, shortly before he died, celebrated Mass there.

[2] Darlington was one of the first Carmelite convents in England.

[3] In 1860, Calvat received permission from the local bishop to return to mainland Europe. She lived for a while in Greece, then moved to back to France and eventually died in Altamura, Italy.

I am in a kind of fairyland here. Just think of the climate at Hyères, that of a garden on the edge of the sea, a lovely valley sheltered from the northern winds by a semi-circular range of mountains with olive, orange, parasol pine, and charming almond trees. Two great palm trees grow near the remote house where I live. It's like being in the Far East! The sea lies in the distance at the end of the valley, bluer than the sky; and out to sea you can see the "Isles of the Blest" about which poets have always sung. A choir of nightingales charms you day and night with their lovely music; and amid all this beauty of nature, not far from my bed, there is a chapel where the Blessed Sacrament is reserved.[1]

He added that he was unable even to compose as much as a bar of music. Did the "choir of nightingales" remind him of the words of St. John of the Cross who described the song of the nightingale in his "Spiritual Canticle."

The breathing of the air,
The song of the sweet nightingale,
The grove and its living beauty
In the serene night,
With a flame that is consuming and painless.[2]

While staying in Castelbello, Hermann was able to renew his friendship with Eymard, who was also convalescing in this beautiful area. In religious temperament and dedication to the Eucharist, they were kindred spirits. In the course of a walk together on April 18, Eymard told him of his plan to devote himself to the work of perpetual adoration and to found a third order of Marists independent of the Marists. This congregation would be dedicated to adoration of the Blessed Sacrament. Cohen was, of course, delighted

---

[1] Beaurin, pp 196-197.
[2] Collected Works, ICS, p. 557.

with this idea. On April 23, he wrote, "Our thoughts and desires coincide, let us both work together for this project." They discovered they had both made the same vow—to preach always on Jesus and the Eucharistic Christ. They both shared a tender but sentimental devotion to Our Lady.

Eymard had been moved by what he perceived to be a great lack in the spiritual lives of French clergy at the time, and this had been communicated to him by some of the clergy themselves. Though there were many "spiritual associations" for laity, many ordinary people were unchurched, and one particular need he saw was that of providing a course of instruction for the First Communion of adults. Later, however, Eymard diverged from Cohen and his friends in his views on the Eucharist, and the disagreement centred on the idea of making reparation to God for the sins of the world. Eymard felt that reparation alone was a limitation on his own vision of a Eucharistic apostolate. This brings us back to the initial movement that Cohen encountered at the Carmelite convent in Paris where Marie-Thérèse Dubouché began an apostolate of reparation in the convent chapel. Eventually, cracks appeared in their original united approach. Cohen tended to go for the big effect, to make it as public and solemn as possible, and by so doing, he hoped to reach a greater number of people. Dubouché wished to cultivate the spirit of Nazareth, which she saw as the perfect form of Christianity. Eymard tended to view adoration in the context of the cenacle or "Upper Room," though he did also favor a degree of external pomp and ceremony in regard to the Eucharist. He visualized any new houses that might emerge as little "cenacles" of prayer giving rise to apostolic activity. These differences caused each of them much suffering.

There was a further difference between Eymard and Cohen on the matter of mixed congregations for night adoration: Cohen favoured men and women taking part in separate adoration sessions, while Eymard disagreed. It is of interest, too, in trying to put together a picture of Cohen's character, that Eymard found him intolerant on this point and was very hurt by his opposition. However, in

1860, Cohen visited his old friend and tried to be reconciled with him but without success. Eymard said he had been too hurt by Cohen's actions and words to renew their friendship. In another letter, Eymard maintains Cohen will always be "La Juive," referring to a contemporary opera, though the wordd mean "The Jewess." Even the saints have their differences.

As it happened, the three different Eucharistic movements, namely, nocturnal adoration, the Reparatrice or "Family of Adoration" movement, and Eymard's Religious of the Blessed Sacrament, all ended up independent of one another. The Reparatrice movement met initially at the chapel of the Carmelite nuns in Paris. Indeed, originally Cardinal Pierre Berulle wished to establish perpetual adoration among the Carmels in France when the Carmelite nuns arrived in Paris in 1604. The founder, Barbara Acarie,[1] an older cousin of Berulle, successfully opposed this because she believed it went against the wishes of St. Teresa. Berulle exerted the full power of his authority on his saintly cousin in quite an abusive way, so much so that she died soon after he had upbraided her on this point in her own convent parlor.

Branching Out

In October, Cohen headed for Montpellier to prepare for the foundation of another Carmelite house, and from there he went to Bagnères to lay the foundation stone of a new church that he himself had designed. In November, he set out to preach at Bordeaux. According to newspaper reports at the time, "He graced

---

[1] The career of Barbara Acarie was a remarkable one. She was instrumental in bringing the Carmelite nuns to France. Barbara Avrillot was born on February 1, 1566, and married Pierre Acarie in 1582, the year of Saint Teresa's death. They had five children. In 1601, she was inspired by St. Teresa to establish the Carmelite nuns in France. After her husband's death, she entered the Carmel herself and is now known as Blessed Marie of the Incarnation.

the primatial chair with the magnificent voice of a Ravignan or a Lacordaire."[1] It was actually his birthday, November 10, and the scene took place before a distinguished gathering in the presence of the cardinal archbishop of Bordeaux. Often on his preaching tours, Cohen would give an organ recital for the poor, usually for the charity closest to his heart, the St. Vincent de Paul Society. From Bordeaux, Cohen went to preach in Angers and Tours, which also proved to be successful missions. In Tours, he was welcomed by Leon Dupont, the "holy man of Tours." According to this witness, the best and most perceptive of the clergy were amazed at his eloquence. For Dupont himself, it cemented a strong bond of friendship with Cohen; and he determined to further the cause of the Eucharist and nocturnal adoration.[2] From Tours, Cohen made his way down south to Marseilles to preach in aid of the Saint Vincent de Paul Society. At that time the local bishop was Eugène de Mazenod, the founder of the Oblates of Mary Immaculate.[3] De Mazenod, who was very devoted to the Eucharist, gave him a great welcome and became a firm friend. It was April 25, 1853, the Cathedral was full and there was a great atmosphere there. Cohen certainly made a lasting impression on the bishop, who prevailed on him to remain a few days.

After this, Cohen went to stay at the Carmelite house in Carcassonne, which provided a brief period of rest and relaxation. Lenten preaching was quite an institution in France in those days. In the following year, 1854, we find him preaching a Lenten series of sermons in the historic city of Pamiers. From there, he made his way to Lyon where, on Easter Thursday, April 20, he preached on behalf of abandoned children cared for by the St. Vincent de Paul Society. Then it was on to Paris, and there he preached in the famous church

---

[1]   Beaurin, p. 203.

[2]   Emmanuel, *Life of Sister Marie.*

[3]   Eugène de Mazenod was beatified by Pope Paul VI on October 19, 1975 and canonized by Bl. John Paul 11December 3, 1995. Julian Eymard initially joined the Oblates.

of Saint-Sulpice. This was the scene of his best-known sermon, which highlighted the dramatic and fervent nature of much of his preaching. Here, he renewed contact with the nocturnal adoration group that he had founded in the church of Our Lady of Victories. He also enjoyed a reunion with his old friends, Abbé Francois de la Bouillerie and Abbé Charles Desgenettes. Cohen noted with satisfaction that the movement for nocturnal adoration was spreading rapidly in Paris. Cohen was now so exhausted from overwork that he was obliged to go to the famous health resort of Bagnères-de-Bigorre near Lourdes with his companion, Louis of the Sacred Hearts, and rest up there until the end of the year. Bagnères had been a popular spa town for centuries where people came to "take the waters" and the "cure."

There was already a Carmelite convent in the town that had been established twenty-five years previously and dedicated to Saint John of the Cross. For a long time before Cohen's visit, Sister Mary of the Angels, prioress in the Carmel, wished to have a foundation of the friars in the Pyrenees just as the friars had established themselves at Bordeaux. Her repeated requests to the superior, Dominic Arbizu y Munarriz, were consistently turned down. She had even contacted Cohen about this while he was still a novice at Le Broussey. Now when he came there for a short rest, she took up the matter again. Cohen felt it was a good place for a foundation and found a suitable site; he invited Father Dominic himself to come and examine the situation. Dominic now agreed that the project should go ahead once they obtained the permission of Bishop Bertrand Laurence, bishop of Tarbes. This church dignitary would later be involved in assessing the apparitions of Bernadette in whose diocese Lourdes and Bagnères were situated. All went according to plan until they were ready to sign over the site, but the Carmelites could not find anyone to stand surety for the purchase. Providentially, an English friend of the prioress was passing through at the time and she came to the rescue. Cohen himself designed the new church and laid the foundation stone.

We need to keep in mind that this was a time of new beginnings for the Carmelite Order in France. The first provincial chapter of the province of Aquitaine had not yet taken place. In regard to the upsurge of growth in the order at this time, Cohen noted that when he first entered the order there were very few French Carmelites—now there were forty! The number of friars had soon grown to a hundred, counting the many Spanish Carmelites who had to flee Spain at this time. Moreover, when Cohen joined there were only four Carmelite houses in France. The new developments at Besançon, Montigny, Montpellier, Carcassonne, and Pamiers[1] added to this number.[2] There were plans for a Paris foundation as well, and in Bordeaux, a large church was in the process of being built. Cohen tends to gloss over his own part in bringing so many new ventures to fruition. This blossoming facilitated the development that would take place in England some years later.

Cohen returned to Bagnères-de-Bigorre in the Spring of 1854 and supervised the completion of the Carmelite church in the town. Sufficient funds flowed in for this foundation. Artists, too, came forward. The famous painter, Horace Vernet,[3] knew and respected Cohen and volunteered to decorate the church with frescoes, though he died before he could complete the work. A sculptor named Jean-

---

[1] The Carmelites first came to Pamiers in 1311. Many years later they returned and took over the old bishop's residence—the headquarters of the Pamiers inquisition. The inquisition into the Cathar heretical movement was conducted by the local bishop, Jacques Fournier, later Pope Benedict XII. The Carmelite sisters opened a convent at Pamiers in 1648, and after subsequent expulsion, they returned in 1804. Fifty years later the prioress, Mother Elisea de Lassus St-Gènies, hoped that Cohen would restore the friars to the town; the foundation did in fact take place but was led by Louis of the Assumption.

[2] Cohen also refers to a projected Carmelite church in Paris. This was later built on the Rue de la Pompe but was taken over in the suppression at the end of the century, It is now a Spanish church.

[3] Vernet was also a "war artist" and accompanied French troops in the Crimean War.

Marie Bonassieu enriched the nave and porch with two beautiful pieces of statuary.[1] The organ builder, Aristide Cavaillé-Coll, out of appreciation for Cohen, gave him one of his best instruments at a reduced price. Bishop Laurence presided at the blessing of the new church on September 2, 1856, amid a great crowd of clergy and people. At the official opening ceremony, a young priest named Abbé Laprie, who later joined the Franciscans, preached for the occasion. He recalled Cohen's conversion and retraced the story of the foundation of the house at Bagnères: "In just two years, a unique monument is being built in Bagnères—a priory and a church. The foundation, which is nearly completed, began with the sign of the cross and was carried through with no other resources except faith and hope, yet it cost 200,000 francs to build. A friar, whom I don't have to name because you know him very well yourselves, said to himself in the manner of St. Teresa whom he calls his seraphic mother: 'Five sous and I are nothing; but five sous, God, and I are everything.'"[2] Cohen continued his apostolate in the south of France. About this time, he received a request from Father Noel Hanset, superior general of the order, to meet him in Belgium and preach there for some weeks. The emphasis was always on Eucharistic devotion, and Cohen reported his joy at visiting Liège where it was believed St. Juliana was inspired to institute the feast of Corpus Christi. He then returned to Le Broussey where, on June 29, feast of St. Peter and St. Paul, he preached for the profession of a fellow Jewish convert named Bernard Bauer. They both thought of themselves as the David and Jonathan of the New Testament.

Cohen was preaching an Advent retreat at Lyon the following December when he learned the sad news of his mother's death. He returned immediately to Paris to be with his family. It had been a disappointment to Hermann that his mother had not embraced

---

[1]   Bonassieu was responsible for the immense statue of the Virgin and Child on an elevation in Le Puy in Haute Loire. It is 16 meters in height and weighs 110 tons. It is very popular with tourists.

[2]   Tierney, p.60

the Catholic faith before she died. He remarked to his family, "We must hope that at the last moment something happened between herself and God of which we know nothing." He told the Curé d'Ars, John Vianney, about his anxiety, and the latter reassured him: "Hope, continue to hope. One day, on the feast of the Immaculate Conception, you will receive a letter which will give you great consolation."[1] Vianney had in fact a high regard for Cohen, and when Cohen visited his church at Ars, he tried to get him to preach. Cohen only consented after insisting the saintly curé give his own usual instruction first. The good curé gave his usual address and then, possibly with more than a hint of good humour, introduced Cohen. He told the congregation an edifying story about a saintly person who prayed that she might hear Our Lady sing. Her prayer seemed granted when a beautiful lady sang a heavenly melody and the holy person was rapt in ecstasy. However, the lady said that she was only the Virgin Catherine and she had yet to hear the real thing. When Our Lady sang, this saintly person promptly died of joy. "Well," said the curé, "you have only been listening to St. Catherine, now you are going to hear the Blessed Virgin herself!"[2]

The curé's prophetic words about Cohen's mother proved true when, on December 8, 1861, a Jesuit priest handed Cohen a letter. The writer of the letter, Leonie Guillemant, who was aware of Cohen's anxiety about his mother's salvation, was a well-known writer on spiritual themes such as the Eucharist, the Sacred Heart, and Mary. The letter contained in effect a private revelation that on her deathbed Cohen's mother had accepted Christ. Cohen took a prudent view of the revelation. He wrote, "So we can accept this good news with reasonable confidence, although without the certitude of faith, which is only granted to canonized saints."[3]

---

[1] Ibid., p. 60.

[2] Charles Sylvain, *Flamme Ardente au Carmel: vie de Hermann Cohen, en religion Père Augustin-Marie du Très-Saint-Sacrement, carme déchaussé* (Flavigny-sur-Ozerain, France: Traditions Monastiques, 2009), p.186 (my translation).

[3] Ibid., p. 60.

When we reflect on the anguish Cohen endured concerning his mother's spiritual state, we realize that people like him at that time did not have the benefit of the teaching of Vatican II (or even Vatican I). In the declaration *Nostra Aetate*,(In this day of ours) on October 28, 1965, both Muslims and Jews have been rehabilitated. It is implied in the doctrine set out there that members of these faiths can be saved without converting to Christianity. As a corollary to that, later in the same year (December 5), the Second Vatican Council issued another document, the Declaration on Religious Liberty. This declaration states, "Freedom of this kind means that all should be immune from coercion on the part of individuals, social groups, and every human power so that, within due limits, nobody is forced to act against his convictions in religious matters in private or in public, alone or in association with others."[1]

The year 1856 was a busy one for Cohen. A large mixed mission team, including no less than five Carmelites, preached a mission for men in the cathedral at Bordeaux, which was packed to capacity for the occasion. He even interrupted his work in Bordeaux to preach in Paris and returned to complete his commitments in Bordeaux. On the Easter Monday after that mission, the Latin Mass in honor of St. Teresa, which Cohen had composed, was sung for the first time.

The Founder

A Carmelite writer, Henri Peltier, referring to Cohen, commented, "In France, the resurgent Order acquired in his person someone brilliant but quite solid: a poet, musician, preacher, and equally capable of negotiating the thorniest business problems."[2]This is a verdict about Cohen that seems to have gone undisputed and

---

[1] Austin Flannery, ed., Declaration on Religious Liberty (*Dignitatis Humanae*), Vatican Council II: The Conciliar and Post Conciliar Documents (Dublin: Dominican Publications, 1975)
[2] André de Sainte-Marie, *L'Ordre de Notre-Dame du Mont-Carmel* (Bruges, Belgium,1910 pp 72-173).

with few exceptions. Another Carmelite author, in a historical study, has this to say: "In France itself, Père Hermann contributed powerfully, by the prestige of his name as well as by his untiring zeal, for the expansion of the Order, which he had embraced with a filial recognition of Mary."[1] Cohen indeed had prodigious gifts and energy as a founder. Father Nicomède, prior of Tarasteix, informs us, "Father Augustine-Mary of the Most Holy Sacrament [Cohen] was the right hand of Father Dominic [Arbizu y Munarriz], in planting and strengthening the vine of Saint Teresa in France. He was a man who seemed prepared in a special manner by Providence, to assist in the growth of our holy Reform."[2]

Carmelites in Lyon

Another of these "vines" planted by Cohen was situated in the Lyon, France's "second city."[3] There, amid tremendous obstacles, including opposition from the local cardinal, Louis de Bonald, he restored the Carmelites to Lyon in 1860. There was a ruined Carmelite priory there from which friars had been evicted during the French Revolution, and a tremendous amount of work was needed to make it habitable once more. As prior in Lyon, Cohen's assistant as novice master was Spanish-born Father Joseph-Louis Vizcarra, who would join him in London in the same capacity some years later. Sadly, Cohen's work in Lyon and elsewhere was undone during the devastation caused by the Franco-Prussian War in 1871. Indeed, the story of Cohen's work for Carmelite foundations resembles that of St. Teresa of Avila in Spain.

---

[1]   Ibid., pp. 172-173).

[2]   Flamme Ardente, p.15. He was alluding to Psalm 80:15 "the stock that your right hand planted." From a Letter of Approbation by Father Luke Ranise, Superior General of the Carmelites.

[3]   Cohen left an account of the foundation of Carmelites in Lyon in a document called "Notice manuscrite de la Fondation des Carmes déchausses à Lyon en 1858." Sylvain, p. 167.

During the course of the mission he preached in Lyon, Cohen had been approached by a wealthy businessman who wished to donate 10,000 francs toward a Carmelite foundation there. (Sister Marchand, superior of the Daughters of Charity, already had a promise of a large donation from a wealthy friend.) At the time, Cohen was embroiled in the work at Bagnères, but he thought about the project and waited for God's good time. Carmelites had flourished in Lyon before the French Revolution of 1789. In 1619, Lyon, the ancient city of the Gauls dedicated to the Blessed Virgin Mary, had welcomed the Discalced Carmelites. They established themselves on the summit of a high rock in the town, overlooking the river Saône, which flowed past nearby, and close to the rest of the city of Lyon. This location was a pleasant, healthy environment.

For almost two hundred years, the Carmelites devoted themselves to the spiritual well-being of the town. But then, like all other religious orders, the friars had been driven out by religious persecution during the revolution. Since the first quarter of the nineteenth century, their old priory was used as an army barracks, and was in a bad state. The church itself had been divided into sleeping quarters for the soldiers. It was also difficult to access, the road leading to the place being very steep. Sister Marchand was the prime mover in the return of the Carmelites to Lyon. In 1853, influenced by an aunt of one of her colleagues who knew and appreciated the Carmelite friars in Agen, she arranged for a Carmelite to preach in Lyon in aid of the St. Vincent de Paul Society. This friar made a great impression on his audience; as a result, one of the diocesan priests there, Abbé Baracan, asked to enter the order. It appears that the fledgling order was creating a favorable impression among the people.

Finally Cohen himself came to preach the Advent retreat in the cathedral of Lyons in 1855, and funds were promised for a foundation. More donations came in, and by 1857, the provincial negotiated the purchase of the old priory due to be released by the government in 1859.[1] However, unexpected opposition arose when a government figure persuaded Cardinal de Bonald to delay things. The cardinal resisted pressure from various delegations around Lyon to allow the Carmelites to set up a house in his archdiocese. But with some ingenuity, the president of the St. Vincent de Paul Society publicized the project, commending the cardinal for his initiative. Reading about this, a high government official, who was a friend of the cardinal, congratulated him for restoring the Carmelites to Lyon. Now, assured of government support, the cardinal promptly dropped his opposition and authorized the foundation for the year 1860. Cohen believed the Curé d'Ars had foretold the foundation and that it would be of great benefit to the diocese. During 1859, Cohen had continued his work throughout France. He returned to Lyon on August 2, a day on which a pilgrimage in honor of St. Francis converged on the convent of Poor Clares to gain the "Portiuncula" indulgence. Many of the people recognized him, and there was an amusing incident when the crowd begged for a public blessing in the street and refused to be put off. An embarrassed Cohen eventually consented to their wishes and then escaped into the church. The incident does highlight the esteem and indeed veneration in which Cohen was held during his lifetime.

Cohen planned to inaugurate the foundation on September 8, the feast of the Birthday of the Blessed Virgin Mary, the twelfth anniversary of his First Communion. The church was duly re-consecrated on that day. It was a difficult time for Cohen and the new community living in unfinished accommodation. They were struggling financially but were helped by their Carmelite sisters in Fourvière in spite of the poverty of the latter as well. Other communities of sisters in the city also generously provided the friars with ready-made meals. In spite of the difficulties, the foundation

---

[1] The building was in a deplorable condition with graffiti-infested walls as well as vermin. Members of a conscription force known as the Gardes Mobiles, fleeing from Paris, had stayed in the building after the revolution of 1848 and vandalized the Carmelite statues in the church.

flourished, and the community was enlarged to meet the demands of the people. As the Carmelites became better known, many benefactors came forward to pay for the work of restoration. By October 15, feast of St. Teresa, great progress had been made, and a solemn Mass took place with numerous guests present from religious communities in the city. Cohen lost no time either in setting up a group of the Third Order of Carmel, now known as the Secular Order. On July 16 in the following year, Cohen set up the Brown Scapular Confraternity. The object of both these groups both now and then is to practice the Carmelite spirit of prayer following the teaching of St. Teresa and St. John of the Cross.

Cardinal de Bonald was due to officiate in the new Carmelite church on November 24, the old feast of St. John of the Cross. Again, many guests attended, including Cohen's friend Father Marie-Alphonse Ratisbonne. The new Carmelite house at Lyons was a great personal success for Cohen. He was appointed vicar of the new community. He would repeat this kind of success in the great city of London just a few years later. The ensuing winter turned out to be a trying time for the community. It was bitterly cold, and the community succumbed to illness. Cohen remarked, "In order that the grain grow and bear fruit, it must be trodden underfoot, crushed, and pressed down under the snow during the winter. We are buried under the weight of suffering and illness, but this makes me hope that the Lord will make use of us as good seed to bear fruit for the harvest."[1]

In the following May, the house was upgraded and allowed to inaugurate a novitiate, and so Cohen became the first prior of the Carmelite house at Lyon. It was indeed a busy time for him with the responsibility of leading the community, together with carrying on an apostolate in the city. There were many notable conversions in the course of Cohen's work in Lyon. Cohen's first biographer, Charles Sylvain, mentions seven prominent examples while implying

[1] Sylvain, p. 173

there were many more. Among them was an influential woman in the city who went to hear the former *artiste* out of curiosity and soon after regained her faith. Cohen's fame as a musician preceded him wherever he went and drew other musicians to him. The first violinist of the Grand-Théâtre of Lyon, M. Baumann fell dangerously ill. His friends tried to persuade him to see a priest, but he refused. After some persistence on their part he agreed to see Father Hermann and talk about music. It was only a short step from there for Cohen to move from music to reconciliation with God. Cohen then arranged for the cardinal to come and give Baumann the sacrament of confirmation. To this event all Baumann's friends were invited, and he passed away peacefully shortly afterward.

Cohen's list of friends reads like a "Who's Who" of musical celebrities of the 19th and early 20th centuries. He had a beneficial influence on many of them. On one occasion, a famous local cellist in Lyon Conservatoire, François George-Hainl, was curious to meet someone who, unlike himself, had renounced worldly success. He decided to visit the new priory and investigate. However, he got cold feet at the last minute, and as he knew Cohen would be out on a Wednesday hearing confessions at a convent, he decided to call on that day in order to avoid a spiritual confrontation. Cohen's appointment happened to be cancelled, and George-Hainl met a friar in the garden and asked to see Father Hermann. "I am he," said Cohen, "and you are George-Hainl." The two conversed for some time, and a few days later, George-Hainl returned and received the sacraments from him at the church of Our Lady of Fourvière.[1]

Cohen's pastoral approach had a surprisingly modern touch to it. For instance, an elderly lady, also gravely ill, had resisted all efforts to reconcile her to the church. When Cohen approached her, she bristled, "I'm not going to confession." "And, Madame," Cohen

---

[1]   George-Hainl was conductor at the Grand-Théâtre in Lyon and later became chief of the orchestra of the Grand-Opera in Paris from 1863 to 1872.

replied, "who says that you must?"[1] It was enough to disarm her, and she too received the last sacraments from Cohen's hands before she died.

There is scarcely any doubt that Cohen created a huge and favorable impression around him—and not just on the faithful. The municipal authorities were so impressed by this man that they were prepared to move mountains for him—well, almost. As noted, the approach to the church was so steep it constituted a danger to the public; at great expense, they carried out levelling work on the gradient and improved the flight of steps to the church. They also opened up an access route to the fashionable area of Fourvière, which provided a pleasant amenity for the public.

It seems that Cohen was receiving a degree of adulation in Lyons that made him distinctly uncomfortable. This was a very different reaction to what he received as a child prodigy. Now he preferred to shun it. With this in mind, he wrote to the superior general, Elisaeus Rayer volunteering for the missions in India[2] Circumstances decreed otherwise.

In October 1856, Cohen was taken up with a travelling apostolate, but at the request of his sister, he went back to Paris to secretly baptize his nephew, George, in the church of the Blessed Sacrament Fathers on Rue Montparnasse. George's perseverance in wanting to become Catholic was remarkable in a boy so young.

---

[1] Sylvain, p. 180.

[2] Carmelite missionaries from Europe went to Malabar, India, in 1656. Noel Hanset, superior general of the Carmelites before Rayer, encouraged missionary work in the Order. He visited Cohen's French Province of Carmelites in 1855 and urged that missionaries go to India. Here he received the best response in the Order with eleven friars volunteering to go to Malabar. Later on, April 1883, Fr. John of the Cross and Brother Peter-Mary of St. Joseph from the Kensington community founded by Cohen, were assigned to the Carmelite community in Quilon, India. They set out for India on October 1, 1883. Members of the Syro-Malabar Province now work in Australia. (De Mendiola, *El Carmelo Teresiano en la Historia*, Cuarta Parte, Vol. 5, pp 58-59)

Soon afterward, when the boy refused to join his father in a Jewish prayer, the father realized what had happened and George admitted he was a Christian. His father then took the boy and put him in a non-Catholic boarding school in Germany under a false name. He refused to divulge where he had put him. When George asked to see his mother, he was told he could see her on condition that he renounced his faith. This he refused to do. His mother prevailed on her husband to take her to see her son, but they were forbidden to mention religion. A few months later, George's father admitted defeat, and the boy was recalled home.[1] A short time later, Cohen's elder brother, Albert, became a Catholic. He remarked that a faith that gave such strength to a child must be from God.

---

[1]   See "Selections from the Writings of Hermann Cohen" at the end of this book for an account of young George's conversion. On his deathbed, Hermann's father, David Abraham, rebuked his son for what he referred to as "the three great faults of your life; becoming a Catholic yourself, making your sister a Catholic and baptizing your nephew." Sylvain, p. 162.

Chapter 8

Music and the Mystic

In this chapter, I will digress a little in order to survey Hermann Cohen's musical output, especially his religious music.[1] Music of course is closely allied to poetry, and in Greek mythology both are inspired by the muses from which the name derives. So poets and musicians are closely linked because both set out to express the inexpressible. We speak about beautiful music, and this suggests that music has the power to evoke in us a sense of the beauty of God and of God's creation. The poet Gerard Manley Hopkins refers to God as "beauty's self and beauty's giver."[2]

Some people regard music as the most elevated of the fine arts—halfway between the physical and the spiritual. Departing from his normal milieu (theology), Hans Kung writes, "In some circumstances, can't musicians, poets, artists, and religious people have an inkling of, glimpse, hear, see, and express in their works realities that burst physical space, the space of energy and time? Can, for example Mozart's music, which is beyond doubt a phenomenon

---

[1] I am indebted to Father Benedict-Marie Bartrez of Toulouse for material in this chapter.
[2] Gerard Manley Hopkins, *Selected Poems,* Nonesuch Press, London 1954, p 70.

of physics, be grasped solely with physics? May the physicist qua physicist want to pass a *final* judgement on the *Jupiter* symphony?"[1] In an old study called "The effects of music" (1927), Max Schoen quotes a writer name Myers as follows: "There are three main lines of activity which take us away from the purely practical, everyday aspect of our experiences." He mentions "play" first, "phantasy" second (which allows full play to the imagination), and "mysticism" third:

> The third consists in mystical experience in which we lose the normal awareness of our own individuality and its relation to our surroundings. The ecstasies (active and passive) of love and religion afford the most striking and undoubted instances of this kind of experience—the lost relation of the self to its environment. I believe that our experience of beauty always partakes in some degree of this mystical or ecstatic character. Nowhere in art or nature as in music do we more keenly feel this "uplifting of the soul" as we term it, "this uplifting of the unconscious."[2]

The Composer Hermann[3]

There were two distinct periods in the musical output of Cohen.[4] Before his conversion to Christianity, his piano pieces were brilliant,

---

1 Hans Kung, *The Beginning of All Things: Science and Religion*, trans. John Bowden (Grand Rapids, MI: William B. Eerdmans, 2007, p. 52.

2 Max Schoen, ed., *The Effects of Music*, London: Kegan Paul, 1927.

3 Cohen was sometimes known to have been introduced to people as the "composer Hermann."

4 "The Banks of the Elbe" was dedicated to the Duchess de Rauzan who would later be his godmother. Some time ago a new discovery of three additional compositions was brought to my attention by Richard Cross: "Introductions and Variations" Cohen), "Fantasia from a Motif (Casta Diva)" (Bellini/ Cohen), and "Fantasia Brilliant" from "Maria di Rohan" (Donizetti/Cohen). These have been performed publicly by pianist Justin Kolb.

very secular, but often of great virtuosity. There was a collection of dances for the piano called "Fleurs d'Hiver," or "Flowers of Winter." Twelve other pieces, published by Ricordi of Milan under the title "Il Messaggiero Musicale II," called for acrobatic virtuosity in the pianist. Then there was his "Reminiscence of I Lombardi," on the theme from Verdi. In regard to that, commentator Benedict-Marie Bartrez, OCD., writes, "It should be noted, nevertheless, that some of these works have a certain religious character closely connected with that vague sadness so characteristic of 'the melancholy Puzzi,' notably a nocturne entitled 'Venetian Night' and 'Schlummerlied, a Lullaby' composed in 1841. One of his best known pieces, 'The Banks of the Elbe,' although sustained by a very marked waltz rhythm, is bathed in gentle melancholy."[1]Here again we touch on "melancholy Puzzi" from a northern melancholy shore. In his younger days, Cohen composed two unsuccessful operas. It's likely he was able to recycle some of these melodies in the dozens of motets he later produced. In spite of his gifts, in this first period Cohen did not make a name for himself in the musical world. As a pianist, for instance, he lacked the exacting and austere training given to Franz Liszt by his father. Also the adulation and indulgence of his mother, among others, would become a great obstacle for the young Hermann in his career as a pianist.

Just a few years after Cohen's death, another gifted young pianist, Elizabeth Catez, now St. Elizabeth of the Trinity, also responded with her whole being to the Lord's invitation to enter into an intimate relationship with him. At the age of thirteen, Elizabeth won first prize in piano performance at the Conservatoire of Dijon. Conrad de Meester, O.C.D., writes, "Several times, she takes part in concerts organized by the Conservatoire in town, and journalists from the local papers promise her a bright future."[2] Elizabeth knew that she vibrated

---

[1] Benedict-Marie Bartrez, *Carmel, La Pére Hermann*, Éditions du Carmel, Avignon, 1989, N.54, p. 23.

[2] Conrad de Meester, *Your Presence Is My Joy! Life and Message of Bl. Elizabeth of the Trinity* (Darlington, England: Darlington Carmel, Undated, p. 7).

like a lyre to the divine touch. In the article I have referred to above, Benedict-Marie Bartrez compares the two Carmelites and sees their roles as essentially that of an interpreter. He writes, "Everything leads us to believe that Hermann and Elizabeth were sincere interpreters: they would live in communion with the work they were to interpret to others—music cannot live without the interpreter."[1]

"A great pianist interprets for us, the audience, the works of the great composers. So it is the composer and the music that make the interpreter and the interpretation. Just as it is not the swallows that make the summer, but probably the opposite is true, so it is not the interpreter that makes the work but inversely the work makes the interpreter."[2]

The composer is sometimes seated among the audience, or is absent or perhaps dead, and the musical instrument is a dead thing in itself. Everything depends on the interpreter bringing this composition to life; so that at the end of the performance, we can say we have experienced the beauty of a work of art. An artist like Cohen could be carried away by the power of his music. I have already referred to the *Memoirs* of Cohen's former girlfriend, Céleste Mogador. It seems that music was the last thing on his mind when they were together late at night in his apartment when his other guests had departed. She asked him to play the piano, and he became so taken up with his music that he seemed to forget all about her. It has been suggested that no art has as much power as music to uplift the soul. In the *Phantom of the Opera*, a popular musical from the eighties by Andrew Lloyd-Webber, the lyrics point to this same phenomenon of the power of 'music of the night.'

> Close your eyes . . .
> Purge your thoughts of the life you knew before;
> Close your eyes, let your spirit start to soar,
> And you'll live as you never lived before.

[1] Benedict-Marie Bartrez, *Hermann Cohen,* Mount Carmel, October,1992, pp. 202-203.
[2] Ibid., pp. 202-203

From this point of view, it is not at all surprising that we have numerous examples of great artists at some point turning wholeheartedly to God, the source of all beauty. One of the best examples is Cohen's own mentor and tutor, Franz Liszt. On one occasion, Liszt gave Cohen a copy of the Bible. His underlying spirituality would have exerted an unconscious influence on someone who was as sensitive and responsive to the maestro as Cohen. Liszt had a well-earned reputation as a worldly and even dissolute person for much of his life. Yet witnesses tell us there was always something mesmeric and transcendental about Liszt as a person. He remained deeply spiritual at the bottom of it all. He described himself as "half-gypsy, half Franciscan," and this seems an apt description. In fact, he later became a Franciscan tertiary.[1] He became a personal friend of Pope Pius IX and eventually took minor orders,[2] was known as Abbé Liszt, and was considered to be a conscientious cleric. Charles de Foucauld is another good example of this kind of conversion; and nearer our own times, the gifted writer Thomas Merton abandoned a worldly life and entered the Trappist monastery in Gethsemane in the United States. All this goes to show that while Cohen's conversion may have come as a surprise to his friends, it was of a piece with the romantic musician searching for truth, beauty, and love. That also goes far to explain why the public perceived in Cohen a pronounced melancholic streak, an inner restlessness that refused to be satisfied with counterfeit happiness.

The Romantic Ideal

Nature and love were the powerful twin themes of the romantics as they reacted to the age of enlightenment, and these they celebrated in music, literature, landscape art, and especially poetry. In regard

---

[1] A Franciscan tertiary is a lay member of the Franciscan Third Order.

[2] Before the Second Vatican Council, there were four minor orders that a candidate received before proceeding to subdiaconate, diaconate, and priesthood. These were preceded by a ceremony of tonsure, which constituted a person a cleric.

to literature, English-speaking readers will immediately think of William Wordsworth, who was inspired by the lovely landscapes of the Lake District and other English scenes. Wordsworth tells us:

> The sounding cataract
> Haunted me like a passion.[1]

Or later in the same poem he writes,

> Therefore am I still
> A lover of the meadows and the woods,
> And mountains; and of all that we behold
> From this green earth; of all the mighty world
> Of eye, and ear . . . well pleased to recognise
> In nature and the language of the sense,
> The anchor of my purest thoughts, the nurse,
> The guide, the guardian of my heart and soul
> Of all my moral being.[2]

Here Wordsworth immerses himself in the contemplation of nature, which he describes in quasi-religious language. St. John of the Cross glorified nature in his lyrical poetry, but for him, the beauty of the "meadows and the woods" were simply the footprints of the Beloved. John's inner ear was attuned to the "silent music" of creation. This was the spirit in which the romantic Cohen would also celebrate nature, and we will look at this again when we give an account of the retreat he established in the beautiful Pyrenean setting of Tarasteix. "Nature draws us away from the dark world," as Cohen says in one of his canticles: "Nature above all is the place of encounter; nature is the pure reflection of God's glory."[3]

---

[1] The Poetical Works of William Wordsworth: "Lines Composed above Tintern Abbey," Oxford University Press, 1911. p. 206.

[2] Ibid. p. 207.

[3] Bartrez, p. 208.

John Keats is acclaimed as one of the foremost English romantics. For him, beauty too, was a component of love. "A thing of beauty is a joy forever."[1] No one better than Keats has given voice to these themes in his magical verse straddling nature and love, and the apparent ending of the latter in death.

> Bright star, would I were steadfast as thou art
> Not in lone splendour hung aloft the night,
> And watching, with eternal lids apart,
> Like nature's patient sleepless eremite.
> The moving waters at their priest-like task
> Of pure ablution round earth's human shores.[2]

The "romantic movement" in music is huge in its scope from the beginning of the nineteenth century on, the period that concerns us. Cohen was part of this developing scene. He was on familiar terms with some of its best exponents: Liszt himself, Mendelssohn, Chopin, and Berlioz. "The romantic is an idealist who pursues love as a dream, often an impossible dream."[3] Later on as a Carmelite priest, Cohen's preaching would be imbued with a romantic streak. His first collection of hymns was called *For the Love of Jesus Christ*, and though the lyrics for these were written by Sister Marie-Pauline du Fougerais, they perfectly expressed his own sentiments.[4] That

---

[1] John Keats, "Endymion."

[2] John Keats, "Bright star, would I were faithful as thou art." It has been made into a movie called after the opening words of the poem. Keats also wrote about "La Belle Dame sans Merci." Sadly Keats died a premature death in 1821, the year Hermann Cohen was born: the last two verses of the poem, presumably also addressed to Fanny, ran: "Still to hear her tender-taken breath, and so live ever or else swoon to death."

[3] Bartrez, *Carmel, Le Père Hermann*, p 33.

[4] For example, this was one Cohen was said to particularly like: "To you, God of love, I make an ardent prayer, Attend to me, fill my desire! May I dwell, O Lord, in your lovely sanctuary, 'til I draw my last breath." Beaurin, p. 228.

was one reason the music for these flowed so rapidly from his pen. Cohen had known the limitations and disappointments of human love in his youth, and now he had turned wholeheartedly to the only love that can truly satisfy. He would devote the remainder of his life to sharing this newfound love with others who were also searching as he had done. He had found this love through Jesus in the Eucharist.

Cohen knew that by entering the Carmelite Order, he was not abandoning what he held most dear; rather, he was responding to a better beauty, to the "silent music" of which St. John of the Cross sings. Again speaking of Cohen, Bartrez continues, "Inspired by love for the Eucharist, inspired also by love for music, for musical beauty—these two poles were perfectly fused—his a true interpreter who effaces himself before the musical reality, a humble instrument who inspires people and so reaches with full freedom into the heart of the public."[1]

Some of Cohen's eminent associates, such as Marie-Thérèse Dubouché and Julian Eymard, criticized the music Cohen played in church as being more suited to the opera than the altar. But this criticism seems to me somewhat unfounded. If a melody is beautiful and uplifting, why not use it to praise God rather than leave all the best tunes to the devil? However, Sister Marie-Pauline du Fougerais seems to have put Cohen's mind at ease on this matter. Again Bartrez sums up the issue: "The poet and the musician have but one heart and one soul. Indeed it is hard to say which inspired the other, the melody is the poetry singing, the poetry the melody speaking."[2]

Religious Music

After his conversion to Christianity, Cohen began a second period of musical output that lasted for about twenty years. He began composing music for Sister Marie-Pauline's poems in November

---

[1] Bartrez, *Carmel,* p. 27. (My translation)
[2] Bartrez, p. 211.

1850, and the work was finished before March 21, 1851. It amounted to forty motets in honor of the Eucharist called *For the Love of Jesus Christ*. Thirty were written in French, and ten were in Latin.[1]

As we look at Cohen's musical work today, we find it very impressive indeed. It consists of four collections of motets in polyphony, for organ or piano accompaniment. Bishop Louis Baunard, writing at the beginning of the twentieth century, referred to them in these words: "The artist (Cohen) was to sing the sweetest, the most mystical and penetrating melodies ever heard in our age."[2] Another critic, Jean Castex, quoted by Beaurin, also commented, "Hermann's romantic impulse never became pretentious. The listener could also sense that there is a high degree of complexity in his piano technique; and there are unexpected chords, which some musical commentators thought had been invented in the 1930's. Even in the 'ritornelle,' there is a great sense of German music."[3]

Cohen also composed a Latin Mass dedicated to his "seraphic mother St. Teresa of Jesus." It was first sung on the feast of St. Teresa in 1852 by three of his musical friends. One of them was an outstanding tenor, Count de Cahuzac.[4] Later, he rewrote this Mass for choirs with solos and duets with organ support. M. d'Etcheverry, organist in Saint Paul's church in Bordeaux, where it was first performed, has described the Mass as follows: "This musical work, executed in 1856 in this town [Bordeaux] is remarkable for the purity and ease of its melody, so easy to remember, something which

---

1 See his Forward or Dedication for this work in "A Selection from the Writings of Hermann Cohen" in Part 2 of this book.

2 Quoted in P. Andrè de Saint Marie, p. 173) Baunard also tells us (p. 173) that at the moment of Benediction in the church of St.-Valère, that occasioned Cohen's conversion, he heard these words that seemed to come from the sacred host: Ego sum via, veritas et vita (I am the way, the truth and the life.) Baunard was a professor at the University of Lille.

3 Beaurin, p. 226.

4 De Cahuzac later joined the Carmelites and attracted crowds to listen to him sing in the Carmelite church.

is becoming more and more rare. The solos are beautiful in feeling. The Kyrie Eleison is reminiscent of the German school, the Sanctus and Agnus Dei are two striking pieces and are indeed inspired."[1]

Bartrez observes, regarding the first baritone solo for the Kyrie Eleison, "We are immediately entranced by the purity and simplicity of the melody: the secret lies in the fact that the composer put all his art into an expression of faith for the glory of God alone."[2] The motets comprise the greater part of Cohen's sacred musical compositions, He became acquainted with the Visitation Sister Marie-Pauline Fougerais in a convent near the Paris Carmel. A talented poet, between the years 1841 and 1842, she had composed thirty-two canticles, which she then put aside for several years. Later, she wished to help a family threatened with financial ruin, and it occurred to her that, if set to music, her poems could be sold in order to help them. Her superior agreed with the idea and, having consulted the Marist superior, he suggested they approach Cohen. He obliged, and so his first collection entitled *Gloire à Marie* (Praise of Mary) was born.

In regard to his second collection of canticles, Cohen began composing music for more of Sister Marie-Pauline's poems in November 1850, and the work was finished before March 21, 1851. Some regard this as his best work. It allows him to express the theme of love, a favorite with the romantics. In 1869, his third collection, *Flowers of Carmel*, was published. This includes the beautiful "Flos Carmeli," which is included in the CD of Cohen's Latin Mass.[3]

His fourth and final collection was called *Thabor*, comprising some twenty hymns and motets in Latin dedicated to the Blessed Sacrament. Most of these were composed in the silence and seclusion of the holy desert he had established in Tarasteix near Lourdes. The lyrics for his last two collections were written by various authors,

[1] Sylvain, p. 230.
[2] Bartrez, *Mount Carmel*, 1992, p. 215.
[3] Mass of St. Teresa of Avila, available from the Carmelite Book Service, http://www.carmelite.org.uk/acatalog.

including his friend Bishop François de la Bouillerie, and Père Louis Nègre, S.J.,[1] and some at least were written by Cohen himself.

One of the testimonies to Cohen's musical genius comes from a lifelong friend and eminent musician, Bavarian-born Joseph Schad.[2] They first met in Geneva where Liszt arranged for the fifteen-year-old Cohen to be installed as professor of music Schad was a fellow professor at age twenty-four. Later, they met up again briefly in Paris on the musical circuit. After spending a long time in Germany and then returning to Paris, Schad tells us, that "Hermann had disappeared." Great was his surprise when he took up a position as organist in Bordeaux cathedral and found Cohen was living in the vicinity as a Discalced Carmelite. "I found my former friend somewhat changed physically and morally. He gave me his collection [of motets] 'For the love of Jesus Christ,' and I transcribed some of them for the piano [*The Collections*]. As to melody and religious feeling, they are very remarkable compositions, and they are based on a harmony that is pure and happily varied."[3]

Cohen is not well known as a composer in spite of his great talents, but at a time of great poverty in church music in the nineteenth century, Cohen's motets were a welcome and original creation adapted to the times in which he lived. Cohen's motets became very popular and were subsequently often sung in cathedrals, churches, and schools throughout France right into the twentieth century. They were also brought by Carmelite nuns to new foundations in the United States. They have, therefore, their place in the history of church music in the 19th century.

---

[1]   His name will crop up in the story of Lourdes where he shows himself skeptical of Bernadette's visions.

[2]   M. Moreau, *Hermann au Saint Desert de Tarasteix* (Paris: R. Haton, 1877). Schad was a prolific composer.

[3]   Beaurin, p. 164.

Endnote

Influence of Sister Marie-Pauline du Fougerais on the Cohen Family

It seems that Cohen had introduced his sister Henrietta, who was married to lithographic artist Raunheim, to Sister Marie-Pauline, who asked her to teach music to her class. Henrietta was a good music teacher herself, but Cohen feared she might display anti-Christian prejudice to the children. Henrietta warmed to this holy and kindly Visitation sister and, as time passed, felt drawn to the Christian faith. She agreed that they would all go as a family (taking her mother, her husband, and her son George) to Agen to visit Hermann where he was now studying for the priesthood.

In preparation for the visit, Cohen sent his sister a letter outlining his own newfound Christian faith and including a copy of biblical passages that pointed to Jesus as the Messiah expected by Israel. He had already enlisted many people in the south of France in a prayer crusade for the conversion of his family. When Henrietta arrived, Hermann took the opportunity of expounding the doctrine of the Trinity at a Mass she attended. By this time, Henrietta's difficulties resolved themselves, but there was a problem. She told her brother that she would rather be lost than separated from her only son George. Here we notice maternal instincts at their most sublime. Her husband was adamantly opposed to Christianity, and she knew he would try to separate her from her child. At this, Cohen used a little emotional blackmail: "I no longer knew what saint to invoke, for I had exhausted all my arguments; so I stopped and challenged her energetically—how will you face Sister Marie-Pauline if she knows you believe but you don't have the courage of your convictions? Is this going to be the thanks she gets for all her efforts, her love, her kindness, and her prayers? This sudden appeal to her affection for the one she called *her* Mother Marie-Pauline caused her considerable confusion. We were in the garden where we had gone to have a heart-to-heart exchange; she walked on and on in silence. A great struggle was evidently taking place within her. After a few minutes, she turned to me and said, "If I can be baptized unknown to my husband, I will be a Christian before I return to Paris." The fifth evening after this conversion, I poured on her forehead the water of new birth and placed in her mouth the delightful bread of the holy Eucharist, the bread of life, whose sweetness those fervent hymns of Mother Marie-Pauline had inspired me to sing."[1]

---

[1] Flamme Ardente, p. 120.

Chapter 9

Hermann Cohen and
St. Raphael Kalinowski

In this chapter, I would like to underline what the two Carmelites - Hermann Cohen and St. Raphael Kalinowski had in common. I will also describe their relationship with mutual friends—members of the Czartoryski and Narischin families. The main lines of congruity between the two focus on the following points. Both admit to a conversion experience at around the age of thirty after many years of indifference to religion. Cohen as a Jewish convert, was more dramatic and more radical, of course, while Kalinowski's conversion resembled more that of Charles de Foucauld in Paris at the end of the nineteenth century. At an early age, both became attached to young actresses and thought about marriage. Both wrote memoirs detailing certain aspects of their lives. Both joined the Teresian Carmelite Order and played a big part as founders and restorers of Carmel in their respective areas of ministry, France and Poland. Kalinowski was the first male Teresian Carmelite candidate to be canonized since that of St. John of the Cross in 1726.

These developments took place after the church had progressed through periods of suppression and religious persecution in both countries. However, Cohen was a Jewish German; and Kalinowski was born in Vilnius or Vilna,[1] Lithuania, of Polish parents. Kalinowski later encouraged Sister Emily Rostworowska to translate Charles Sylvain's French biography of Hermann Cohen into Polish.

As sons of St. Teresa of Avila, both had the interests of the whole Carmelite family very much at heart, and they worked hard to promote the growth of both the Carmelite sisters and the Carmelite Secular Order. Both Kalinowski and Cohen strongly supported the work of the St. Vincent de Paul Society. From the point of view of devotional orientation, both focused on the Eucharist and dedication to Our Lady. Both had links to members of the same family—in this case the aristocratic Czartoryski family, heirs to the Polish throne. This noble family found themselves in exile in Paris because of their role in an insurrection against Russian czarist rule over Poland in 1830, as a result of which they were forced to flee their country.

In addition, both were associated with two sisters, Catherine and Natalie Narischkin. The sisters had been members of the Greek Orthodox Church but later converted to Roman Catholicism in Paris.[2] Raphael Kalinowski lets us know in his "Memoirs" that he knew these women and admired them. He recalled, "I knew Catherine Narischkin, a convert from schism to Catholicism. She was an angel of mercy like her sister Natalie, a daughter of Saint Vincent de Paul."[3] It is not stated where Kalinowski met the sisters, but they were widely traveled as was he. It is interesting that Natalie was involved in the foundation of the Sisters of Charity in the town of Gratz or Graz in Austria some years before Kalinowski entered the Carmelite house there as a novice.

---

[1]   Also known as Wilno.

[2]   Narischkins were a noble Russian family related to the Romanovs. Natalie's family was related to the mother of Peter the Great.

[3]   Joseph Kalinowski, *Pologne, Russie, Sibérie: d'après ses mémoires et sa correspondance: influence contraire du Catholicisme et du Schisme moscovite sur la Civilisation* (Liège, Belgium: Arts et Mètiers, 1923).

At one point, Cohen became Natalie's spiritual director in Paris. They may have met because Cohen liked to visit yet another famous shrine of Our Lady situated at 140 Rue de Bac in Paris where the Daughter of Charity Catherine Labouré (now canonized) received the revelation of the Miraculous Medal from the Blessed Virgin. Natalie became superior of the convent of Daughters of Charity situated in the nearby Rue Saint-Guillame. Natalie and her sister were born in St. Petersburg to parents Gregory Narischkin and Princess Anne Mestchesky. Natalie was born on August 6, 1820, the year before Cohen. In addition to Catherine, whom she addresses as "Kate" in her letters, she had a brother and two other sisters, Marie and Elizabeth. Cohen visited Natalie in Paris whenever he passed through. On August 9, 1854, Natalie wrote to her sister Catherine, "I have seen the Father [Hermann] in our chapel, where he said Mass, during which his own Eucharistic canticles were sung and which everyone who hears them agrees are most beautiful. He turned away from a worldly life and in an instant was transformed into a St. John of the Cross, by the sudden and all-powerful strength of the divine Eucharist."[1]

A contemporary novelist, Pauline de la Ferronays, who wrote under her husband's name, Augustus Craven, knew the Narischin family well. The above quotation comes from her French biography of Natalie written in 1877, a few years after Natalie's untimely death. Natalie and Ferronays's younger sister, Olga, were exactly the same age and inseparable friends. Natalie, as a sister of Charity would dedicate her life to Christ and the sick. She was particularly close to a *notable* person at court, Count Xavier de Maistre and his family.[2] When Natalie was invited to attend balls and functions hosted by de Maistre, she would often take refuge in the house chapel with

---

[1] Madame Augustus Craven, *La Soeur Natalie Narischkin, fille de Saint Vincent de Paul* (Paris: Didier et Cie, 1877). This writer was born Pauline de la Ferronays.

[2] He was a brother of the famous Joseph de Maistre, an ardent monarchist and champion of the papacy. His work had an influence leading up to Vatican I, which proclaimed papal infallibility.

one of the de Maistre daughters where they would pray quietly, away from the glare and glitter of the ballroom. Here her behavior resembles that of Elizabeth of the Trinity in similar situations later in the century.

In her biography, Craven refers to some Jesuit priests and others who gave Natalie spiritual direction. Then she goes on, "In the first place, among these must be mentioned Father Hermann, whose conversion touched Natalie in a special way. She never tired of giving an account of this graced event of which he [Hermann] had been the recipient. In her letters, she mentions the great joy it gave her when he appeared one day in the motherhouse to say Mass."[1] Again in the biography, she tells us, "In 1862 this admirable and holy religious spent fifteen days in Paris; and during his stay, he came to say mass every day in the little convent on the Rue Saint-Guillaume. These two people, so worthy of each other, would engage in a direct and intimate exchange. But nothing we may say about these encounters can equal the tone in which Sister Natalie herself gives witness, not only to the holiness of her guest, but also to the atmosphere that she herself radiated around her."

Again, Natalie wrote in a cover note, enclosing a photo of Cohen,

Chère [Dear] Kate,

How can I thank you for your generous gift? It is in your name that I am enabled to carry out these good works of charity. As for myself, I'm poor; I am unable to recompense you, but this image carries a signature, which is that of a *saint* (writer's emphasis). My companions here are overjoyed and covered by the perfume of such virtue. Yesterday, in signing this little image which I'm sending you, he remarked to me, "Truly I don't deserve to visit this house; I sense Jesus everywhere, in the holy sacrament, in the chapel, in your

[1] This and the next four citations are taken from Craven, *La Soeur Natalie Narischkin*.

hearts, in the rooms, everywhere; in a word, one breathes Jesus, our love, in this dear house." Our hearts radiate happiness and thankfulness; and you yourself, dear Kate, do please thank God with us for the graces which the visit of this Father has brought us.

Craven adds, "The opinion which Father Hermann had of Sister Natalie was hardly different from what she had of him; and in speaking of her he said "that in his judgment, she was one of the most beautiful souls in the church." After Natalie's return from Gratz, she wrote to her other sister Elizabeth: "These days at Gratz spent in the parlor of our little convent produced in me almost the same effects as a dream . . . and these moments when I had the happiness of finding myself close to you, seemed to pass quickly and are now far distant. Needless to say, the sisters are happy at my return; my only regret is having to leave our good Father [Hermann]; just seeing him is enough to inspire in me the desire to practice all the virtues."[1]

Writing to her friend Mathilde, the Countess des Cars, Natalie says: "Cholera has returned to Paris. You know how it has ravaged everywhere, and death is rapid. Pray for all the people who so suddenly go before the tribunal of the Sovereign Judge. If you hear that it has come this way, won't you have Masses said for the salvation of my poor soul? And would you let Father [Hermann] know.[2] As it happened, it was Narischin herself who would be informed of Cohen's death in Berlin in 1871 by a Vincentian colleague of hers who nursed him in his last illness.

At the beginning of 1902, in a letter to his friend Sister Mary Xavier, Kalinowski gives us these interesting details: "She, Catherine

[1]   Timothy Tierney, *Saint Raphael Kalinowski (Apprenticed to Sainthood in Siberia)*, Balboa Press, 2016, p. 316.

[2]   Craven, p. 371

Flambeau translated all of your records on French convents. As a token of gratitude I send her a small relic of the hair of Sister Thérèse of the Child Jesus. Fr. Herman [*sic*] was the spiritual director of this sister before she joined the Order."[1]

In 1903, Kalinowski was busy reading and correcting the translation of Craven's biography of Natalie Narischkin that he had received from his friend, Wenceslas Nowakowski (later known as Albert) a Capuchin. Kalinowski thought that the example of Sister Natalie and the reading of her biography could help bring back to the Catholic Church many Russians of good faith. Kalinowski did his best to promote this biography. In 1898, Kalinowski published a booklet that gives us an interesting description of Natalie Narischkin. The booklet tried to show, in the thinking of the times, that for him, a person can find true happiness only in the Catholic Church. He continues, turning to the work of Emily Rostworowska, who had translated Sylvain's biography of Hermann Cohen into Polish:

> I happened to read this biography of Herman [*sic*] and welcomed the opportunity to further explore these two converts and it was impossible not to admire them. . . . Ah, the source from which flow streams of love and strength that brought a previously unknown outpouring of joy—was holy faith. . . . It was only in the one true Catholic Church, and in the Church alone, that each of these two converts drank from the source of living water, thirsting for truth and searching for God Himself. The presence of the Lord Jesus in the Blessed Sacrament won over Herman, and his presence in the Church gained Natalie. Herman was her spiritual director who designed the final shaping of the beauty of her soul. They met each other providentially, as if the hand of providence brought those two into the

---

[1] Jean-Baptiste Bouchaud OCD, *Miłość za Miłość*, Wydawnuctwo Karmelitow Bosych, Krakow, 2006.

bosom of the Church, coming as they did, from different expressions of hostility to the Church. The former, after a baptism of penance leading to a life in Carmel and dedicated missionary work, by the generosity of his ministry became a martyr to the French prisoners in Spandau during the Franco-Prussian War. This was the end of his life in exile. The latter—Natalie . . . preserved her innocence in a safe refuge in the Congregation of the Daughters of Charity. This was a time of social upheaval (1848–1874) and she worked, sometimes heroically, to assist others in the most varied needs, and continued to sacrifice herself to the last moments of her life. Faithful to her call and mission she could say with Saint Paul, Apostle: "*Cursum consummavi, fides servavi*" [I have finished the course, I have kept the faith]. The Catholic faith united them and was the source of their happiness.[1]

Reflecting on the example of their lives Kalinowski continues: "This reminds us that above all, it is impossible not to ask the question: why Herman left the world and did not look for repentance in Judaism? . . . Where the source of the love of God was baptism for Herman, (sic) an unknown hand directed Natalie to the bosom of holy Church."[2]

After her reception into the Catholic Church Natalie wrote:

"Venice, August 18, 1844.

A date forever memorable for me, my dear friends, my dear sisters . . . yes, I can tell you now I am a Catholic! My friends, my good Father Aladel, my good sisters at the Rue de Bac, all of you, whom God and the Holy Virgin *has charged to watch over me, you must rejoice today. . . for you have been*

---

[1] Bouchaud, p. 416.

[2] Ibid.

heard! [Natalie's emphasis] I am happy at last! Yes happy to have returned to the fold, but sad to be so unworthy."[1]

Kalinowski only quotes this part of her letter, but I am adding the remainder taken from the biography of Natalie already referred to:

> Can you imagine how God has given me this grace? . . . Yes, you can, because you have unfortunately such a good opinion of me; but I myself who knows what I deserve and to what degree I am miserable and ungrateful, I cannot understand such a mercy. . . . My friends! What a memory I will keep of this day! It seems to me again that I'm not sufficiently grateful. But God has, and will again have pity on me. How can I thank you, all you to whom I owe my happiness! Circumstances delayed my conversion, until this day consecrated to the Holy Virgin. Will she not protect me all my life as on this day of her glorious Assumption? I have been enfolded and watched over, what more can I say. I only want to tell you of my happiness. Thank the good God for me![2]

In another letter to her sister, Natalie writes, "Good Father Herman arrives on Monday. . . . What a delight to love Jesus, love him as holy people do. . . . Love like a fire envelops and permeates him like rays surrounding his heart."[3] Narischkin didn't expect, when she wrote these words, that he would make a similar assessment of her. After his conversion and even before joining the Carmelite Order, Cohen called her "one of the most beautiful souls in the Church."[4] Natalie Narischkin died a saintly death on her birthday, August 6, 1874, Feast of the Transfiguration. She was surrounded

---

[1]   Craven, p 50.

[2]   Ibid.

[3]   Beaurin, p. 213

[4]   Ibid., p. 213.

by her community and the priest who gave her the Last Rites. Her last words were, "We shall meet again in heaven, and pray for me."[1] She was buried in the area reserved for the Sisters of Charity in Montparnasse cemetery.

Cohen's Influence Spreads to Poland

On November 1, 1895, Sister Emily Rostworowska, a nun from the Monastery of Our Lady of Mercy at Lagiewniki, near Krakow, turned to Kalinowski and asked him to supply her with details of the life of Cohen. She wrote:

> I am not allowed to talk a lot [she was very ill] but instead dedicate myself to the work of our vocation. To profitably use these long free hours I decided on a Polish translation of some good and edifying book if could get my hands on the life of Father Herman [*sic*], a Carmelite, who seemed to me wonderfully fired with the love of God and therefore worthy of translation. The work is almost finished, you may live to see it published, but the question is whether published or not, this Father is well-known. . . . I come to you, Father, in need, and at the same time ask if your own recollections could add something to this story? In Paris, you could easily have known the Carmelites or at least heard of Father Herman [*sic*].[2]

In fact, Kalinowski did not personally know Cohen, but his colleague Bartholomew Diaz de Cerio knew him well in the novitiate of the Order in Le Broussey, near Bordeaux. Another colleague, Jean-Baptiste Bouchaud was actually given Cohen's room next to the chapel in the novitiate at Le Broussey. Because of her illness, Sister Emily was unable to correct the defects in her translation of

---

[1] Craven, p. 210.
[2] Bouchaud, pp. 419-420.

the biography. But the situation was saved when she asked Cohen's sister, who was the owner of the book, for permission to publish her translation, despite its shortcomings. Printing costs would be covered by the congregation of Our Lady of Mercy.

The above-mentioned friars knew a lot about Cohen, of course, so Kalinowski was able to satisfy Sister Emily's wishes. In January 1896, Cohen's sister Henrietta Raunheim wrote to Carmelite Father Athanasius who acted as a go-between: "I would be very happy if the biography of my beloved brother, Father Herman [*sic*], is translated into Polish. This book is my own now, because I had to pay a considerable sum to P. Sylvain [author] and M. Oudin [the publisher] for it. Can the good Father of Czerna [Kalinowski] ensure that the Polish translation is accurate and well done? Will I be able to show it to Polish experts who would be able to judge this matter? My wish is that no word should be changed. This book has already been translated into German, English and Italian."

In another letter a month later Henrietta explained why she was so concerned to make sure that the translation of the biography of her brother was authentic and accurate. The biography written by Father Sylvain was done under the guidance of the late lamented Father Martin [Felix Fronteau, 1827–1894, who was a general councilor of the Discalced Carmelites in Rome]. Father [Martin] was a priest in the diocese of Tours, and a professor of rhetoric. He heard a sermon by Father Hermann speaking of the inexpressible happiness which he felt at being a Christian and a friar. Under the influence of this sermon, he joined the recently restored Order and the province of Aquitaine as Father Hermann did, and he was one of the pillars of the Province for fifteen years. After his release from the office of provincial, he was appointed to the hermitage in the solitude of Tarasteix, founded by Father Hermann. Father Martin introduced the eremitical life there in 1869.

In 1872, Father Martin was appointed general councilor and held that office for eighteen years. No one in Carmel knew Hermann better than he, and Henrietta was right when she wrote that in a sense he was the author of the biography of her brother, especially the second part, for which he provided Sylvain with the necessary information. Henrietta was really coauthor of the first part because the information came from her. It was understandable then that she wished the translation to be faithful to Sylvain; so she at first refused permission for a Polish edition. She had learned that it was very inaccurate, and two chapters had been omitted altogether. Not having the energy to redo the work, Sister Emily then said she would give it up.

However, her work was of great value and could have done much good, so this development worried Kalinowski, and he wrote again to Henrietta. She replied graciously, "Please do what you consider to be appropriate. Hermann means the same to you and to me. I agree that the work of beloved Sister Emily be transmitted as it is and I repeat that it's better than nothing. Let us ask Our Lady of Mount Carmel that the Polish edition will do as much good as it has done in other languages. Please tell her Sister Emily that I am united with her in Jesus Christ."[1]

So in this way Cohen began his mission in Poland, where so many Jews lived. Certainly it brought joy, comfort, and courage to those Jews who had converted to the church and to many other Polish people. Kalinowski thanked God for all that, but he was not yet satisfied. He wrote to Natalie Narischkin and asked her to write down everything she knew and remembered about Cohen. Natalie complied with his wishes, and her work was published by Kalinowski in the *Chroniques du Carmel*. At the end of the booklet, Kalinowski addresses Sister Emily: "May those who read your work hopefully bear the fruit desired by you. May the life of Father Hermann and Sister Natalie Narishkin who were first enlightened outside the church, demonstrate that only in the Holy Catholic Church can faith offer eternal life."[2]

---

[1] Tierney, *Saint Raphael Kalinowski,* p. 319

[2] Ibid.

The Czartoryskis.

Paris became a mecca for political dissidents in the nineteenth century. Because of his musical reputation, Cohen was invited to the Hôtel Lambert where he made a great impression on the Czartoryski family and became a personal friend of Princess Amparo. He would have met her in the southern French town of Bagnères-de-Bigorre where there was a community of Carmelite friars, which Cohen had helped set up. Here the exiled Spanish royal family occasionally frequented the spa waters. Cohen acted as chaplain to the family on these occasions. Princess Mary (later Mother Mary Xavier OCD, Krakow) and Duchess Marcelina were greatly impressed by this humble friar. Princess Mary later wrote:

> In reading the *Chronicles of Carmel* . . . I asked myself after my entrance into Carmel, from where could have come this strong affection for our fathers; because before this, I had not known the Carmelites . . . Father Hermann was the first Carmelite that I had the opportunity to meet. I remember how I was struck with admiration for this religious whom I saw for the first time, so holy, so humble, only recently miraculously converted. I saw him enter the stately gilded hall, which contrasted so much with this holy and humble Carmelite, dressed in a heavy habit and white mantle. . . . After he had greeted everyone, he sat down at the piano and played so beautifully that it made a lasting impression on us.[1]

Princess Mary (Mother Mary Xavier) and Duchess Marcellina, greatly influenced by Cohen, would later exert considerable influence in their turn on Joseph Kalinowski.

---

[1] Beaurin, p. 213.

Le Père Hermann photographié vers 1868 en compagnie de l'abbé Roziès face à la Grotte de Lourdes

Sainte Bernadette Soubirous
(1844 - 1879)
Protégée par le Père Hermann
dès le début des apparitions

Chapter 10

Hermann Cohen and
St. Bernadette Soubirous (1858)

The shrine of the Virgin Mary, situated in the town of Lourdes in the south of France, has perhaps been the most influential place of Marian pilgrimage in the history of the church. The year 2008 marked the 150th anniversary of the apparitions at the grotto of Massabielle, a jubilee year. There, the Virgin Mary appeared to the young peasant girl, Bernadette Soubirous, who is now honored as a saint. The story is well known to many Catholics, so we can presume widespread awareness of its basic facts. I would like, however, to describe Hermann Cohen's connection with the story of Bernadette, which is generally not known. It will highlight Cohen's devotion to Mary, tell us something about nineteenth-century spirituality; and force us to confront the unusual or even the miraculous on the journey of faith.

Cohen's association with the shrine encompasses a period of ten years, 1858 to 1868. The following chapter will deal with the intervening period, in the course of which Cohen restored the Carmelite friars to England after they had been absent for a number of years. Following this he was given permission to return to the holy desert of Tarasteix in the vicinity of Lourdes. The current convent of Discalced Carmelite nuns in Lourdes traces its foundation to 1876.

It is situated almost directly opposite the shrine on a low hillside on the far side of the Gave. There is an even older Carmelite convent in Nevers, the city where Bernadette's remains are now venerated. The most obvious link between Carmelites and Lourdes is that the eighteenth and final apparition took place on July 16, 1858, the feast of Our Lady of Mount Carmel. In this context, there is some evidence to suggest that Bernadette herself subsequently wished to enter Carmel. However, she decided against this and, in any case, ill health would have prevented it. The Carmelite connection I wish to refer to here revolves around three very different people: Cohen himself, his future confrere Hyacinthe Loyson and St. Thérèse of Lisieux, who prayed earnestly for Loyson's conversion. In addition, we have the story of the Martin family and the place Lourdes held in their lives.

Though there is evidence of a small group of women processing to the grotto with lighted candles at an early stage, Cohen was the first Catholic priest to lead a pilgrimage in Lourdes. This in itself is some kind of distinction if we consider the countless thousands of priests who have followed in his footsteps. Some books on Lourdes are unaware of this fact and describe the first pilgrimage as taking place sometime later. There are few references to Cohen in literature on Lourdes.[1] However, we do have references to him in an account of Lourdes by the great French Marian scholar René Laurentin. Similarly, the detailed witness of Antoinette Tardhivail, a friend of Cohen's, is often overlooked.

New venture

During his year in the novitiate at Le Broussey in France in 1849, Cohen would have studied the contemplative origins of the Carmelite Order, which he had joined a short time previously. There he would have learned about the tradition of holy deserts,

---

[1]   Of the dozens of banners commemorating various saints and holy people strung around the Basilica of Pius X, there is none of Cohen, who was involved there from the beginning.

which were intended to preserve the original inspiration of prayer and contemplation begun by the first hermits on Mount Carmel early in the thirteenth century, or some time previously. It is quite remarkable that in only five years as a Carmelite priest, Cohen had attained a sufficient spiritual maturity and drive to take on the tremendous challenge of founding a holy desert.

The Primitive Rule given to the first Carmelite lay hermits by Albert, patriarch of Jerusalem, counseled the hermits in the imitation of the prophet Elijah, traditionally regarded as their father, founder, and inspirer of their way of life. Elijah's disciples and those of his successor, Elisha, were known as the "sons of the prophet." The rule required the Carmelites to remain in their cells (rooms) in order to "meditate on the law of the Lord both day and night and to watch in prayer." The hermits were called the "Brothers of the Virgin Mary, Queen of Carmel." Occasionally, they came down from the mountain to communicate the fruits of prayer they had received from God in solitude to the people living in the surrounding area.

After the Saracen invasions, the hermits emigrated to Europe where they were to officially become mendicants like the Dominicans and Franciscans, leaving their solitude to preach and work in the apostolate under its various forms. They would now be known as friars rather than monks. These early Carmelites may have brought Byzantine images or icons of Mother and Child with them to Europe, images that later influenced artwork relating to Our Lady of Mount Carmel. Indeed, it would seem that it was an image of Mary like "Our Lady of Grace of Cambrai," given to the Cathedral of Cambrai in France in 1450, that most appealed to Bernadette. On one occasion, a priest visited Bernadette with an album of pictures of Mary; and this was the one she selected. She seems to have preferred this over the now-famous statue of Our Lady of Lourdes by sculptor Joseph Fabisch still in position in the grotto. Bernadette was known to have disliked this image; she said it was beautiful, but very far from the real thing!

One of the most popular Carmelite images of Mary in France was known as "La Bruna" or "The Dark One," and it was based on the icon of Cambrai. It had been venerated in the Carmel of Naples and is thought to have been painted in the first half of the thirteenth century. Throughout the fourteenth and fifteenth centuries, the Carmelites always looked back to the origins of their sublime vocation in solitude. Some tried to retain the original form of the life in silence and contemplation. In time, hermitages, often called holy deserts, were established to facilitated this style of life, by contrast with the houses carrying on a more active apostolate.

In 1856, In the *Haut Pyrenees,* Cohen discovered a vast wooded solitude at the village of Tarasteix about twenty kilometers from the then unknown town of Lourdes. A letter written in 1857 shows us what Cohen was thinking: "I can't tell you how much I long for the solitude of Tarasteix. I am collecting funds to pay off the debt here [Lyon], and then I shall make my way there."[1]

Cohen found Dominic Arbizu y Munarriz sympathetic to the idea of a mountain retreat. By this time Dominic had become superior general of the Italian Congregation of Teresian Carmelites. Munarriz was himself ready to abandon everything and even resign as superior general to join him there. As it turned out, Cohen was to spend only two years at Tarasteix before his death.

The Holy Desert of Elijah at Tarasteix

Cohen's choice of location for the holy desert could not have been better. It would have appealed to his spiritual father, John of the Cross, who loved beautiful settings that could promote contemplation and union with God. We have a description of the place left by the last Carmelite to reside there before religious were again expelled from monasteries toward the end of the nineteenth century. He writes: "Here one can only see the sky and wooded areas, and one hears only the murmur of a fountain flowing under the trees nearby. Imagine a chain of wooded hills stretching from north to

---

[1] Sylvain, p. 205.

south, from Maubourgnet to Lourdes, about thirty five kilometers long, and four to six kilometers wide. There are tranquil valleys lying between the hills, evergreen and dotted with clusters of oak trees. From Tarasteix, the forest is deep and dense."[1]

Cohen chose a site on high ground but sheltered by the highest peaks. It would not be too cold in winter, while in summer it would be cooled by refreshing breezes. It is difficult to imagine a more beautiful spot for the cells of the hermits, as regards both the views from there and the purity of the air—two things that St. Teresa looked for in her foundations. From Tarasteix, in fact, you can see the whole range of the Pyrenees extending in all directions and broken only by a gap through which the green fields of the Ariège district can be seen.[2] Another account described the setting of the holy desert in these words: "It would be difficult to find a more agreeable site, more in accord with the solitary life. The solitude, the silence, the separation from the world, that circle of woods with their cool shade, the purity of the air, the murmur of fountains with their waters falling to the valley; the flowers, the birds, the stillness of nature, all carry the heart to God, detaching it from creatures."[3]

Here, too, in this neighborhood, the shrine of Lourdes can be found. At the time when Cohen was surveying the area, a fourteen-year-old child near the hamlet of Bartrès was tending sheep for her former wet nurse in the hills overlooking Lourdes. She wished to make her First Communion and prevailed on her parents to allow her to return to her home in Lourdes in order to learn her catechism in preparation for this event. Cohen could not have foreseen that two years later he would have the privilege of meeting Bernadette, the future visionary.

---

[1] Tierney, p. 66.

[2] This was the area inhabited by the sect known as Cathars in medieval times. They were an esoteric, gnostic-type group that was pursued by the Inquisition and incurred the condemnation of the church.

[3] Beaurin, p. 275.

The Apparitions at Lourdes: 1858

While Cohen was still involved with the Carmelite houses at Bagnères and Lyon, "a beautiful lady" first appeared to Bernadette on February 11, 1858.[1] Cohen seems to have heard the news from one of his friends in March 1858. Antoinette Tardhivail was a frequent visitor at the nearby Carmelite convent at Bagnères. Laurentin suggests that Tardhivail later took Bernadette to visit the Carmelite convent in Bagnères.[2] Certainly she did visit there in 1862. On March 25, 1858, the feast of the Annunciation, the Virgin Mary appeared again to Bernadette and said, "I am the Immaculate Conception," using the local *patois* that Bernadette spoke. This was just four years after the dogma of the Immaculate Conception of Mary had been proclaimed by Pope Pius IX on December 8, 1854. On Tuesday, April 7, Tardhivail, with her two sisters, Marie and Theotiste, were present at the seventeenth apparition to Bernadette. She has left a precise, truthful, simple, and convincing account, which goes as follows:

> Since the feast of the Annunciation, the little girl had not returned to the grotto until yesterday. I witnessed one of her ecstasies, which according to Doctor Dozous, who was

---

[1] It's interesting that Bernadette herself did not claim to have seen Mary; rather, she referred to *aquero*, meaning "it" or "that thing" in the local patois.

[2] Antoinette Tardhivail was assistant sacristan at the parish church in Lourdes. It would seem that Thérèse's mother, Zélie, spoke at length to her when she visited Lourdes in search of a cure. Antoinette had noticed in one of the apparitions that Bernadette appeared to be holding her candle in such a way as to burn her fingers. However, there were no burn marks discernible. She later tested Bernadette in the sacristy with a lighted candle, and Bernadette withdrew her hand very quickly. She also mentions the fact that Bernadette refused gifts of money. When people proffered her forty or twenty franc coins, she pushed them away. Antoinette sent reports of the apparitions to Rome.

observing her closely, lasted an hour. I finally reached the place, but I had left home before four o'clock in the morning; and she only arrived at about seven o'clock. On arriving, she fell on her knees beside the Gave just a few yards from the grotto, and from there, she was beginning to see the Blessed Virgin on the rose bush near the entrance. At that moment her ecstasy began. We noticed her smile then become serious and thoughtful and sometimes sad, in tune with what Our Lady was telling her. We saw her greet Our Lady; and then she began to talk to her, but no one could hear anything. You could see her lips moving, and she followed all the movements of Our Blessed Lady. Yesterday, she asked her to work a miracle so that unbelievers would accept all she said, but the Blessed Virgin only replied by a very sad smile, which made the child sad as well. Everyone shows great respect for the young person when her ecstasy begins until it is completed. The men uncover their heads, and people go down on their knees to pray. I am sending you a little piece of the rose bush near which Our Lady stood. I managed to get it with a great deal of trouble because I thought if anyone saw me taking the cutting, I would be in trouble![1]

Cohen returned to Tarasteix in May, but he did not go immediately to the grotto, according to Tardhivail. She had described to him what she witnessed. Since April 7, the apparitions had ceased. People got involved in unusual phenomena, and there were plenty of bogus reports circulating, including alleged visions of Mary. One of these turned out to be nothing more than a stalacmite in the interior of the cave which vaguely resembled a lady dressed in white!

The authorities also got worried and started to dismantle the grotto and prohibited people from drinking at the spring. Finally, they were ready to take the original advice of the police commissar

---

[1] Beaurin, pp. 2279-280.

Dominique Jacomet and close the grotto altogether. So on June 15, barricades were set up. The parish priest of Lourdes, Abbé Peyramale, intervened on July 8, the bishop got involved on July 11, and calm was restored. People started to pray at a distance from the grotto. Bernadette herself must have suffered a lot with this turn of events. She did not attend the grotto. She made her first Holy Communion at this time, but she had no apparition on that day. Bernadette advised people not to go to the grotto because the barricades had been erected. Then on July 16, the feast of Our Lady of Mount Carmel, the "beautiful lady" appeared to her for the last time. At sunset, Bernadette had felt an impulse to go to the grotto in spite of the prohibitions of the authorities and thus respond to Our Lady's invitation. She disguised herself and went with her aunt, Lucile Casterot, but did not go directly to the grotto. She crossed the River Gave and remained on the right bank. She knelt down and began to recite the rosary. In spite of the distance and the twilight, she had no difficulty in seeing Our Lady. She raised her hands in a gesture of joyful greeting. In the semi-darkness several people noticed Bernadette smile. Someone lit a candle, and people could see the joy on Bernadette's face. In the lovely light of the setting sun, people began to join in the rosary. After her ecstasy, Bernadette was questioned by Antoinette, and she said, "I did not see the Gave or anything else. I only saw her. I have never seen anybody as beautiful as she is." The apparition bowed toward the humble visionary as though in a farewell greeting and then disappeared. In her farewell, Our Lady of Lourdes, in a sense, left one final message—and that was "silence"—for she appeared without saying anything!

The Aftermath of the Apparitions

The authorities, for various reasons, tried very hard to contain a phenomenon, which to them seemed to be getting out of control. That was the reason for the barricades. It seems, however, that when some visiting journalist wrote favorably about the apparitions, some local women known to the Soubirous family took the matter into their own hands with a view to easing the restrictions imposed by the authorities. They spread false reports, for example that Napoleon's wife, devout Spanish lady, Empress Eugènie, had sent Bernadette a gift and asked her to pray for her. The authorities overreacted and took the women to court where a light fine was imposed. The women appealed, and the case went to a higher court in Pau. The defendants were acquitted. It became a "cause célèbre," and the women became local heroes.

Soon two more distinguished visitors became a catalyst for change. While Hermann Cohen was engrossed with the foundations at Tarasteix and Lyon in the summer of 1858, his friend, the famous Ultramontane lawyer and journalist Louis Veuillot was on a visit to the health spa at Bagnères. He was extremely influential and something of a prize-fighter in the conservative Catholic cause. Like Cohen, he experienced a deep conversion from an irreligious lifestyle some years previously. He passed through Lourdes during the month of July and spoke to the Abbé Peyramale, Bernadette's parish priest. After initial hostility, the priest had been won over by Bernadette's sincerity, as had the local bishop and two others. Veuillot interviewed Bernadette and was deeply impressed with her. He called on Cohen, and they were both disposed to believe in the apparitions. Both were afterward to defend Lourdes—Veuillot in his frequent articles in the Catholic newspaper *L'Univers* of which he was editor, and Cohen at the grotto itself, by leading the first pilgrimage there. Accompanied by Abbé Rozies of Tarasteix, on September 20, 1858 – just two months after the final apparition- -Cohen led hundreds of people in front of the grotto, although it was still enclosed behind barricades and access was forbidden by the civil authorities. On the same day, Amirale Bruat, governess to the emperor's son, visited the grotto. Laurentin writes, "On September 21, 1858, she had met a renowned Carmelite, Père Hermann. This musician, a convert from Judaism, whom many called a saint, had stirred up great excitement in Lourdes with his *loud and hearty* rendition of the *Magnificat,* and one of the psalms, and then by preaching at the forbidden grotto. He had made an impression on Bernadette. In February 1865, when she received his picture, she announced. 'I've really wished to have this.'"[1] At this time, Bishop Bertrand Laurence of Tarbes was studying the dossier on the apparitions and was soon to give a favorable decision.

Abbé Rozies had been a great help to Cohen in providing hospitality during his initial work of planning the holy desert. On one particular visit, the two priests were met by Abbé Peyramale, who offered them hospitality. Cohen went to see the mayor to ask permission for a visit to the grotto, and it was reluctantly given— and then only provided they went before dawn. Cohen and Rozies celebrated Mass at 3:00 a.m. and then went on their way to Massabielle accompanied by Dr. Pierre Romaine Dozous who had drawn up an official report of several miracles that had taken place there the previous month. Abbé Rozies describes the visit:

> We arrived at the grotto at dawn, but we were already meeting some people returning from there reciting the rosary and carrying water with them from the grotto in jugs and decanters. Something unusual happened to Father Augustine [Cohen] when he bent down to drink from the spring at the grotto; and as he did so, his breviary fell into the basin. A lady quickly tried to retrieve it from the water, and the priest also looked to see if the pages had gotten wet. There was one particularly beautiful picture of Our

---

[1] René Laurentin, *Bernadette Speaks: A Life of St. Bernadette Soubirous in Her Own Words* (Boston: Pauline Books & Media, 2000). In part 2, chapter 5, of his book, Laurentin gives an account of a long interview between a certain Abbé Pierre-François Junqua and Bernadette. Like Loyson, Junqua later left the church. "For this reason," Laurentin suggests, "the pious literature of the day, out of a sense of decency, attributed his memoirs to a believer in Lourdes, a Pére Hermann. But Pére Hermann who also questioned Bernadette, did not leave any notes." Laurentin, p. 165.

Lady, which he expected to find soaked. But not only was the colored picture of Our Lady not spoiled, but a perfect copy of it was imprinted on the blank page of his breviary. Cohen remarked, "Holy Virgin, you have done me a great favor, instead of one picture of you, you have given me two! We then returned to the village to meet up with other people who had received favors from Our Lady. Among them was a man who had lost an eye and had been in a lot of pain for two years. His pain ceased after washing in the spring at the grotto."[1]

The next day, Cohen wished to return to the grotto and told Abbé Peyramale, but he had no official permission, and the abbé told him to be careful. He replied, "I have not seen Our Lady, but I experience the same sensations at the grotto that I received at my conversion."[2] There is a report by the Commissar Jacomet dated September 20, 1858, and addressed to the prefect, which tells us about that pilgrimage the night before, as noted by Laurentin above: "Early this morning, there was a lot of agitation at the grotto caused by Father Hermann and Doctor Dozous who left the town together and went to the grotto; and there, surrounded by a curious crowd who had come with the Carmelite, Father Hermann, they sang the 'Magnificat' and another psalm so loudly that his voice could be heard on the way to Pau."[3]

The report reminded people that access to the grotto was forbidden except with the formal permission of the mayor. The above official also confirms the historical accuracy of Abbé Rozies's account. That same day, Cohen had a long talk with Bernadette. His friend Tardhivail had very quickly won the confidence and affection of Bernadette; Tardhivail became her teacher and taught her to read at the end of the year 1858. Bernadette, in fact, was not

---

[1]   Beaurin, pp. 284-285.
[2]   Ibid., p. 285.
[3]   Laurentin, p. 165.

too eager to meet priests as she had been grilled so much by some of them. In fact, on July 30, she was interrogated by the famous preacher Hyacinthe Loyson.[1] Loyson, who at this time had not yet joined the Carmelites, visited Lourdes with ecclesiastical approval and interviewed Bernadette in his hotel room. Antoinette tells us he questioned her in French but distorted everything the illiterate child said. Loyson cynically remarked, "The lady would have done better to teach you to speak." With peasant pride and much astuteness, Bernadette shot back: "What she didn't teach me was to make fun of people who don't know any better"![2]Loyson later left the Carmelite Order and the church; he figures in the story of Saint Thérèse as we shall see later. Bernadette was also interviewed by Père Louis Nègre, S.J, a friend of Cohen, between July and August 1858. He believed the apparitions were false.

In her interviews with various people, Bernadette was usually accompanied by Antoinette Tardhivail. But it would have been different perhaps in the case of this priest, Cohen, a Carmelite who was spiritual director to her teacher (who herself had spent some brief time in a Carmelite convent) It is not surprising, then, that Bernadette spent a long time talking to this sympathetic priest who was himself so devoted to Mary. We can assume, too, that Bernadette was glad to meet a Carmelite, recalling the last apparition on July 16. In fact, Bernadette's aunt wrote in regard to her vocation to religious life, "From the beginning, her attraction would have taken her to Carmel—she wanted to be a Carmelite."[3]Bernadette's mother Louise, her aunt Basile, and Abbé Peyramale, however, advised her to join the Sisters of Charity of Nevers, as they feared her health was not good enough for the strict Carmelite way of life. And Bernadette, in fact, went to Nevers some years later. On her way, she called to see the Carmelite students in Bordeaux. But she also had a certificate of

---

[1]   Loyson would later become a Carmelite confrère of Cohen, as will be mentioned later.

[2]   René Laurentin, *Bernadette of Lourdes*, p.130

[3]   Tierney, p. 71.

affiliation to the Carmel at Rennes given her by the prioress of that convent. For his part, Cohen never forgot Bernadette. He wrote from London in 1865, "I was so pleased to hear that young Bernadette is as good and humble as ever." In 1871, he remarked, "I am very glad that Bernadette has become a religious—she will be protected from many dangers."[1]

Going back to that first pilgrimage, Cohen gave a parting address in September 1858 to people who were gathered around. "People of Lourdes: The Blessed Virgin has done great things in your city. I have traveled a lot, and I would like to tell you that I have not found a church like yours anywhere else bearing witness to your great devotion to the Blessed Virgin. In fact, in your basilica, I have not found a single altar that does not represent a mystery in the life of the Blessed Mother of God. You have received a great grace."[2] Cohen was referring to the many altars of Our Lady in the parish church of Lourdes. Nine days after Cohen's visit, Napoleon III lifted the ban on visiting the grotto. The church where Bernadette was baptized has been completely renovated, and very few of the original furnishings and statues remain. However, a wooden statue of the Virgin with outstretched arms was in place in the parish church at that time. Bernadette would have venerated this statue, which is now situated in "Le Cachot," Bernadette's home for two years from 1856 to 1858.

In the years immediately following these momentous events the phenomenon of Lourdes gained momentum, with crowds visiting the shrine and bringing their sick to bathe in the spring at the grotto. Many healings were reported from the very beginning. Meanwhile, Cohen continued his Carmelite apostolate in France, being in great demand as a preacher throughout the country and further afield. But with great regret, he had to abandon his hope of living in the Pyrenean holy desert in 1858.

---

[1] Ibid., p. 71.

[2] Ibid, pp 71-72

Interior of Carmelite Church, Kensington,London

Chapter 11

Restoration of Teresian Carmelite Friars and Nuns to London (1862)

We now turn to the next phase of Hermann Cohen's life just a few years after the events at Lourdes. The Carmelite Order, like all other religious orders at the time of the English Reformation, suffered the consequences of the Act of Suppression or dissolution of the monasteries by order of Henry VIII. This "Stripping of the Altars" was carried forward in England during the sixteenth century.[1] Although a few unsuccessful attempts had been made, the ancient Carmelite Order would not be restored in England again until the arrival of two Irish Carmelites in Aylesford, Kent, in 1925.

In the meantime, the Carmelite Order on the continent of Europe underwent a reform movement that originated in Spain in 1562 through the work of St. Teresa of Avila. The newly reformed order, open to women and men, would be known as Discalced (or Barefooted) Carmelites. Eventually the "Discalced" group separated from the parent order and became a religious order in its own right.

---

[1]   This is a reference to Eamon Duffy's book of the same name (New Haven, Conn.: Yale University Press, 1992).

Carmelite Friars

At the beginning of the seventeenth century there was also great interest in introducing the male branch of the Discalced Carmelite Order to England. The great Thomas of Jesus restored the order in northern Europe after initiating the concept of the desert house for an eremitical community at Bolarque (Spain) in 1590. This was in keeping with the earliest traditions of Carmel. However, Thomas also became converted to the idea of a missionary dimension when he founded the second *holy desert* in Las Bateucas (Spain) in 1599. In his *Life of Teresa*, published under the name of Diego de Yepes, he added a chapter outlining Teresa's approval of the missionary vocation. As a consequence, he had to leave Spain and live in Rome where he helped set up "Propaganda Fide, the Congregation for the Missions."[1]

Thomas of Jesus founded a Carmelite house in Brussels in 1610, and then started the missionary college of St. Albert in Louvain. Here, young men from England, Ireland, and Holland studied to become Carmelite friars with a view to returning to their own countries as missionaries. The English mission began in 1614 in London. During the course of the centuries, many Discalced Carmelites managed to carry out a ministry in England under difficult and dangerous circumstances. The first of these missionaries to reach England (in disguise) was Thomas Doughty, who became known as Father Simon Stock, appropriate for such a new beginning in England.[2] Doughty's native area was Lincolnshire. He was under the auspices of the Spanish ambassador Count de Gondemar, and that to some extent ensured his safety; but he seems to have largely worked as a chaplain to one of the Roper families. These were relatives of the martyred "Man for all Seasons," St. Thomas More;

---

[1] Cardinal Newman later attended the college set up there in association with the congregation.

[2] St. Simon Stock, an Englishman, was an early Prior General of the Carmelite Order.

the family had a house in Holborn, London. Doughty moved about with extreme caution in order to celebrate Mass, encourage people in their faith, and reconcile others to the church. He also wrote some inspirational pamphlets. However, his movements and activities were noted; and a government report dismissed him as the author of "divers late and foolish pamphlets; his lodging is in the lower end of Holborn." Doughty became involved in the idea of sending a Carmelite Missionary team to a new colony which would be named Avalon, in Newfoundland, North America. The project was planned through a friend George Calvert (Lord Baltimore), who was possibly a convert of his. This project ended in failure, but these details about Doughty demonstrate how the English Carmelite Mission looked toward the New World from the very beginning.

The second Carmelite missionary to England after Doughty was William Pendryck and he, together with a later arrival John Ruddgley, worked for many years from the cathedral city of Wells in Somerset. There was a Carmelite monastery for women here for many years. This is not far from Wincanton where the second Carmelite foundation after Kensington was later made. In the succeeding decades dozens of Carmelite missionaries ministered in England. Cohen's pioneering work in England has an indirect bearing on the presence of the Carmelite family in English-speaking countries in the California-Arizona Province in the USA, in Australia, and the Philippines. Over the years, some friars who had been based in the English region have served in all of these areas.[1]

Near the end of the eighteenth century, a Discalced Carmelite named Francis Willoughby Brewster began his ministry in England.[2] By coincidence, like Doughty, he too was from Lincolnshire and labored in his native area of Market Rasen for over fifty years. After a nine-week illness, he died there on June 11, 1849, at the age of

---

[1] The Washington Province, however, had made a foundation of friars in the Philippines before friars from the Anglo-Irish Province went there.

[2] Father Benedict Zimmerann O.C.D, *Carmel in England*, Ch. 5, Burns Oates, London,1899.

seventy-nine years. On January 17, he was buried near the altar in the chapel he built. Seven priests and a great crowd of people attended his funeral. When he retired from ministry in 1847, he spent his time as a beekeeper and in a life of contemplation. There was a long epitaph on his gravestone in Latin ending with the words, "Ave et Vale in Pace," or "Hail and farewell in peace." But in spite of individual heroic missionary exploits, no one so far had set up a Carmelite community in England.

With the death of the last Carmelite, the order had effectively died out in England. But two years before Brewster's death, something was happening in Paris that would restore the broken continuity and indeed put the order on a firm footing in England. And it would also put the order on a par with about fifteen other orders of male religious including Jesuits, Benedictines, Dominicans, Oratorians, Franciscans, Passionists, Oblates, and many others that had become established there in the preceding decades.

A Providential Meeting.

So once again Cohen was called upon to undertake a great new initiative and in a very different environment. In England, he would be cut off from family and friends—a loss he would feel keenly. Cardinal Nicholas Wiseman of Westminster met Cohen in Rome in 1862 when both attended the canonization of the Japanese martyrs, Saint Paul Miki and Companions. Wiseman would have known Brewster, the last Carmelite in England. The Cardinal was born in Seville, Spain, of Irish parents and although a brilliant scholar in biblical and oriental languages, he abandoned the academic world to renew the Catholic Church in England.[1] After eventually

---

[1] Wiseman met John Henry Newman in 1832 when Newman was on his "Grand Tour" of the Mediterranean and called at the English College in Rome. Wiseman later encouraged the future Cardinal-to convert to Catholicism, though he wasn't responsible for Newman's conversion. He was in fact disappointed that Newman delayed doing so for four years.

becoming vicar apostolic in 1840 (preliminary to the establishment of a hierarchy), Wiseman was appointed cardinal archbishop of Westminster by Pope Pius IX in 1860, the first to be so honored since Cardinal Reginald Pole. The name Westminster was chosen because of the great medieval Benedictine Abbey, which was now in the hands of the Anglican Church, adjoining the Houses of Parliament. The Cardinal had been actively encouraging religious orders to establish themselves in England after the centuries-long break. He recognized in Cohen the qualities of a founder and was aware of his record as such in France invited him to do the same in London. Cohen's name in religion was Augustine Mary of the Blessed Sacrament, and his Eucharistic piety, which centered on nocturnal adoration, also appealed to the Cardinal. Against the wishes of the superior general of the order, Father Elisaeus Rayer, who felt he could not spare Cohen, the new mission was undertaken with the express permission of Pope Pius IX.

On Cohen's visit to Rome to receive permission, the pope gave him a rather fulsome blessing with the words, "I send you to convert England as, in the sixth century, one of my predecessors also blessed and sent the monk, Augustine, the former apostle of that country."[1] This visit to Rome was a significant one for Cohen, not only because of his meeting with the pope, but also because of a reunion and reconciliation with his former tutor, Franz Liszt, who received Holy Communion from his hands in the church of Santa Maria Vittoria.[2] They had parted bitterly many years earlier when Liszt accused Cohen of defrauding him of concert earnings, an accusation he always denied. Liszt would also meet the pope.[3] On a previous visit to Rome during his work in Lyons where he had

---

[1] Sylvain, pp. 184-185.

[2] Bernini's famous sculpture of Saint Teresa in ecstasy is displayed here.

[3] Indeed Pius IX has often been portrayed as a gloomy figure, prisoner of the Vatican, but he had a lighter side. Liszt had led the dissolute life of the "artiste," but in later years had experienced a profound conversion and took minor holy orders. When making a protracted confession to Pope Pius IX,

also set up a Confraternity of Thanksgiving, Cohen presented the pope with a long shopping list of indulgences for the new society. Pius interjected, "Father, you are asking me for half of paradise," to which Hermann responded, "Yes, Holy Father, but you have the keys." When the afore mentioned Dominic Arbizu y Munarriz was elected to the highest office in the order and was introduced to him, the pope he remarked; "Here is my polyglot General. He will have the energy of Spain, the ardor of France and the diplomacy of Italy"![1]

Mission to England

Cohen then promptly left for his new work in the spirit of the missionary: with no financial resources whatsoever. He set out for England from Paris on August 5, 1862. His friends in Paris supplied him with the price of a ticket; in all, he had only 180 francs, and with this small sum he inaugurated the Discalced Carmelites in England. He arrived in London on August 6, the feast of the Transfiguration. One of the things that he found difficult was having to abandon his religious habit and instead dress in a black frock coat and stiff white collar in which he felt imprisoned. He commented in a letter to Bishop Dupanloup of Orleans, "Here I am at my post, charged with establishing a new Carmel. I beg your grace to recommend me to Our Lord and His holy mother. This project appears to me to be very difficult and takes from me all the support I felt in France."[2]

Catholicism in England was undergoing a new awakening at this time after centuries of intolerance. In a sermon, Cardinal John Henry Newman (now Blessed) commented in regard to an earlier period, which he himself remembered, "No longer the Catholic Church in the country; nay, no longer, I may say, a Catholic community; but

---

the pope is reported to have cut him short, "*Basta* (enough), Liszt, go tell your sins to your piano!"

[1] Peter-Thomas Rohrbach O.C.D, *Journey to Carith*, ICS Publications, Washington, D.C., 2000.

[2] Beaurin, p. 297.

a few adherents of the old religion, moving silently and sorrowfully about, as memorials of what had been." Newman preached this, which was possibly his most famous sermon, on what he called the "Second Spring" at the first synod of bishops called by Wiseman in 1852. And calling on his considerable powers of oratory, Newman would also say in the course of his sermon, speaking to the text from the Song of Songs, "Arise, my love, my dove, my beautiful one, for winter is now past, the rain is over and gone":

> A second temple rises on the ruins of the old. Canterbury has gone its way, and York is gone, and Durham is gone, and Winchester is gone. It was sore to part with them. We clung to the vision of past greatness, and would not believe it could come to nought; but the Church in England has died, and the Church lives again. Westminster and Nottingham, Beverley and Hexham, Northampton and Shrewsbury, if the world lasts, shall be names as musical to the ear, as stirring to the heart, as the glories we have lost; and saints shall rise out of them if God so will, and doctors once again shall give the law to Israel, and preachers call to penance and to justice, as at the beginning.[1]

Newman was superior of the Birmingham Oratory, which he had founded. Wiseman himself was largely responsible for the restoration of the Catholic hierarchy to England. When Cohen arrived in London, things had changed significantly from previous years, but it was still very difficult, and prejudice and social discrimination were still rife. It might be true to say, however, that Cohen had harbored some prejudice against what was seen from the continent as a very Protestant country. He would later be able to shed much of this bias as he encountered an unexpected degree of tolerance from English people.

---

[1] John Henry Newman, "Second Spring," in *Sermons for Various Occasions* (London: Longmans, Green, 1908)

Revisiting

In his first hours there, Cohen must have recalled his visit twenty-five years earlier in the company of the famous Italian operatic tenor Giovanni Matteo Mario. How things had changed, with Cohen, the former musical celebrity and reformed gambler, returning to London as a humble Carmelite friar. But Cohen, the "artiste," was still remembered; people wished to see him, and he was offered numerous invitations to preach. Indeed, his reputation as a preacher had preceded him and was probably a factor in Wiseman's choice of him in the first place, as well as his obvious zeal and spirituality. Many people from what was known as London society would later flock to hear him preach, perhaps out of curiosity. It could be said, however, that Cohen the convert was not altogether unknown in London. A few years before this, the influential Catholic journal *The Rambler* had carried a story about his conversion, quoting extensively from a contemporary account by Jean-Baptiste Gergères, "Conversion of the Pianist Hermann." The article assumed that many of its readers would be familiar with his story.

So, in London once more, Cohen was launched into a busy apostolate. In September he was joined by friars from Bagnères - two lay brothers, Stanislaus and Arnold, and a priest, Sebastian Viney. In October an Italian Carmelite priest arrived – Fr. Felix from La Scala in Rome. In the following year Spanish-born Joseph-Louis Vizcarra arrived in Kensington and was appointed novice master. He would succeed Cohen as prior.[1] The Assumption Sisters gave Cohen the use of a small house that belonged to them in the corner of Kensington

---

[1] The friendship between Cohen and Joseph-Louis seems to have later soured later. Writing to the Carmelite general from London in 1866, Cohen stated, "I regret to say that the intimacy that existed between our prior and myself has disappeared and has changed into a reciprocal 'malaise.'" He then went on to ask the general for alms for a projected preaching mission in Paray-le-Monial, France. Presumably he didn't wish to ask the prior for money. He further expressed an "immense need" to spend a week with the

Square.[1] (It is situated on what was for many years later the campus of Heythrop College, a Jesuit Catholic theological school of the University of London.) The sitting room could accommodate about forty people, and this was used as a chapel. In those early days, the friars were extremely impoverished; they had to resort to using flower pots in lieu of cooking utensils. On October 15, 1862, feast of St. Teresa of Avila, Teresian Carmelite friars made their first foundation in England.

The solemn opening of the new foundation took place in the presence of Cardinal Wiseman as well as future cardinals, Henry Manning and Edward Howard. Frederick William Faber, the famous spiritual writer and composer of hymns such as "Faith of our Fathers," also attended.[2] Cohen sang the High Mass in the little chapel of the house together with his new community. The Archbishop welcomed the Carmelites with joy, and he had great expectations of this order dedicated to Our Lady, Queen of Carmel, and which in the past had such an honored place in England.

---

father general in Rome, presumably to unburden himself. Vizcarra died in London on November 8, 1869.

[1] It's interesting that they were listed as 'The Convent of the Assumption of the Perpetual Adoration of the Blessed Sacrament.' This was Cohen's great devotion. The Sisters have preserved a tradition—often a common narrative among other women's congregations who worked with male religious and clergy, that the friars were somewhat demanding, expecting them to wash their clothes, provide vegetables for them from their garden, and so forth.

[2] Faber was the exact opposite of Newman, who was a sober and reticent Englishman and abhorred any form of external display. Though Faber was a convert, son of an Anglican clergyman, he exuded nineteenth-century French and Italian "piousness." He would have much more in common with Cohen on this account. Indeed, Cohen often wrote at the top of his letters, "Tout pour Jesus" (All for Jesus). At the same time, Cohen and Newman also had something in common—both had Jewish ancestry, both were musically gifted, and both introduced new religious groups to England. Faber founded the London Brompton Oratory while Newman founded Birmingham.

About this time, Albert Cohen, Hermann's brother, visited him in London and was received into the church by Cardinal Wiseman. He donated a significant amount of money to the new foundation. Cohen placed the new beginning under the protection of St. Simon Stock, thus making him the patron of the present English region of Teresian Carmelites. Indeed, the mission was under the protection of Simon Stock from the early days of the seventeenth century. The precious relic of St. Simon Stock (one of the saint's tibia bones from his tomb) was entrusted to Cohen who had returned to Bordeaux to collect it and take it to Kensington to be installed in the projected new church. The ornate casket, containing the relic, is still displayed in Kensington Priory, having been rescued from the ruined church during World War II. The relic was a gift to the Carmelites from the Archbishop of Bordeaux.[1]

Cohen was certainly very busy in his new apostolate. As he was the only one in the community who could speak English, he had to do everything himself, even buy the daily provisions. Even so, his English was not fluent, and it took a long time to prepare his sermons. Soon, German-born Cohen discovered a large expatriate German Lutheran community in Brighton, and he went to visit them. He went there quite often, and at the end of Lent 1863, many of them became Catholics. He later spoke of Brighton as "his little diocese."

Expansion

From its beginning in England, the Carmelite mission was aware of the need for a novitiate house to ensure the future of the venture. Interested lay people such as Thomas Walmesley became involved; he offered a site at Galley Hill in Kent in the vicinity of Aylesford, where St. Simon Stock was reputed to have received the brown

---

[1] Domingo A. Fdez. De Mendiola, *El Carmelo Teresiano en la Historia*, cuarta Parte, Roma 2015, p.63.

scapular.[1] When this didn't work out, Walmesley suggested another place on his estate at Lilystone Hall in Essex, which had a Mass Centre for local Catholics. The village was appropriately enough called Stock. Lilystone Hall, together with two other local manor houses, was owned by an old Catholic family, the Petres. Walmesley had married into this family. He had made contact with Cohen when he arrived in London. Indeed, it appears from a letter of Walmesley's that Cohen's initial intention was to start with a novitiate house in a rural spot outside London, in keeping with his practice in France. In all these proposals, Walmesley had the full backing of Wiseman. He launched an appeal for funds in 1863 and sent out a letter together with a letter of endorsement from the cardinal.[2] For some unknown reason, possibly from a lack of sufficient funds, all these projects were abandoned, and Cohen turned his attention to consolidating the Carmelite presence in London.

It now became a priority to obtain a bigger house suited to community life. They discovered such a house and garden on the market off present-day Church Street, Kensington. It belonged to octogenarian Stephen Bird, chairman of Western Rail who, it was known, was not favorably disposed to the Catholic Church. He had relinquished the big house for a smaller one across the street. The house had originally belonged to Sir Isaac Newton, the great mathematician and formulator of the law of gravity.[3] However, Cohen entrusted the matter to St. Joseph, went to see this gentleman, and succeeded in renting the house. But Bird baulked at

---

[1] In fact, a more authentic tradition would place this vision at the old Carmelite priory in Cambridge. In an earlier letter dated August 22. Cohen had written, "Mary Immaculate gave the holy scapular to St. Simon Stock in a place quite near to London [Aylesford]. Since that time, she has taken possession of England in a very real way."

[2] See "Selections from the Writings of Hermann Cohen" in Part 2 of this book.

[3] The apartment block next door to the church at the present time is called Newton Court and was built in the garden of the property.

the idea of actually selling his house to the Carmelites. Apparently he had been intimidated by the local Anglican archdeacon who lived nearby. Again on the feast of St. Teresa, October 16, 1863, they took possession of this "rented priory."

Predictably, the presence of Catholic friars met with opposition from the residents and passersby (windows were broken on occasion by local boys), but gradually things improved when the local police chief intervened. And as the Carmelites became better known, they began to be more appreciated. Cohen sent reports to Rome about applications to the order. One was nineteen-year-old Francis Foley, "son of Michael Foley and Henrietta Madden, his legitimate spouse."[1] Francis was born on November 7, 1843, and he wished to enter the Order on the coming month of February 7. Cohen also mentions a second postulant named Edward Pope. On March 8, 1863, a novice, Edmund Sharples, was received into the community in the little chapel. This was a significant step forward and a sign of hope for the future.[2]

Cohen was kept busy in his new situation. In a letter, he mentions that he preached in English but also sometimes in French, and in German to the group in Brighton. He also heard confessions in all three languages. He preached incessantly in the chapel; many people began to frequent the place, and there were several converts to the faith. In addition to this work, Wiseman also gave him the task of

---

[1] The parents of an applicant to a religious order at that time needed to be validly married.

[2] Edmund Sharples would be a key member of the English region in the future. Sharples has left us a short account of the beginnings, "The Foundation of Kensington Carmel" (Kensington Archives). Cohen kept Carmelite headquarters in Rome informed of developments. Writing in French on April 20, 1863 he observed, "An English novice has left after nine months of novitiate. In a moment of temptation to pride, he left and said nothing to us." He also went into detail of what we might regard as minutiae. Writing to the general on November 8, 1863, Cohen enquired, "When should we start cloister?"

spiritual director to his clergy and engaged him for their retreats. Moreover, the cardinal, aware of Cohen's Eucharistic devotion, put him in charge of the Eucharistic apostolate in London. Cohen remarked, "Anything to do with the Blessed Sacrament is dear to me. The cardinal knows my preference very well."[1]

Cohen began to involve himself with preparing children for their First Communion. At that time, due to anti-Catholic sentiment in this officially Protestant country, there was necessarily very little outward solemnity attached to this ceremony. Cohen instructed the children in their faith. He held a one-day retreat for them, and the cardinal himself came to talk to them. Cohen was ill at the end of summer in 1863, but by spring he was able to travel to Paris to preach a retreat to the nocturnal adoration group at the church of St. Thomas Aquinas.

Notable Event – "Flowery Land Pirates"

Soon the Carmelites received permission to exercise their ministry in public. Cohen was summoned to the infamous Newgate prison to give spiritual assistance to eight Catholic sailors, one of whom was Spanish and the others Filipinos. They had been convicted of piracy and murder on the high seas in a notorious case that became known as the "Flowery Land Pirates." This was the name of the British vessel on which they served. This group had mutinied and brutally murdered the captain and some of the crew. When captured and brought to trial, five of them were sentenced to death and three were exonerated. Their defense was that all had been ill-treated on board. Father Joseph-Louis visited them during the course of a month and was able to converse with them in Spanish to their great consolation. On the morning of the execution Cohen and two colleagues went to visit the prisoners at the Old Bailey, London's place of execution for centuries, and he found the conversion of these men the most

---

[1]   Sylvain, p. 188

moving experience since his ordination. Indeed, he was so affected by the experience that he included a lengthy account of it in the speech he would give later at the Malines Congress.[1]

Before the executions were carried out, Governor Jonas, having ascertained that the men had become docile, granted Cohen three requests from the condemned: they could wear badges of their religion, including the brown scapular; the priests would accompany them to the place of execution (previously refused); and they would be allowed to say goodbye to each other. Cohen was amazed that the crowd showed no anti-Catholic feeling; rather, they showed the priests every mark of respect. *The Times*, in an evening edition, thought it worthwhile reporting the fact that three Roman Catholic priests, tonsured and wearing stoles round their necks, mounted the scaffold and attended the condemned men. Nothing on this scale (five executions at the same time) had happened at the Old Bailey for forty years, and the whole episode was widely reported; five scaffolds had been erected in a row, and there were thousands of curious spectators, some of whom had hired out rooms adjacent to the scene to watch the spectacle.

It should be mentioned in favor of British tolerance in general that Cohen was amazed at the courtesy extended to him by the governor of Newgate and his staff. They were even given refreshments in the governor's rooms after the event. He reflected that he might not receive similar treatment in many Catholic countries.

Eucharistic Congress at Malines

The following year, Cohen was invited to give a talk at the above-mentioned Malines Congress at Malines, present day Mechelen, in Belgium. It was a kind of general assembly to which Catholics from all over Europe came to discuss religious and other matters. Famous

[1]   This was a landmark gathering of Belgian Catholic leaders in 1863 that eventually evolved into one of the first Catholic political organizations in that nation.

speakers were invited, such as Count Montalembert and Bishop Felix Dupanloup of Orleans. Cardinal Wiseman was a key member of the congress, and in one of his speeches, he outlined at length the current position of Catholics in England and did not mince his words in regard to the post-Reformation period.

Cohen's talk, entitled "Catholicism in England," was delivered on September 3, 1864, and was also in the style of the day using the polemics of his time.[1] In his talk, he also consciously tried to counter the liberalism of Montalembert. He referred to the situation in England in these words: "But in England, the Real Presence of Jesus Christ in the Eucharist has been for three centuries the special object of insult and blasphemy...."[2] much of his speech was in similar vein. But he also spoke at length about the case of the executions at the Old Bailey, indicating the tolerance he met with from the crowd.

The speech was published in a newspaper, *Independence Belgique*, which also made a personal attack on him, calling him a "mediocre musician, always playing the same fugue and preaching the same sermon."[3]Perhaps Cohen was an easier target for the press than the cardinal at that time.

There was additional fallout from Cohen's lecture at Malines and this incident throws additional light on Cohen's character. The archbishop of Paris was personally offended by a passage in his talk, and the superior general of the Carmelites asked him to write a letter of apology. Cohen's first reaction was to reply to the general,

---

[1]   "Catholicism in England," address delivered at the Catholic Congress at Malines, September 3, 1864, in Catholicism in England, (London: E. Dillon, [1864]). "The great obstacle to progress is that the Lord has been left out of legislation, out of constitutions, and out of the governing process. People have maintained, 'our laws deal with human matters, God doesn't count.'" Pope Emeritus Benedict XVI echoed this thought in his criticism of the European Constitution. Cohen's talk is interesting as it is the longest document we have from his pen.

[2]   Father Hermann, *Catholicism in England*, E. Dillon, London,1864, p. 10.

[3]   Beaurin, p. 308.

"People say that the Holy Father will be pleased to know someone has spoken out against the liberalism of Montalembert."[1] It seems that the matter in contention was a remark he made about problems in the relationship between secular and regular clergy. Cohen wrote to the archbishop:

> Today then, as we celebrate the solemnity of N.P. [N.P. stands for "Notre Père," or "Our Father"] St. John of the Cross, I received a letter from N.R.P. [Our Reverend Father] General who asked me to send an apology to V.E. [Your Eminence] for a passage in my discourse to the Congress of Malines. The voice of my superior is for me the voice of God. I do accept, my Lord, that I made an allusion, even if only incidentally, to certain developments relating to religious orders, outside England [speaking of some disagreements in certain Catholic nations between the secular clergy and the religious], in the sense that I was asked to air their grievances—well founded or not as the case may be. However even if the religious orders had entrusted me with the task of pleading their cause, Malines was not the place to speak about it, but Rome. . . So then I humbly come to express my regret at the feet of Your Excellency and confess that I should not have made public my feelings in this regard. I hope you will pray that Our Lord will give me greater prudence in the future and that you will impart the favor of your blessing to me.[2]

Donald Cave comments on his letter, "It seems clear in view of the above letter that Cohen was thoroughly convinced of his position, in no way revoking it in this apology."[3]

---

[1] Op.Cit., Donald Cave, *L'Oeuvre eucharistique pour les Hommes*, p. I-19.

[2] Cave, *L'Oeuvre encharistique*, (quoted in Italian; my translation).

[3] Ibid. Cohen appealed to the support of Dom Prosper Guéranger of Solesmes for his stance. The two met at Mons, and Cohen insisted, "The

Part of his speech was also published in *The Times* in London. Apparently Cohen's remarks did not endear him to his host country. However, the attack had beneficial results for the Carmelites. The crusty old Stephen Bird had a fair and honest side to his character, and when he read the report in *The Times*, he summoned Cohen from across the street. "Well," he said, pointing to the newspaper he was reading at breakfast, "I see they have some nice things to say about you here. Please sit down. I have sent for you today to tell you that I am in much more of a hurry to sell this house to you than you are to buy it. This article has changed my attitude so much that I want to get down to business straight away and close the matter with you. You never know, maybe I might change my mind later!"[1] Needless to say, Cohen was delighted; the contract was signed, and the Carmelites became the owners of the house and large garden in Duke's Lane, Kensington.[2] Later on, the address of the new priory would be Carmel House, 5 Vicarage Lane.[3]

Soon Cohen was writing to one of his friends, "We must now build a church in the garden. Have a word in St. Joseph's ear. Why not? He has already built several."[4] And St. Joseph did oblige, as he had done in France. On July 16, 1865, Cardinal Henry Manning laid the foundation stone of the new church. He had succeeded

---

secular clergy in part shows great hostility to us, even publicly. I have never encountered such passionate jealousy" (Carmelite archives, Rome).

[1] Sylvain, p. 200

[2] The house cost 3,000 pounds sterling. There was, however, only one thousand pounds in the kitty, so the chapter requested the loan of 2,400 pounds from Gabrielle de Musset at 5 percent interest. The organ cost 1,000 pounds. The benefactors were the Countess of Villenueve from Lyon, friend of Cohen, Joseph de la Bouillerie, nephew of Cohen's friend Bishop de la Bouillerie of Bordeaux, as well as some members of the Spanish family of Christopher de Murieta, friends of the prior Joseph Louis who were resident in London.

[3] "Carmel House" would be changed to Carmelite Monastery in 1867 (41 Church Street is the address of the present priory).

[4] Ibid., p.201

Wiseman, who had died earlier in the year.[1] It was designed by the eminent architect Edward Welby Pugin, son of "God's architect," Augustus Pugin, who was responsible for many of the new churches at the time throughout England and Ireland. Father Dominic Arbizu y Munarriz, superior general of the order with whom Cohen had worked in the restoration of Carmel in France, was present.[2] Cohen rightly felt that great progress had been made. "Now we can really say that the Order has been established in England as there is a corner of the land which the Carmelites can call home."

Meanwhile, work went ahead on the new church, which was completed in only a year by July 16, the feast of Our Lady of Mount Carmel, in 1866.[3] In a letter dated June 29, Joseph-Louis, now prior and writing to a friend, outlined the program for the solemn opening. "We will begin with the solemn transfer of the precious relic of N.P. St. Simon Stock." Cohen who had left Kensington at this stage returned for the opening ceremony. The solemn opening duly took place with Cardinal Manning, a convert of Wiseman, presiding. He had been a former member of the Oxford Movement along with Newman. Bishop Thomas Grant of Southwark sang the High Mass, and the sermon was preached by Father Peter Gallwey,

---

[1] A member of the community, Sebastian Viney, preached a long and eloquent sermon on the occasion of Wiseman's death. It was printed by E. Dillon and ran to twenty-three pages. It was titled "What Are the Duties of Catholics in England after the Death of Cardinal Wiseman?" He took for his text the passage from Luke's Gospel where Jesus sets his face for Jerusalem.

[2] Dominic took the opportunity of his visit to London to carry out a visitation of the Irish houses. He was not at all pleased with what he saw. There was no common life in Dublin or Loughrea. Relaxation in all its forms had crept in. By an authoritative act, he replaced the superiors with more worthy ones. He gave many exhortations and appeals for the religious to return to their duty and show themselves true Discalced Carmelites. He was successful. This canonical visit was a time of renewal for Carmel in Ireland (Blanc, *Un Grand Religieux*).

[3] This church was destroyed by incendiary bombs during World War II in February, 1944; a new one designed by Sir Giles Scott was built to replace it.

the Irish-born Jesuit. Cohen told his sister, "Our celebrations to mark the inauguration were splendid, consoling and well attended. We have a beautiful church and an excellent organ by Cavaillé, and many debts! However, those are St. Joseph's affair."[1]

Cavaillé-Coll was the most innovative organ-building firm of the day. Out of regard for Cohen's reputation as a musician, they had given him an excellent instrument at a reduced price for the church he built at Bagnères in the south of France some years earlier. During this opening Mass, the choir sang Mozart's "Ave Verum" and Arcadelt's "Ave Maria." The church was dedicated to Our Lady of Mount Carmel and St. Simon Stock. What a magnificent achievement by a man who arrived in London only three years previously with twenty dollars in his pocket and who was so poor that he used flower pots as crockery!

Cohen, as we know, was on intimate terms with the greatest musicians of the age, beginning with Hungarian-born composer Franz Liszt. Liszt is regarded by many as the greatest pianist of all time. The installation of the Cavaillé-Coll organ was marked by the playing of organ solos by the two most renowned organists in France, Charles-Marie Widor and Alexander Guilmant, friends of César Franck who, like Cohen, composed sacred music. Cohen meanwhile was in great demand as a preacher, traveling to Ireland, Scotland, France, and Prussia. About his visit to Ireland, he wrote, "I received your letter in the south of Ireland in Waterford, where I found to my great joy, a people fired by a great Catholic spirit, so alive that I could have believed I was living among the early Christians. Yesterday I had 9,000 listeners. I have never seen such great faith."[2] Cardinal Wiseman's family was from Waterford, and perhaps he had given him some contacts there. Cohen also visited Dublin, where he preached in St. Teresa's Carmelite church on Clarendon Street.

---

[1] Ibid., p. 201
[2] Flamme Ardente., p. 211. It's interesting that Cohen drew such an enormous crowd in a country he had never visited before. His reputation must have gone before him.

Carmelite Nuns in England

This account would be incomplete without also mentioning Cohen's part in bringing the Discalced Carmelite nuns to London. Cohen first suggested this idea to Cardinal Wiseman, who agreed with the venture but died before it could be put into effect. Cardinal Manning went ahead with the project with some modification (he insisted that the nuns be under his jurisdiction).

Cohen sought the cooperation of the Carmel of Lyon where he was well known, and it was agreed that Mother Teresa (Aragones d'Orcet), with four other sisters, would set up a Carmelite community in London. One of the four was English-born Marie-Thérèse Browning. They set out from Lyon on December 18, arrived in London on December 23, 1863, and were given accommodation in a convent near the Carmelite priory. Perhaps through her aristocratic background, Mother Teresa enjoyed the patronage of Helen Selina, Lady Dufferin, Marchioness of Londonderry.[1] In February, the sisters moved to St. John's Wood, and one of the lay brothers at the priory, who was a skilled carpenter, provided them with furniture.

They moved again on September 13, 1867, and on the following day, they settled into a new convent in Lillie Road, Fulham. Mother Teresa commented in a letter to a friend, "There was not a great deal of solemnity, rather everything was done very simply, but it appears to us that we have accomplished the work of the good God in all the accompanying circumstances, and it gives us a real confidence that we will achieve His work in spite of the difficulties." She continues, "We arrived about six o'clock the previous evening; and on the

---

[1] Lady Helen Selena Dufferin was the author of some well-known Irish songs like "The Emigrant's Farewell," about a typical Irish emigrant to the U.S. Given her status as a musician, it is likely she heard Cohen giving concerts in London in olden days. Her husband was a diplomat well acquainted with the Paris scene. She was a granddaughter of the Irish playwright, Richard Brindsley Sheridan, Lady Dufferin died in 1867. Dufferins are related to the Guinness family.

following morning, we had our first Mass in honor of the holy name of Mary. We were in a similar position to our holy Mother Teresa; on arrival, our priority was to arrange the altar, of which we had been deprived for two days, then to have holy Mass celebrated and reserve our sweet Jesus, our life and our all. One cannot live in Carmel without Jesus."[1]

Mother Teresa mentioned in her letter that the prior Cohen) acted as interpreter and arranged for them to have the services of a notary, Mr. Arnold, who was a convert to the church. He would not accept any remuneration for his work, and she tells us that he spared no pains to help the nuns. Later the nuns moved temporarily to Isleworth while a new convent was being built. The next move made by the sisters in 1908 took them to Bridge Lane, Golders Green.[2]

Less than ten years after Cohen's death, there was a kind of "Cambrian explosion" of Carmelite monasteries for women in England. But this development came about through the instrumentality of a "mulier fortis," a strong woman named Mother Mary Dupont. She was a member of the Carmel on the Rue d'Enfer in Paris, where Cohen used visit for prayer; this community originated in the first mission of Venerable Anne of Jesus to France. Mother Mary Dupont led a foundation from Paris to St. Charles Square near Notting Hill in London in 1878. Due to unusual circumstances, she remained prioress until her death in 1942 at the age of ninety-one. She founded thirty-three Carmels in Great Britain between 1907 and 1938—more than St. Teresa herself in Spain.

Carmelite Secular Order

It is worth noting also that Cohen, during his time in London, promoted and encouraged the Carmelite Third Order, now known as the Secular Order. In recent years, it has been acknowledged more than in the past that Carmelite Seculars are an integral part

---

[1]   This letter is kept in the Archives, Kensington.
[2]   This community no longer exists.

of the Carmelite family. He refers to Third Order members in some of his letters. In fact, most of the extant letters in Kensington were addressed to Cornelia Freeman, who was a member of the Carmelite Third Order. In them, he gives her spiritual direction and advice on practical matters, such as the appropriate education of her son. The seed was well and truly planted, and the Carmelite Secular Order continues to meet in Kensington down to the present day.

Continuation of Apostolate after London

It was a keen disappointment to many people that Cohen was recalled to France after three years, though he still remained a member of the Kensington community. Father Dominic insisted he was needed back in France, so when Cohen's term as prior at Kensington expired, he set off for France in October 1865 to preach an octave for the feast of St. Teresa in the Carmel at Rennes. From there, he went to Saint-Pern to the novitiate of the Little Sisters of the Poor, where the founder, (now Saint) Jeanne Jugan, resided. By Advent, he had gone to Berlin where he was well known, and there he preached both in German and French. Between the years 1866 and 1868, Cohen traveled throughout Europe and especially France. His last visit to London was in the year 1867. By Lent 1868, we find him back in Berlin, and it was here he received the news that he could now return to the holy desert or eremitical house at Tarasteix near Lourdes, which pleased him greatly. He wrote from Berlin at Easter, April 11, 1868, to thank his successor, Father Joseph-Louis, and to ask the prayers of the community, which he was now definitively leaving:

> In ceasing to form one of your communities, it is my duty to offer my grateful thanks for all the love shown to me by you and to ask forgiveness for all the faults I have committed. I also express my gratitude to all the fathers and brothers, and my regret that I should so often have given them

bad example and made things difficult for them by my temperament. I pray that you, Rev. Father, and the religious will ask the Lord Jesus to forgive me and change me. The station now ended has been satisfactory for the people I have seen. My health is good. Again, I wish you a happy feast. I start tomorrow for Posen [now Poznan, part of Poland]. Give me your blessing![1]

At this point, the Carmelite community in Kensington was well set up, and soon eleven friars were working to a busy schedule. The English Catholic Directory gives details of the community in 1871, the year Cohen died. The church was situated in an important area in Kensington. The pro-cathedral for Westminster was at the adjoining church of Our Lady of Victories on High Road, now High Street, Kensington, though it later moved to Moorfields in the East End.[2]

In 1871, Stanilaus Viney, a member of the first community, was now prior. Masses were celebrated each Sunday on the hour from 7 to 11 a.m. There were long sessions of confessions every day, morning and afternoon, except Monday; and many devotional exercises. There was Nocturnal Adoration of the Blessed Sacrament took place once

---

[1] Another of Cohen's legacies was a strong musical tradition. One of London's best-known musical conductors, the late John McCarthy, OBE, was director of music for many years. He made a recording of Cohen's Latin Mass of St. Teresa sung by the Carmelite choir.

[2] However, the cardinal's residence was in Broadstairs, Kent, well known as the setting for Dickens's *Olde Curiosity Shop* on a corner and *Bleak House*, which dominated the village. Famous candle maker and supplier of oil for sanctuary lamps, Francis Tucker had his business in Kensington. This was an old firm founded in 1730 and was an exclusive supplier to the Church. In 1906 managed to secure a deal with the Church which required 65 percent beeswax in candles, as he could not compete with alternative methods developed by the giant Price Company, which later took over the firm about 1910, as well as that of Charles Farris supplier to the Anglican church.

a week - a devotion that was Cohen's legacy everywhere he went. It should be said, however, that such was the fervor of the growing community of Catholics in England that other churches in London had similar heavy schedules, although there seemed to be sufficient priests to meet them. The Catholic Church expanded greatly in these early years and, of course, it became very much an international community. Soon there were Italian, French, and German centres in London with their own chaplains. The Carmelites heard confessions in English, French, Italian, and Spanish.

The need for a second house, while recognized, was shelved for the time being. As things turned out, it would take twenty more years before the dream could be realized and a new foundation could take place. This happened on December 21, 1882, when a foundation was made in Wincanton, Somerset. Together with the Kensington Priory, these two houses made possible the establishment of the English semi-province of Discalced Carmelites. This foundation was closed in May 1991 after 120 years of ministry in the area.

Endnotes.

Note A:

Brother Alfred Lapham, who was a member of the Kensington Community wrote an account of Cohen, which began, "It was in 1916 when I was sent to join the Carmelite Community in Kensington, and there I met Brother Louis Joseph; he died after great suffering in 1928 at the great age of eighty-five. He entered the Order at Montilimart, France, and was transferred to London in November 1863 during the priorship of Father Hermann Cohen. Hence, Brother Louis was able to tell me much of that great friar, of whom I intend to write." Though contemporaries, he is to be distinguished from the Joseph-Louis Vizcarra who became prior.

Note B:

The Carmelite Order, the Carmelites of the Ancient Observance, had a well-known pre-Reformation church in London, which was located in

Whitefriars Street. The crypt of this church has been preserved in the new building development on this site. The *Daily Mail* offices in Fleet Street were known as "New Carmelite House." In a revolutionary move, Australian Rupert Murdoch, now a citizen of the United States, moved his printing presses from Fleet Street to the East End of London in 1988, against great opposition from the unions. By coincidence, his Northcliffe House publishing firm moved to Kensington, not far from the present Carmelite church.

Note C:

A piano presented to Cohen by the famous piano makers, Erard, is still preserved at the Kensington Priory.

Chapter 12

Back to Lourdes and the Pyrenees (1868–1870)

The desert will blossom like the lily.

We remember that Hermann Cohen, with great regret, had to abandon his hope of living in the Pyrenean desert at Tarasteix in 1858. Father Dominic, the superior general, was anxious to get the holy desert established with regular observance, and this came about under Father Martin in 1867.[1] Now in 1868, after a visit there, Dominic gave Cohen permission to take up residence as a hermit. Cohen wrote to his nephew George informing him that as he was planning to leave for the holy desert. He was not sure he would succeed in his plan as his colleagues were anxious to hold on to him in Le Broussey where his presence was invaluable. If successful, he would not be allowed to correspond with him for the time being. However he did receive the necessary permission and just before leaving, he wrote to a colleague in Paris:

---

[1] Father Martin (Felix Fronteau, 1827–1894), a former secular priest, was a general councilor of the Order for many years. He would have given Abbé Sylvain most of the information on the religious life of Hermann Cohen; he included this in his biography.

172

Dear Father,

You asked me to send you a line before leaving for the Promised Land. I can only say that I feel great joy as I approach the place of my rest. As you say, this period will be decisive for me. Our Lord awaits me there to form me according to his will; and if I leave myself flexible in his divine hand, I shall at last become what I have for a long time wanted to be, a son of St Teresa and conformed to the image of the son of God crucified by love. O happy solitude! Yes, the happiness found in solitude.[1]

So Cohen was eventually on his way to Tarasteix to stay.[2] As the hermit drew near, the bells rang out to welcome him. Candles were lit and the "Veni Creator" sung as he prostrated himself in the middle of the choir. The Carmelite desert is constructed like a Carthusian monastery. The desert at Tarasteix was designed for about twenty people. The main buildings consisted of a chapel, sacristy and a chapter hall. Each hermit lived in a unit comprising four small apartments – oratory, workroom, bedroom and utility room. These were clustered around the cloister. These units were completely separate from one another. Cohen's stay in the desert began in the month of May when nature was awakening. Though the hermits were allowed to gather socially occasionally, Cohen preferred to remain alone in his garden. He particularly liked to watch the bees at work. Once a fortnight the prior summoned the community together in chapter for a period of mutual spiritual

---

[1] Ibid., p. 343

[2] Religious were expelled from monasteries in France at the end of the nineteenth century. Tarasteix fell into utter ruin and decay. It was used as a prisoner-of-war camp for three thousand German soldiers during World War I. It became a restaurant for some time in the 1950s. It has now been restored by an ultra-conservative Catholic group who hoped to bring Hermann Cohen's remains back there and make it a centre of pilgrimage.

sharing and encouraging one another in living a more intense life of prayer.

Even within the desert complex, there were two hermitages — further away from the main buildings, after the manner of the old anchorholds. These were used by designated friars for a solitary retreat during Advent and Lent. Here the Carmelite hermit was completely on his own and cut off from even the usual minimum contact with his brothers in normal desert life, such as reciting the midnight office in common in the chapel. At those times when the rest of the community assembled for prayer in common, each of the hermits rang a bell in his own hermitage to synchronize with the main services.

Spiritual Link through the Eucharist to St. Thérèse of Lisieux

During his time at Tarasteix near the end of his life, Cohen, with the permission of the prior, composed a collection of motets titled *Thabor* (1870). He had to do so without any instrumental resources, which were not available there. One of these in particular on a Eucharistic theme called, "The Divine Prisoner's Little Flower," for which Cohen himself partly composed the words, greatly influenced St. Thérèse of Lisieux.[1] The subtitle of this canticle is: "My nard gave forth its fragrance".(S of Sgs:1:12)[2] The first verses of this canticle are as follows:

> Between two cold bars there grew a humble plant,
> Which brightened the tedium of the prisoner
> Who cultivated it with love.
> And in exchange for his care,
> He saw the humble plant
> Emit the fragrance of its flowers
> With all its energy.[3]

---

[1] See Part 2 (end) for full text of the canticle.

[2] St. John of the Cross comments on this verse in Stanza 17 of his "Spiritual Canticle."

[3] Tierney, p. 89.

These hymns composed by Cohen were very popular in France for many years. We will recall that some years later in another part of France, Thérèse of Lisieux would refer to herself as the Little Flower. Her autobiography begins with the words, "The springtime story of a little white flower."[1] The idea of Jesus being a "prisoner of love" in the tabernacle would have appealed greatly to Thérèse's romantic nature. There are secular love songs with this title. One of her poems in fact treats explicitly of this theme:

> A speck of dust (not more) I've made
> My place—from which I do not stir—
> The sanctuary's holy shade,
> So close there to love's prisoner.[2]

Thérèse's devotion to the Eucharist was typically Carmelite, a devotion Carmelites inherited from the one they called their holy mother, St. Teresa of Avila. Cohen had an extraordinary devotion to the Eucharist and referred to himself as a "convert of the Eucharist."

Cohen played a key role in founding the movement for nocturnal adoration of the Eucharist in the church of Our Lady of Victories in Paris, as we saw earlier in the story, and this movement became widespread in France. In his work of adoration, Cohen enlisted the support of likeminded people such as Cyrille de Bengue. The latter much later on organized Eucharistic devotion in a little chapel on the hill of Montmartre, the highest point in Paris, on September 6,

---

[1] Here again we have a clear spiritual link with Hermann Cohen and Thérèse of Lisieux. In *Story of a Soul* Thérèse mentions a holy card illustrated by her sister Celine which she kept on this theme though she does not quote the hymn. The sentiments of the hymn were very much her own however, and indeed in popular devotion, she has been best known as the Little Flower. The story of the flower plucked by her father in the garden of Les Buissonets had great significance for Thérèse (*Story of a Soul*, p.71).

[2] Thérèse of Lisieux, *The Collected Poems of St. Thérèse of Lisieux*, trans. Alan Bancroft (Leominster, UK: Gracewing, 2001)

1878. This was the period when the great basilica known as Sacré-Coeur was being built on this site. Thérèse would later send her gold bracelet to be used in the fashioning of the tabernacle of the new basilica. She would have inherited her love of the Eucharist from her father, Louis Martin, who attended adoration of the Eucharist whenever possible, and in fact had his weekly hour watching in prayer at nocturnal adoration in Lisieux.

First Healings at the Grotto of Lourdes

Cohen's nephew George received a letter from Tarasteix on October 1 in which Cohen mentioned he was having trouble with his eyes, although otherwise everything was going fine. This was a bad omen for life in the desert with the onset of winter, and indeed his health deteriorated. At this turn of events, Cohen looked with confidence to Our Lady of Lourdes. For nearly ten years now, healings were being reported from the grotto. And so Cohen set out for the grotto as a pilgrim once more. This is how Cohen himself reported his visit in a letter to the members of the Confraternity of Thanksgiving:

Bagnères-de-Bigorre.
November 6, 1868.

My dear friends in Jesus Christ,

I have just received a fresh token of Our Lady's tender love for her children, and I am really happy to tell you about it. Since last year, my sight was growing weaker due to fatigue. I spent the last six months in that lovely solitude of the desert in the Carmel at Tarasteix. There I had an unexpected attack of ophthalmia [a serious inflammation of the eye often indicative of more serious conditions], and I was advised to go to Bordeaux to consult a specialist. About a month before that, I was banned from reading. The specialist thoroughly examined my eyes and found them in a bad state—it was a complicated case. I was threatened with glaucoma and the loss of my sight. The doctor said inflammation was inevitable, and I would have to undergo an operation to excise the iris— an operation pioneered by Doctor Greafe of Berlin, the same man who treated my brother Louis.[1] When I left Bordeaux, I had to wear dark glasses with biconvex lenses, a green eyeshade, and take other precautions as well. Any light was unbearable, even that of a candle. It was very painful to try to read anything. At this point, someone suggested that I make a novena to Our Lady of Lourdes, who had already cured several people of blindness. This suggestion appealed to me and all the more since I did not look forward to an operation, which in any event might not be successful. I recalled that it was twenty-two years since Our Lady had obtained for me from the Lord of the Eucharist, a cure far more important than that of my bodily eyes. The novena began on October 24, the feast of St. Raphael who had cured Tobit of his blindness. I bathed my eyes every day in water brought from the miraculous grotto, and I prayed to my Immaculate Mother as did a lot of other people. On the sixth day of the novena, I walked from our house in Bagnères to Lourdes as I thought this was the best way to do the pilgrimage. In fact, already at Bagnères, I felt an improvement in my eyes each day of the novena as soon as the Lourdes water touched them. I even made a point of checking this improvement through the ophthalmoscope so that the doctor could see that the congestion of the visual organs was gradually diminishing— and I used nothing but Lourdes water. Finally, the last day, which was the feast of All Saints, I arrived at the grotto itself close to the spring. My pain was gone as well as all the

---

[1] Albrecht von Graefe was perhaps the most eminent Ophthalmologist of the 19th century. He was a pioneer of surgery for glaucoma and cataract.

symptoms of the illness. Since that day, I have been able to read and write as much as I like without glasses and without precautions, without effort and without fatigue. I can look at the sun or at gaslight or candlelight without feeling the slightest discomfort—and I have got my greatest wish—to continue my life as a hermit at our desert. So, I am completely and totally cured! It is my inmost conviction that this cure is a miracle due to the intercession of Our Blessed Lady. So for that reason, I need to proclaim in public as much as I can the goodness of the heart of Mary. I ask all of you who love our dear Mother to thank God for me, and I entreat all of you who are suffering to go to her with full confidence because no one has ever invoked her in vain.[1]

Miraculous Cure at Lourdes

Medical science confirmed Cohen's inmost conviction that he was miraculously cured at Lourdes. Here is what Dr. Gustave Boissarie said: "Among the events, which took place between 1868 and 1871, four have caught my attention particularly. One of the first cures to be published in the Annals of Lourdes is that of Father Hermann. Quite ill, he went to Bordeaux to consult a well-known specialist who formally diagnosed the presence of glaucoma and proposed the excision of the iris. On his return from Bordeaux, the illness deteriorated every day."[2] Boissarie repeats the train of events mentioned by Cohen himself and concludes, "We are not accustomed to cures as complete and instantaneous as this. They are quite outside the rules and traditions of our art. For my own part, I don't know how to contest or interpret this happening."[3]

---

[1] Sylvain, pp. 210-211.

[2] Tierney, pp. 91-92

[3] Gustave Boissarie, *Lourdes depuis 1858 à nos jours* (Paris: Sanard et Derangeon, 1894), pp. 136–38 (Quoted in Beaurin)

Cohen returned to Lourdes on November 12 to offer a Mass of thanksgiving. The annals of Lourdes mention this private ceremony. "There were only a few people present. Very few in the town knew that he was there. But he wished to express his very deep gratitude. 'What shall I render to the Lord,' he asked and then invited the people to help him pay his debt. He was very emotional and did not try to hide it. He expressed it eloquently making us share his gratitude with him. He was like one of the people Our Lord cured and who went out among the crowd singing his praises."[1]

In a letter dated November 22 addressed to the Countess of Villeneuve,[2] he said, "I could write volumes to you describing all the details of my cure, showing how supernatural it was, and ordained by God to proclaim the power and goodness of his revered Mother."[3] Cohen then returned to his desert life. On January 6, 1869, he wrote to his sister: "I believe that with God's help I shall eventually become a contemplative. Our Lord is favoring me to this end. May the eyes of everyone be opened to see where happiness is really to be found."[4] And in another letter he wrote, "I am very happy to live this contemplative life. It is very clear to me that God's company and conversation are to be preferred much more to that of human beings, and here one is always free to enjoy them."

From the desert he wrote to a friend, a Sister of Charity in Paris, Hermann of Jesus, on January 13, 1870:

> Help me to thank our loving Master and to return him love for love. One day you said to me in the parlour, "How much

---

[1] *Annales de Notre-Dame de Lourdes*, year 1 (quoted in Beaurin).
[2] She was related to the Bonaparte family and. Her ancestor suffered horribly during the French Revolution. Cohen probably met Cohen her through Liszt–as they were connected by marriage with the Sayn-Wittgenstein family. Caroline Sayn-Wittgenstein was Liszt's partner after he left Marie d'Agoult.
[3] Beaurin, p. 353
[4] Ibid., p. 353

the Lord loves you!" I never appreciated these words as much as I do now. I didn't realize that the Spouse of souls chose mine specially. But now for some time, whenever I have the experience of the Lord's love, your words come back to me; and I realize that you already have an intimation of what Our Lord plans to do for me. I can't help feeling that you were right. I protest deep down, "O Jesus how you love me, but what do you see in me? Nothing but weakness and unfaithfulness and yet you are content to favor me so much." I have these experiences normally when I am not even thinking of God but am busy reading or writing or working in the sacristy. Then whether I wish to or not, I have to stop what I am doing. If I don't I feel overwhelmed—if reading, my eyes close involuntarily—until I go before the Blessed Sacrament on my knees and abandon myself to God. It is impossible to resist the torrents of delight that fall on me or the gentle fire that penetrates my heart. I sometimes remain there for hours in keen delight, and the hours pass like minutes.[1]

The First Vatican Council

Those of us who have lived through the Second Vatican Council, popularly known as Vatican II, will resonate with the events leading up to Vatican I.[2] The council set out to confront what it saw as modern errors. It is best known for proclaiming the doctrine of papal infallibility. This was a very divisive issue at the time. In fact, the great Cardinal John Henry Newman thought the definition "inopportune." In the end, it did lead to groups of Catholics leaving the church to form what were called the "Old Catholics," much like the French archbishop Marcel Lefebvre after Vatican II.

---

[1] Beaurin, p. 354
[2] The First Vatican Council opened on December 8, 1869.

Cohen wrote to his nephew George in 1869, "Could I ask you to cut out all the passages dealing with the Council in *L'Univers* and send them to me? It is important for me to be in touch with a movement like that."[1] Again, he wrote to Cyrille de Mont de Benque, his former collaborator in nocturnal adoration:

> St. Teresa's children must take part in this Council by a life of prayer and sacrifice. St. Teresa said that we must support the Church in this way to obtain from God light and strength for those who lead us in faith. So you see that without going to Rome, you and I can take part in the work of the Council . . . and if we offer ourselves single-mindedly to God in the fire of his love, we are doing more for God than some of those forceful prelates near you who try to give lessons to the fathers of the Council in advance. Here I don't have much news, but I did hear of the trouble some people were trying to stir up on the eve of the Council.[2]

In another letter to George, he wrote: "We must continue to pray hard for the Council. The Holy Spirit has promised his assistance; but by prayer, the light of truth may come to a particular Council so that certain controversial questions may be unraveled and that the weak may know what a Catholic ought to believe, and the totality of revealed truth is not diminished."[3]

Cohen had no great theological interest or expertise in the leading questions of the day. He simply urged obedience and fidelity to the church. If he had been alive during Vatican II, he would have been firmly aligned with the conservatives—although by a strange twist, the doctrine of papal infallibility was resisted by conservatives. Cohen had no sympathy with those who were "stirring things up," and he remarked, "The Gallicans cut a sad figure just now, and our

---

[1] Beaurin, p. 356

[2] Tierney., p. 93.

[3] Ibid., p. 93.

Holy Father preaches humility on every occasion. May we obtain, and always possess, this lovely and precious quality. The Gallicans introduce us to another figure whose story intersects with that of St. Thérèse and also St. Bernadette but in a more negative way.[1] One of the staunchest promoters of the Gallican position at the time was a Carmelite priest named Hyacinthe Loyson. I mentioned him earlier as one of the first priests to interview Bernadette, and it would appear aggressively so. He was only six years younger than Cohen, but Loyson did not join the Carmelites until 1860. He first joined the Sulpicians and later the Dominicans. He was a charismatic preacher, perhaps the most famous in France in his time.

Like Cohen, Loyson was a protégé of the great Dominic Arbizu y Munarriz. On one occasion, he left Rome with Loyson on a sea journey back to France; and it turned into a drama-packed voyage. During the night, a soldier who had taken ill jumped overboard. Dominic happened to be on hand to give absolution and recite the final prayers as the tragedy took place. This incident slowed up their progress; so when they arrived at Marseilles, they found that their train had departed. However, at some distance from Marseilles, the train was involved in a crash with an express train and many passengers were killed. They continued their journey the next day, thankful for their escape; and they made their way to Avignon where they stayed in the Carmelite convent for two days. Dominic invited Loyson to preach on devotion to the Sacred Heart. He was so eloquent that his mentor was most impressed and told him; "Father Hyacinthe, keep to that style of preaching; it's really good. You won't be courting danger, and you'll do a lot of good."[2] Later, they called at the Carmel of Montelimar. At the grill in the convent parlour, Dominic placed his hand on Hyacinthe's shoulder and addressed the

---

[1] Gallicanism was the adopted position of those who favored a kind of national French church as opposed to the Ultramontanes, who represented strict adherence to the view that the Supreme Pontiff was in fact supreme! Gallicans held that an ecumenical council was above the pope.

[2] Henri Blanc, *Un Grand Religieux*, p.176.

nuns, "Ask the Lord to make him very humble and very obedient. He is a great preacher, people will applaud him. But this kind of praise can turn heads. Make sure you pray for him then." Loyson replied, "Yes, Sisters, if I follow the advice of our Father General; I'm sure I will never go wrong."[1] When things didn't turn out exactly as Dominic had hoped, we recall that about twenty years later a young French nun in Lisieux would do just that: would pray for Loyson and would continue to do so after her death!

Loyson was opposed to the Franco-Prussian War and said so at the time, which sounds very modern to our ears. More importantly from a theological point of view, he opposed the impending definition of papal infallibility. When he was attacked by Bishop Felix Dupanloup of his native diocese of Orleans, who urged him to repent, he retorted, "What you call a great fault committed, I call a great duty accomplished." Hyacinthe Loyson left the Order (where he had been superior of the Paris Carmel) and the Roman Catholic Church just before Vatican I. He entered into a civil marriage with an American lady named Emily Butterfield, the widow of a man called Merriman. He founded a "Catholic Gallican church" in Paris in 1879 complete with a liturgy he himself had composed or adapted. Hermann Cohen, like Thérèse later in the century, was deeply concerned about Loyson's salvation and wrote a poignant letter to him on September 27, 1869, from his solitude in Tarasteix.[2] One of Loyson's staunchest opponents was the journalist Louis Veuillot, who was a friend of Cohen. It is highly likely that he was referring to Loyson when he mentioned the "Gallicans cutting a sad figure." Vatican I was adjourned abruptly in 1870 because of the outbreak of war between France and Prussia.

Cohen was anxious that Eucharistic devotion might be propagated at all times, and he makes a request of de Benque to tell

---

[1] Ibid., p. 177.

[2] A Selection from the Writings of Hermann Cohen at the end of this book for the text of this letter.

the bishops about nocturnal adoration so that it might spread from France throughout the whole world.

Cohen seems to have had some premonition of his early death. In the course of a walk at the beginning of the year 1870, he said emphatically to the brother with him, "I feel that God has called me here to the desert to prepare me for my death. If you only knew how, for some time now, he has been detaching me from everything."[1]

On October 28, 1869, he confided to someone in a letter:

> The good Master, our lover, wants to possess my heart for himself alone; and not only my heart, but also my memory, my mind, my thoughts, and my attention. He does not want me to initiate anything, he does not want me to work in his service by preaching or other enterprises. He wishes me to give myself and remain hidden, silent, forgotten, so that having been in some way a public figure with acclaim from a lot of people, I should now retire into obscurity through self-effacement and disappear as though I were dead so that my life may remain hidden in God with Jesus Christ. I have never felt called as clearly as this. I enjoy great peace doing this though by nature I am expansive and given to continual activity.[2]

Here Cohen shows a true insight into his own character. He acknowledged that it occasionally pushed him toward extremes in his work. At the Carmelite Provincial Chapter in May 1870, Cohen was elected first councilor of the province of Aquitaine. He was also appointed novice master, which meant he would be based at Le Broussey. However, Cohen after a short time requested permission to return to the desert; and this request was granted. He was even assigned there for life. But as things turned out, he was never to benefit from this concession. Within two months of his arrival at

---

[1] Beaurin, p. 359.
[2] Ibid., p. 359.

Le Broussey, war broke out between France and Germany—that is, between his native country and the country of his adoption. He stayed on at Le Broussey for a while until the Battle of Sedan that signalled the end of the Napoleonic regime and the founding of the Third Republic. Religious persecution followed. The priory at Agen was destroyed, and that at Lyon was looted. The Carmelites were evicted, some of them imprisoned.

This was naturally a great blow to Cohen who had done so much to establish the Lyon house. He knew he would have to leave France, and he was given some final days of quiet at Tarasteix. There is a valuable comment extant from the famous scholar Father Benedict Zimmermann, from the Kensington Priory, which Cohen had founded. "In London where we made our novitiate, Father Hermann's memory is still alive. Two of our brothers lived with him in the desert [Tarasteix], and they are never tired of telling us about him."[1]

Thérèse and Loyson

We now move on to the year 1897, and we find the name Hyacinthe Loyson cropping up in the story of St. Thérèse. It is well known that she offered her last holy Communion for the conversion of this renegade priest on August 19, which was the feast of Saint Hyacinthe. Thérèse had made Loyson's salvation a priority in her prayer for most of her brief religious life. She made him the subject of a letter to her sister Céline as early as July 8, 1891. His preaching in Normandy at this time was reported in the press and Thérèse writes: "The unfortunate prodigal went to Coutances where he started over again the conferences given at Caen. It appears he intends to travel throughout France in this way. His wife follows him everywhere."[2] Then she urges Céline to renewed prayers for his conversion.

---

[1] Benedict Zimmermann, Carmelite Archives, Kensington.

[2] *Letters of St. Thérèse of Lisieux*, Volume II, translated by John Clarke, OCD, ICS Publications, Washington DC., p. 728.

In January 1911, the year before he died, the Carmel at Lisieux sent Loyson a copy of the *Story of a Soul*. Part of his reply stated, "I was touched, very much touched by many of the things I read in this book."[1] Lest we be too quick to rush to judgment ourselves, we could do well to remember this line from the same letter to Céline: "I have been mistaken more than once in my life, but I am convinced that what God condemns in man is not error when this is sincere, but selfishness, pride, and hatred."[2] Touché! Céline (Sister Geneviève) pursued a correspondence with the former Carmelite for the last year of his life, sending him articles on the progress of Thérèse's cause. He apparently died a pious death on February 9, 1912.[3]

In this chapter, I have surveyed some details that suggest a Carmelite link with the story of Lourdes as it evolved. I have shown how Thérèse of Lisieux fits into Cohen's story. Her spirituality in regard to the Eucharist, and the Little Flower theme, echoes that of Hermann Cohen, the confidant of Bernadette. And Thérèse's subsequent zeal for the spiritual welfare of Hyacinthe Loyson, sometime colleague of Hermann Cohen in the Carmelite Order in France, links together the two most popular female French saints of modern times. Thérèse refers to Lourdes several times in her correspondence. On May 10, 1890, she wrote to her sister Pauline (Mother Agnes of Jesus). "How happy I am to be always a prisoner in Carmel; I have no desire to go to Lourdes to have ecstasies."[4] She was probably referring here to the consolations received by her sister Céline during her pilgrimage to Lourdes in October 1890. The story of Lourdes and Bernadette itself initially concerned the French church of the nineteenth century, but it has had much wider repercussions for the church universal.

1 Ibid., p. 730.
2 Ibid., p. 730.
3 P. Stéphane-Joseph Piat, O.F.M, *Céline,* Ignatius Press, San Francisco, 1997. p. 175.
4 Ibid., pp. 620.

Many years have gone by since the English priest and novelist, Robert Hugh Benson, remarked that physical pain and water are the most common things in the world. And yet the phenomenon of Lourdes shows no sign of abating. Pilgrimage to and prayer at Lourdes has brought untold hope to millions of sick and weary human beings from the beginning. We thank God for this outpouring of healing grace that began as a muddied trickle of water between Bernadette's fingers and is now a torrent in full spate. The whole Church was united with Pope Benedict XVI in September 2008 in acknowledging the unassailable place that Lourdes has in the hearts of the faithful.

Endnote

As far back as 1914, Robert Hugh Benson, an English convert to Catholicism who later became a priest wrote a book that he simply called *Lourdes*. He wrote: "There is at Lourdes, not a marriage feast; but something very like a deathbed. The mother of Jesus is there with her Son. It is she again who takes the initiative. "Here is water," she seems to say, "Dig, Bernadette, and you will find it." But it is no more than water. Then she turns to her Son, "They have water," she says, "but no more." And then he comes forth in his power. "Draw out now from all the sick beds of the world and bear them to the Governor of the feast. Use the commonest things in the world—physical pain and common water. Bring them together and wait until I pass by." Then Jesus of Nazareth passes by; and the sick leap from their beds, and the blind see, and the lepers are cleansed, and devils are cast out. (Robert Hugh Benson, Manresa Press, Roehampton, 1914.

Hermann Cohen`s tomb in Le Broussey

Chapter 13

Final Mission (1870–1871)

Chaplain at Spandau Prison

*T*he following is the sequence of events that placed Hermann Cohen on the road to the prisoner of war camp in Spandau near Berlin, the scene of his last labours. After leaving the 'desert house' at Tarasteix in 1870, Cohen spent some time at the Carmelite priory of Bagnères-de-Bigorre, as he prepared to leave forever his adopted country. In fact, he had permission from the prefect of Bordeaux to remain in France but did not pursue this option. From Bagnères he went to the priory at Carcassonne. Then he left for Switzerland. The Franco-Prussian War was now raging, and Cohen was on the run. Bishop François de la Bouillerie says that for Cohen this meant being guilty of the "double crime of being a friar and a German!"[1] He reached Grenoble where he was physically attacked, being taken for a spy. Eventually, he reached the safety of Geneva. From there he went to Montreux, a lakeside city popular with tourists. After the revolutionary events of September 4, many refugees poured in. Like many refugees today they were fleeing from both the Germans and the revolutionaries. Cohen was asked by Bishop Gaspard de

---

[1] Beaurin, p. 364.

Mermillod of Geneva and Fribourg to take care of the spiritual needs of these refugees. So on October 7, Cohen opened a little chapel to minister to the group.

Then later on, in the month of November, the bishop sent for Cohen again. The French prisoners needed a chaplain, but the Prussian government would not allow them to have a French priest. Cohen received permission from his superiors to comply— at the same time as his permission to retire to the desert at Tarasteix came through! So instead of leaving for his beloved retreat, he had to leave instead for Berlin. He did so on November 24, the old feast day of St. John of the Cross.[1] He wrote to his sister:

> I shall say Mass for George on November 24, the feast of our father St. John of the Cross. On that day, I am leaving to minister to the French prisoners interned in Germany. French priests who wished to go were refused permits. I felt I could not refuse this mission, since Jesus says to those he rejects, "I was in prison and you did not visit me." People think I am suited to the work because I have relatives in Germany. So I am setting out under the protection of Jesus, Mary, and Joseph. I am looking forward to bringing some consolation to these prisoners who are in such great need.[2]

When he left Montreux, Cohen made this prophetic statement: "Germany will be my grave."[3]

When Cohen arrived in Berlin, he took up the chaplaincy of Spandau prisoner of war camp,[4] about nine miles from the capital.

---

[1] With the renewal of the liturgical calendar, the feast of St. John of the Cross was moved to December 14, which now corresponds to the actual date of the saint's death.

[2] Beaurin, p. 367.

[3] Tierney, p. 97.

[4] Spandau camp was later a prison for Nazi war criminals, including Rudolf Hess, who died there.

There were 5,300 French prisoners in the camp. While ministering to their spiritual needs, he also didn't overlook their material ones. He would arrive at the camp armed with parcels of clothes and linen, which he distributed to those in need during the bitter Berlin winter. Again he writes to his sister: "I am at Spandau where you made your First Communion in the sacristy. I vest in this sacristy every day to say Mass and preach to the French prisoners. About 500 of them are ill with typhus and dysentery. About 400 attend Mass every day, and I preach to them. Then I visit the hospital to minister to the sick; and in the afternoon, I visit the barracks to see those who are well. Pray earnestly for their conversion; many of the healthy have not been to confession yet."[1]

On December 12, he wrote to his sister-in-law: "The prisoners are beginning to ask for confession. This evening, I had eight in my room. You see the Lord gives me plenty to do! I have never had such a vast harvest from which to win people to Christ." He wrote to her again on December 22: "The prisoners besiege me from eight o'clock in the morning until evening, and I try to serve them; and they make use of me! They are allowed to come to the presbytery. I must say they are grateful for my devotion to them."[2] To another friend he confided: "I have received no answer to the fourteen letters I sent to France; so I presume they have been confiscated, although there was nothing political in them; but I receive letters from Geneva very regularly. I am asking you if you will be so kind as to take care of my correspondence. I enclose stamps for 4,80 francs."[3]

Cohen must have felt isolated in Germany, cut off as he was from France where his much-loved sister and nephew lived, as well as his Carmelite brothers and many friends. But he did not complain. A last fragment of a letter from him has survived. It was addressed to either George or his mother but was found in George's

---

[1] Tierney, p. 98

[2] Ibid., p. 98.

[3] Ibid., p. 98.

papers. George has noted on it, "'N.B. End of a letter written on 11 December in Spandau, twenty days before his death.' Let us love Jesus more every day! Father Augustine. An unworthy sinner who wishes to be converted for the new year that is beginning. Amen."[1]

Cohen's health deteriorated in the harsh climate at Spandau. He never mentions the tiring mornings in the bitterly cold church, saying Mass and hearing the confessions of about fifty prisoners. George wrote to him on January 8, three days after Bismarck had ordered the bombing of Paris: "If Prussia believes it can demoralize our people by the despicable bombing of women and children, the first time in history this has been done, it is much mistaken. In spite of the 396 victims, the courage of the Parisians, men, women, and children is admirable and indomitable."[2]

We have an account of Cohen's last labours from Father Henri de la Billerie, a Capuchin priest, who met him in Berlin at this time where Cohen was shopping for clothes for his prisoners: "I spent a lot of time with him that day. . . . I found him old and worn and very pale. I also noticed an unhealthy looking spot on his left hand, which seemed to be the result of contagion in the hospital. I went to visit him again in the evening in his room in St. Hedwig's presbytery where he used to stay when he visited Berlin. As he spoke to others present, I studied his face; and I became convinced that he had come to the end of his laborious career."[3] This intuition was only too well justified. On January 9, Cohen contracted smallpox while anointing two of its victims. His family afterward believed that he did not have the spatula with him with which he usually anointed the sick. He had a scratch on his finger through which he contracted the disease. Father de la Billerie tells us:

---

[1] Sylvain, pp.286-287.

[2] Tierney, p. 99. George could not have foreseen that 'bombing women and children' and other innocents would become the rule, not the exception in our own times.

[3] Sylvain, pp. 287-288.

On Friday, the 13, Father Hermann was ill. We went to his room, and his eldest brother Albert had come from Montreux. He was being looked after by a Sister of Charity. "Well Father, I need you," he said to me. "I have smallpox and shall be in bed for three or four weeks. I shall be unhappy if the work I have begun is not continued. Besides, the Lord can take me. You will be there to take my place." "Father," I said, "I hope God will leave you still longer in your ministry." But he looked at his crucifix and said, "No, I don't think so, I hope the Lord will take me this time."[1]

Cohen had been authorized to go on this mission by Father Luke Ranise, successor as superior general of the Order to Cohen's old friend, Dominic Arbizu y Munarriz. The request itself came from the Bishop Gaspard Mermillod (later cardinal) of Geneva and Lausanne. It was a most onerous ministry in depressing circumstances. His day began at eight in the morning and lasted until late in the evening as he reported in one of his letters. It was bitterly cold at that time of year. On January 15, he grew worse; and after a seizure, the parish priest of Spandau decided to give him the last rites. Cohen accepted them with joy and peace, which impressed everyone present. Then he renewed his Carmelite vows. He joined in the "Te Deum," the "Salve Regina," and the "De Profundis." Then he saw his brothers Albert and Louis for the last time and asked Louis to see that he was buried in the vaults of the Cathedral of St. Hedwig in Berlin. Two days later, his condition deteriorated. On January 19, the sister asked if he wanted her to call a priest. Cohen replied, "So I am going to die. May God's holy will be done; besides, if I were cured, I would have to witness distressful things."[2] How right he was. Eight days after his death, Paris fell to the Prussians. The Franco-Prussian War had turned out an unmitigated disaster for France, his adopted country.

---

[1]   Ibid., p. 288.

[2]   Ibid., p. 290.

Cohen was not the only musical genius to be buried in Berlin. I have described Cohen's relationship with Franz Liszt at some length, but another famous name occurs here though I have only given him brief mention in the earlier part of this book. There was an uncanny similarity between the lives of Cohen and famous composer Felix Mendelssohn, born only a few years before Cohen. Both belonged to Jewish banking families, whose fathers bore the forename "Abraham." Both were child musical prodigies. Both converted to Christianity. Both were true romantics. For both men, the earthly dream ended in Berlin, where both were buried, though not in midsummer. And both would have known by experience what it was like, in the words of one of Mendelssohn's most popular pieces, to rise momentarily above this bleak earth "On Wings of Song."[1] Cohen would have enjoyed too, Mendelssohn's oratorio *Elijah*, uncompromising inspirer of the spirit of Carmel. And reflecting on Shakespeare's play "A Midsummer Night's Dream", set to music by Mendelssohn, Cohen would have no trouble, and neither would Saint John of the Cross or St. Thérèse de Lisieux, in weaving Shakespeare's poetry into an allegory of spousal love:

"Yet mark'd I where the bolt of Cupid fell:
It fell upon a little western flower,
Before, milk-white, now purple with love's wound,
And maidens call it love-in-idleness.[2]

Here is a pointer to that "idleness" that bespeaks the Carmelite ideal, "Vacare Deo," to waste time with God:

---

[1] The lyrics were written by a mutual friend of Mendelssohn and Cohen, famous writer Heinrich Heine. Heine once made the prescient remark in view of the Nazi future: "Where books are burned, people will be burned next."

[2] The Complete Works of William Shakespeare. *Midsummer Night's Dream*, Act 2, Scene 1, p. 224, HarperCollins, 2006, Glasgow. Millions of starry-eyes couples have walked down the aisle to the strains of 'Wedding March' from Mendelsson's musical version of 'Midsummer Night's Dream'.

"O living flame of love
That tenderly wounds my soul
In its deepest center."[1]

And so on a frosty morning in the course of a Berlin winter, January 20, 1871, Hermann Cohen yielded his generous soul into the arms of eternal love. In those final days, as his life ebbed slowly away, did the memories also come flooding back? As he lay dying back in his native Germany, we may fancy whether a kaleidoscope of his eventful life played itself before him. Did he revisit those dazzling days in the Paris salons where he mingled with his rich and famous contemporaries? They would sit spellbound listening to the music that flowed effortlessly from his fingers. Did the memory of the charming Celeste whom he first saw wowing the idle crowds at the Paris Hippodrome intrude itself upon him? And as he later admitted, did he recall how his heart raced in unison with Celeste in a race he could not win? Did his memory echo again the emptiness of the life of the "artiste," who knows that the applause he or she most lives for, must eventually fade into silence? And did he recall again those quiet moments in the churches of Paris when Jesus, the Christ, began to knock on the door of his heart and hold out to him the promise of a love that never fades?

And then there was the memory of that final concert in the capital, which he gave to pay off the many debts he had incurred during his gambling days. At that point, Cohen was about to leave the concert stage forever, but later he would ascend the pulpit as a Carmelite friar and preach the love of Jesus and Mary all over Europe in French, German, and English. Indeed, in that very first public sermon in Paris after ordination, he combined aspects of the artist and the priest. Having delivered a visionary and eloquent sermon in the church of Saint-Sulpice on his favourite topic,

"Christ, the 'Fairest of the children of men,'" [Ps 45:2] he sat down at the keys of the magnificent organ, Cavaillé-Coll's masterpiece.

---

[1]   St. John of the Cross, "Living Flame of Love," in *Collected Works*.

One of Cohen's circle, Henri Perreyve, no mean or impressionable critic, but an artist and musician himself and professor at the Sorbonne, commented: "It seemed that the protégé of Liszt reappeared for a moment: all the notes of the organ sang, accompanied by deep bass notes like thunder. The chords ran triumphantly in supreme harmony, then calm returned; as though to assure the triumph of love, the last chords were soft and veiled, the very last sound almost a sigh."[1] It was a prelude to the "silent music" of St. John of the Cross, which like Cohen's music, is also "almost a sigh."

There remained, then, only the quiet murmured prayers of his friends around his bedside and his final words, "Into your hands, Lord, I commend my spirit." Then before the darkness finally descended, perhaps the well-loved verses of St. John of the Cross were playing over his fevered consciousness.

> "Now Consummate! if it be Your will;
> Tear through the veil of this sweet encounter."[2]

We recall, too, the verses of Cohen's great contemporary Blessed John Henry Newman reflecting on the passing of his poetic creation 'Gerontius,' in reality a meditation on his own death:

> "I hear no more the busy beat of time,
> No, nor my fluttering breath, nor struggling pulse;
> Nor does one moment differ from the next....
> This silence pours a solitariness
> Into the very essence of my soul;
> And the deep rest, so soothing, and so sweet,
> Hath something, too, of sternness and of pain."[3]

---

[1]   Beaurin, p. 238.

[2]   Ibid.

[3]   John Henry Newman, *Dream of Gerontius,* Burns Oates, London, 1951, pp. 13-14.

Cohen's last hours do remind us of what St. John of the Cross wrote in his "Spiritual Canticle": "Death cannot be bitter to the soul who loves, who finds in her all sweetness, delights of love. The soul looks upon death as her friend and spouse, and thinking of her, rejoices as on the day of her espousals. She desires the day and hour when death will come, more than the kings of this earth desire their kingdoms."[1] He gave a last blessing to those around him at their request—his attendants, the Sister of Charity who looked after him,[2] and a Jesuit coworker. Cohen survived the night and died quietly the next morning at about ten o'clock. He was forty-nine years of age. It was a truly heroic end to a life that, after conversion, was completely dedicated to Christian and Carmelite ministry. He was indeed a martyr of charity.

His friend Natalie Narischkin, writing to her sister from Paris on February 14, 1871, refers to the news of Cohen's death in Spandau. "Oh! happy, blessed Father Hermann! We have heard of his death promptly and directly from Abbé Le Rebours. It was on January 20 that this beautiful soul took flight to heaven. May he obtain for us the grace of a fervent love for Jesus! That is everything. Oh! What an insignificant thing life is without that sacred love."[3] Then on March 4, 1871, Natalie wrote again:

> I wished to write with all the news at this time, but letters came in from all sides and I had to show some sign of life! [by replying] I had a great desire to give you some details of the final moments of our seraphic Father Hermann. One of our sisters was privileged to look after his final needs and receive his last sigh. Sensing that the end was near, the

---

[1] The Collected Works of St. John of the Cross, ICS Publications, Washington DC, 1979, p. 451.
[2] The Sister of Charity mentioned wrote an account of Cohen's final hours in a letter to his friend, Sister Natalie Naraschin.
[3] Augustus Craven, *La Soeur Natalie Naraschkin*. Didier et Cie, Paris, 1870, pp. 395-396.

saintly Father asked if she knew how to sing the *Te Deum*. "No," she said. "And the *Salve Regina*?" "Oh, yes," said the sister. "Very good, let us sing it together," said Father, and he intoned the ancient antiphon with the sister; and as they sang it, the voice of the dying saint became more feeble before it ceased altogether in order to give rise to new life. Oh, if I ever committed the sin of envy in my life, it was not to have been that privileged sister![1]

Hermann Cohen was buried according to his wishes in the crypt of the Cathedral of St. Hedwig, Berlin. The funds to build this cathedral had originally been collected all over Europe by a Carmelite priest name Mercenati. This cathedral, like so many others, was reduced to rubble by Allied bombs in 1943. Coffins from the vaults, including the one containing Cohen's remains, were reinterred in the city municipal cemetery in East Berlin, just inside the former Berlin wall, which would later on be built through the cemetery – and later, 1989, famously pulled down. And so ended a life that in many ways resembled a shooting star that consumed itself in spreading the kingdom of Christ in the vineyard of Carmel. In the words of one of the Psalms in the Hebrew Testament which every Jewish child would have prayed or sung:

> We have escaped like a bird
> From the snare of the fowlers;
> The snare is broken,
> And we have escaped. (Ps 124:7)

---

[1]   Ibid, p. 402.

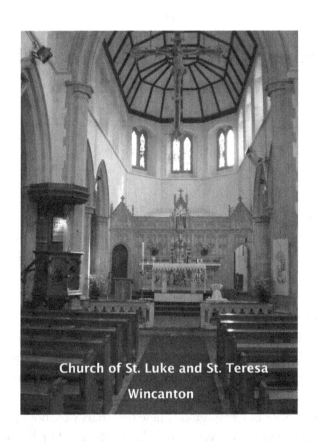

Church of St. Luke and St. Teresa
Wincanton

Chapter 14

Hermann Cohen`s Legacy in England: Wincanton (1882) and Gerrards Cross (1915)

*C*armelite friars were associated with the town of Wincanton, Somerset, in the southwest of England from 1882 until 1995. The Church of St. Luke and St. Teresa in Wincanton celebrated the centenary of its opening in October 2008.

The life and ministry of Hermann Cohen is linked to Wincanton through his work as a founder in London. Furthermore, the first two English Carmelites and first two priors of Wincanton were Father Edmund Sharples and Father Mary-Edward Badger; Sharples may have been in Le Broussey, in Cohen's time and Badger seems to have initially approached Cohen about a Carmelite vocation while the latter was prior of Kensington. These two friars were both products of the new wave of converts from the Anglican Church who were influenced by the Oxford Movement initiated by Newman and his colleagues. Cohen of course did not live to see the opening of this second foundation in Wincanton. As things turned out, after the opening of Kensington Church and later the priory, the dream of a new house was shelved and it would take another twenty years before the new foundation took place. However, we know from a report to Rome by Sebastian Viney on June 6, 1881, that growth in the English region was catching up with that of the older established Irish region. At that point there were nine professed friars in Kensington and eight students, of whom five were already priests. In Ireland, there were thirteen priests and five brothers plus one novice.

The new development that originated in Kensington came about on December 21,1882, when a second foundation was made in Wincanton. Together with Kensington Priory then, these two houses made possible the establishment of the English Semi-Province of Discalced Carmelites. The semi-province was dedicated to St. Simon Stock. In 1880, Father Luke Ranise, superior general of the Order, was on a visit to the Carmelite Priory in Kensington, London. Bishop William Clifford of Clifton made contact with him and invited him to Wincanton to discuss the matter of a foundation in his diocese.[1] The foundation was accepted, and the first Carmelites, under Father Edmund Sharples (a native of Newcastle-on-Tyne), together with another priest and brother, came to Wincanton in late 1881.(They also briefly served in the neighbouring county town of Yeovil, but then the decision was taken to develop Wincanton instead.) The Catholic Mission centre, based in Acorn House, was handed over to the Carmelites. By 1885, a priory was constituted, and full observance of the Carmelite life inaugurated. As time went on it became evident that a new building was not only desirable but necessary. For a number of reasons this would have to take priority over the building of a new church.

The work of the Carmelites in Wincanton continued to prosper. The foundation stone of the monastery was laid on July 16, 1888, the Feast of Our Lady of Mt. Carmel, and the building was completed by August 18 of the following year. As is customary on such occasions,

---

[1] The fact that there was a community of Carmelite nuns in the cathedral city of Wells may have influenced the decision to go to Somerset, in Clifton diocese. The community later merged with that of Darlington, Co. Durham, but both are now closed.

the priory was open to the public for a few days, and then it was solemnly blessed by Bishop Clifford. Father Benedict Zimmermann, OCD., a well-known writer and historian of the Order, who spent many years in Kensington and some time as prior in Wincanton, wrote two articles for the French *Chroniques du Carmel* describing the new priory. In the July issue, he wrote, "A year has passed since that Solemnity. Today the monastery is nearly completed: an artistic work in its poverty and its Teresian simplicity. . . . We often visit the buildings during recreation, where one can view the splendid countryside which stretches out from the windows of the cells."[1] He was alluding here to the magnificent sweep of the Blackmore Vale, of which the priory commanded an outstanding view.

The Priory

The priory was an imposing, three-floor building, with a large basement, and the house was fitted with fine mullioned windows of Bath stone.[2] At the solemn opening, twenty-six persons received the sacrament of confirmation from the bishop. That meant that the number of Catholics had doubled since the outset of the mission, which is evidence of the progress made. On December 29, 1902, the novitiate of the English Semi-Province was transferred from Kensington to Wincanton.

---

[1] Benedict Zimmermann, *Chroniques du Carmel*.

[2] Fr. Antonine Newman carried out an extensive refurbishment of the Wincanton Priory during his term as prior in the 1950's. He also purchased Tout Hill house, next door to the Carmelite priory and this later became a private school. This school was administered first by the sisters of the Little Company of Mary and later by a group of Sisters of Christian Instruction under the title of Our Lady's Primary School. This school received state funding in 1975 and is still thriving. During his time in Wincanton, Fr. Antonine launched a quarterly magazine called *Mount Carmel*. The magazine is still running under much the same format under successive editors as it has for the past sixty years. He was a great devotee of Hermann Cohen.

By 1907 the financial situation of the community seems to have taken a turn for the better. The friars now turned their attention to the building of a new church that would be a fitting house of God. It was to be built on the site of Acorn House, adjoining the old chapel on South Street, now St. Luke's Hall.

Finale

Sadly the involvement of the Carmelites in Wincanton came to an end in May 1995 after 122 years of Carmelite presence and parish ministry in the West Country. This sadness was felt by a great many of the local people, irrespective of religious denomination. The wars of religion were now a distant memory, and the Carmelites were held in great affection by the people of the town, Catholics and non-Catholics alike. No doubt they were also proud of the imposing church and priory that was a landmark for miles around.

Further Expansion

The English Semi-Province meanwhile was consolidating the Carmelite presence in Britain. Already in possession of a motherhouse in Kensington and novitiate in Wincanton, a house of studies was more than desirable. Joseph Ostendi (Joseph Dominic of the Crucified Christ) was a member of the first community in Wincanton. By the year 1908, he was vicar general of the English Semi-Province and prior of Kensington. At this time he approached Bishop Frederick Keating of Northampton with a view to establishing a third Carmelite presence in England. So in the following year some Carmelite friars came from Kensington to the town of Chesham Bois, Bucks and ministered there and in the nearby Chalfonts for some time before they made a definitive move to Gerrards Cross. Here I would like to point out another link with Cohen, the founder of the first house in Kensington. It is very likely that Cohen knew the famous soprano Mathilde Grouman in Paris, to whom he would have been introduced by Franz Liszt. In addition, Grouman came from a Jewish background. Her daughter Blanche would become a great benefactor of the Carmelites in Gerrards Cross. Pamela Bacon, in her account of St. Joseph's Parish, Gerrards Cross, takes up the story:

> Another name which was to become important in the development of Chalfont St. Peter as a Catholic centre, [was] Madame Blanche Marchesi. She was the daughter of a minor Italian nobleman, a lawyer, who took up singing and for a time enjoyed popularity in the concert halls of Europe and the United States. His fame was largely due to his marriage in 1852 to a celebrated soprano and singing teacher, Mathilde Grouman, whose fame reached the notable music centers of Paris and Vienna where, for a time after her marriage, she became Professor of Singing at the Conservatoire. She could claim that she had trained Nellie Melba, Luisa Tetrazzini and Emma Calvi—the foremost operatic and concert singers of their day—and had become acquainted with Liszt, Wagner, Chopin and Verdi (who had offered her the leading role in many of his operas). With such a background their daughter, Blanche, who was born in Paris in 1863, turned instinctively to a musical career. She trained first as a violinist, but then assisted her mother as a singing teacher. In her own right, she had a considerable reputation as a singer, giving a recital in the Queen's Hall, London in 1896 as well as appearing in Berlin and Brussels. But she so loved London that she decided to live there and build up her career as a teacher.[1]

---

[1] Pamela Bacon, *The Flowering of Carmel: The Story of St. Joseph's Parish, Gerrards Cross, and Chalfont St. Peter* (Gerrards Cross, UK: Carmelite Community, 1990),

Due to her devotion to St. Gerard, Blanche took a fancy to
Gerrards Cross when travelling through the rail station there and
bought a property in Chalfont St. Peter not far from the home of
Captain Ford and his wife Jessie Rose. She struck up a friendship
with the couple, possibly because of the wife's musical talent.[1]
Blanche and Captain Ford collaborated in furnishing the new Mass
Center, which would be dedicated to St. Gerard, and she became a
long-term benefactor of the Carmelites. The Mass Centre would be
a temporary location, and suitable sites were sought.

Friar Francis and his brother Percy Lamb were, like Sharples
and Badger, also converts from the Anglican Church through the
Oxford Movement. Francis hesitated about buying the first property
that appeared suitable and soon found there was a more desirable
site available on Austenwood Common, nearer to Gerrards Cross.
The house was named Malherbe and was on an elevated site that
was eminently suitable for a church. Due to the tragic circumstances
of the death of the previous owner, Philip Moore, there were no
immediate takers for the property in spite of a bargain price tag.
Moore was a popular character, brother of the lord of the manor
of Chalfont St. Peter. Finding himself in financial straits, however,
he was expecting a check from his brother to be delivered in the
post. On Easter Sunday April 7, 1912, he was looking out for the
postman, but he passed by his drive. In a fit of depression Moore shot
himself on the doorstep of his home. (A bullet mark is still visible in
the brickwork.) The postman returned soon after but too late with

---

[1] Jessie Rose trained with the famous Carl Rosa Opera Company in London.
This was founded by a man called Carl Rose, like Cohen, a native of
Hamburg, Germany. He later used the similar name *Rosa*. I do not know if
Jessie was related to him, but it is quite likely. Jessie sang in various operas
in London. On November 11, 1901, she sang the role of Lady Rosie Pippin
in Sir Arthur Sullivan's *An Emerald Isle*. In the 1970s, the present writer
who ministered in Gerrards Cross from 1972 to 1982 used to visit Poppy
Pearce, an old parishioner at that time, who remembered the Fords and
Marchesis.

the life-saving cheque and discovered the body of Moore on the doorstep. Eighteen months after the owner's death, the Carmelites were in possession of the property, renamed *The Priory*.

Percy Lamb, architect brother of Francis, was commissioned to design a church in the style of Pugin similar to the one Cohen had built in Kensington. Due to the outbreak of World War I in 1914, the church was left incomplete and a temporary church was constructed. What had been already achieved, however, was of a high order with a beautiful mortuary chapel. The master craftsman for mosaics was the Italian Signore Formelli, who was also responsible for the mosaics in the London Brompton Oratory. Above the side altar adjacent to the mortuary chapel, there is a very beautiful reredos. The gilt figures represent St. Joachim, St. Anne, St. Elizabeth, and St. John the Baptist. These all look toward a similarly gilt figure of Our Lady and Child under a carved gilt canopy. Above the white marble tabernacle there is a gilt crucifix flanked by four candlesticks. The whole panel was regilded with the completion of the new church in the 1960's.

St. Joseph's Church (the name was now changed) was officially opened and blessed on July 29, 1915.

Part Two

Introduction to the Writings

In Part Two I have collected and edited those writings of Hermann Cohen from various sources that have come down to us, though it must be said that much of his writing may have been lost, due to the persecution suffered by the church in the period preceding his untimely death in 1871. Be that as it may, many of Hermann Cohen's sermons, talks, and letters have been preserved, and they help to give us an insight into his spirituality. Sermons, of course, are meant to be heard, and they lose a lot of their impact when merely read. Most of the material here has never before been published in English. The following passages are extracts from these sermons, lectures, homilies, letters, and dedications.

Hermann Cohen was primarily a Romantic musician and used the language of harmony to communicate his love of God to people. Though an effective preacher he often fused his music with his preaching – either preceding his sermons by way of introducing and interpreting his themes on the church organ, or after the sermon by playing for Benediction, which was sometimes the setting for his sermons in those days.

Here then I present many of Hermann Cohen's extant writings and letters, though there are many more of the latter that remain unpublished. The Carmelites in France, Italy and England together possess more than 200 of these. Cardinal Newman stated in a letter to his sister Jemima: "It has ever been a hobby of mine (unless it is a truism, not a hobby) that a man's life lies in his letters."[1] This is true of Cohen.

---

[1] A Packet of Letters, *John Henry Newman* (Edited Joyce Sugg), Clarendon Press, Oxford, 1983, p. 135.

Sermon Fragment on the love of Jesus.[1]

*M*y God, is it possible to have lived without thinking of Jesus, without loving Jesus, without living for Jesus and in Jesus? Now that your grace has awakened me, now that my eyes have seen, my hands have touched, my ears have heard, my heart has loved—yes, I love Jesus Christ. I shall take care not to hide it. I am in honor bound to proclaim it before the world. I love Jesus Christ—that's the secret of my immense peace which has gone on increasing since the first moment I began to love. I love Jesus Christ—this is what I want to proclaim to the ends of the earth. I wish that the walls of this temple would expand to include the millions who live on the earth, so that my voice could reach and penetrate the depths of their hearts, making them vibrate in unison with mine, all responding together in one great hymn of joy and triumph, echoing from earth to heaven, "we too love Jesus Christ." . . .

Everyone wants happiness. But Jesus Christ who is the source of happiness is not loved. We seek pleasure and greatness but Jesus

---

[1]   Sylvain, pp. 222-225. This fragment speaks of the love of Christ in accents that were perhaps more appropriate in the French style of his day, which characterized all his preaching. Many of his sermons would revolve around a typically romantic theme of the elusive nature of happiness. He would point out that this can only be found in Jesus Christ as he himself found it.

Christ our greatest joy and the splendor of the father is not loved. I want to avenge your misunderstood love. Yes, I want to punish my unfaithful and deceitful heart. Yes, heart of mine, if you have been foolish enough to prefer an empty love to the dove of charity, from now on you will find no more satisfaction on earth. I will deprive you of all consolation here below.

I will deprive you of the tenderness of a mother and the blessing of a father. I shall tear you away from all who cherish you. I will consign you to solitude and there I will purify you every moment of your life. You will no longer act except at the will of another. You will no longer enjoy the shared friendship and concern of others; you will become like ice or marble in regard to all that formerly pleased you. But, O sublime vengeance, O generous exchange, O happy fault, all these privations will win for you in return a new love and a divine life. Like the phoenix you will rise from the ashes, a pure flame will emerge within you, and he will renew your youth with the wings of an eagle, and with those wings you will fly to undreamt of realms. You will rise above the clouds of faith and pierce them. You will ascend to a lofty region, to a supernatural world and there you will see what no eye has seen, you will hear what no ear has heard and you will feel what no one's hands have ever touched, what the heart has never conceived. You will learn secrets which must remain hidden from the wise and prudent. You will be enkindled with a love for the beauty of all beauty that cannot fade, the light from light, true God from true God. You will love Jesus. Can you understand now, my brothers, that I became a monk so as to avenge this unknown love."[1] In another

---

[1] Sylvain, p. 275. In the following passage there is an uncanny similarity between what Cohen wrote here and Thomas Merton's reflections on becoming a monk at Gethsemani Abbey, Kentucky, recorded in his first influential book, *The Seven Storey Mountain. (Elected Silence)* "Everything that can be desired will sear you, and brand you with a cautery, and you will fly from it in pain to be alone. Every created joy will come to you as pain, and you will die to all joy and be left alone. All good things that other

place in Cohen wrote: "Leave to others, "he seems to say to me, "the care of their development, the pleasure of gathering in their fruit - leave Lyon, Bagnères, London,...and set yourself to some new work. And thus you see how, in spite of my conversion, I am always the Wandering Jew."

people love and desire and seek will come to you, but only as murderers to cut you off from the world and its occupations."(Thomas Merton, *The Seven Storey Mountain*, Harcourt Brace and Company, Florida, 1948, pp. 422-423.)

Sermon in Bordeaux Cathedral, 1852.[1]

Medius vestrum stetit quem vos nescitis.
In your midst stands one whom you do not know. (Jn 1:26.)

Happiness then where can you be found? Tell me where you are and I will sacrifice all for you: health, fortune, the days of my life, all, all for you. How is it that all are born for happiness if so few can possess it? The problem is we are stymied in our searching by will-o-the-wisps. At length I myself found it, and after that discovery I am overflowing with joy. My heart cannot restrain this eruption; can I ask you to share with me the fullness which overflows in me? But let me now tell you where I have found it.

Happiness consists in the unchanging possession of the only true Good; this true Good must be the most perfect thing imaginable. This supreme good, uniquely contains in himself all perfections: such is the infinite, such is God. Yes indeed, an insatiable heart requires the infinite, an infinite that will allow a person taste the most delightful joys, greater than all pleasures, which lifts one up to heights surpassing all heights. Search out the make up of your

---

[1] Carmel, *Aux Éditions du Carmel*, Marseille, 1989, pp. 67-69. Sermon text: "Among you stands one whom you do not know." This was preached before the Archbishop of Bordeaux on November 10, 1852, which was Cohen's birthday.

hearts—you will be like Alexander who complained that he had no more realms to conquer. Or think of pleasure in terms of Horace and you will cry out with him: "Fleeting pleasure carried away by the years!"[1] Then you realize that perfect undying happiness is none other than God. But, you might ask, how can we encounter God! My answer is that reason raises us up to him, reason which makes humankind here below distinct from all creatures orientated towards earth by their very transitory existence. Reason lifts one's gaze to Heaven and one's understanding seeks out a first and all powerful cause which is Being without beginning. She [reason] raises us to our glorious God, good and just.

In order to know God we must go beyond the creature to the Creator. But what is God in himself? Here, faith raises us to a point where reason rests on its laurels and God's nature is revealed to us, including the mystery of God's fatherhood and sonship [in Christ] which are found in him. Reason hides away, somewhat shamefacedly. Faith makes the splendors of the thrice- Holy God radiate upon us. There is one word which can cause monumental change, a word which can be called a key, a light, a firebrand, love, happiness, glory, freedom, eternity, immensity: that word is Jesus Christ, Son of God and himself God. Sin blunts all our energies; Jesus Christ has descended so that we can rise. He has given himself to us, he lives among us. Jesus Christ himself is the one we can possess. He has done so in order to make us happy.

Faith shows us how to find happiness in God and in Jesus Christ God's son. It is a mystery which pride cannot grasp. But to find Jesus Christ one must watch and pray. Scripture says, "Happy is the one who watches at the doors day and night," that is to say, who watches at the door of his heart to find Jesus Christ. Faith shows us God's goodness in Jesus Christ his Son. That's a mystery

---

[1]   Possibly a reference to one of Horace's odes, for example, book 2.14: "Eheu Fugaces, Postume, Postume, labuntur anni": "Ah, see how they glide by Postumus, Postumus, the years, the swift years."

which pride cannot penetrate. And the thing that proves that this truth comes from God is the fact that humankind does not invent something which it does not understand! When I did not believe in Jesus Christ, a time when I was lost in the darkness of error, of night, of deep anguish, Jesus Christ sent peace and calm into my heart and the wisdom that replaced error on the horizon of my understanding. Whatever is not carried on in the world in the name of Jesus Christ cannot be wise for he is the source of wisdom.

The seraphic St. Teresa sought in prayer the eternal light which illumined her. So, pray, ask and you will receive this intoxicating wine of immortality which flows from the winepress of prayer. Raise yourselves to the summit of Carmel. Take part in the sacred banquet of the poor to which the lowly are invited. Eat the bread, drink the wine which I have prepared for you. By prayer we humble ourselves, we contemplate the distance which separates us from God. Prayer imparts faith. Look at the makeup of the person of prayer, there you will read peace and contentment. It is by prayer that we become engaged and captivated by the divine will which is true freedom. Let us not confuse freedom with license. Freedom is the absence of all obstacles that can hamper the will in the accomplishment of good. Those obstacles are our passions. The divine will is directed to goodness and those who bend under the sacred yoke of that joyous will which is true freedom, fly to God in complete openness.

Faith is acquired through prayer which, united to faith, imparts peace, love, wisdom, light, freedom—all of which are contained in Jesus Christ. It is not possible for someone who does not love Jesus Christ to be happy. We love happiness, and Jesus Christ, our sole happiness, is not loved. We love wealth and Jesus Christ, eternal sufficiency, is not loved. We love pleasures and celebrity and Jesus Christ, the most desirable one, splendor of eternal glory, is not loved. Look, you who now listen to me, how is it that it takes a Jew to come here and beg Christians to adore Jesus Christ? Sun, refuse to shine, clouds cease to pour down rain, melt away you rocks of granite! Daughters of Sion, holy virgins, take up the discipline, cover yourselves in ashes, weep, fast, keep vigil, Jesus is not loved, because he is not known! We study, we know everything except Him. And even so missionaries carry his name to the ends of the earth. Even so martyrs die on the scaffold. For him thirty young Daughters of Charity leave tomorrow from the very house for which you have suggested that I make a fundraising appeal, and they will say goodbye to France to go and face the dangers of a long sea journey. Under the direction of Lazarist [Vincentian] religious they will make a foundation in Chile which will carry even further the name of St. Vincent de Paul!

Who then is Jesus Christ? Who is he? Listen to the prophet. *"Qui pourra reconter sa generation?"* (Who can declare his generation? Is 53:8) God infinitely good, infinitely holy, infinitely powerful, infinitely one, desires to communicate with his finite creature; God must communicate to the godhead and the name "Father" fits well here. Can the Father of all living things who reproduce themselves according to his laws, not give rise to another self by means of the fruitfulness of his blissful and perfect nature? It is from this need to communicate Godself that God the Father has engendered a Son perfect like himself from all eternity. . . . God from God, light from light, true God from true God, from all eternity like him.

Only things which are subject to change belong in time: God is unchanging. God was from the beginning. God can produce from himself another self and doesn't need to associate with anyone else in doing so. *"From the womb before the dawn I have begotten you."* (Ps. 101:3.) That unique child exhausted the total divine fruitfulness. The Father has given us that same Son of God, and likewise God, in whom he is well pleased; this is also why God has loved the world so much. Yes, indeed, he who is the unspeakable happiness of the angels comes down from heaven smitten with love for humankind and becomes man. And God makes himself like us in order to love us. He has descended from the heavens because of his immense love and for our salvation. It was for the sake of humanity alone that he took up a life of privation and suffering; for them he endured humiliation, outrage, calumny; to them he announced the Good News and suffered the most frightful tortures; for them he died amid the most degrading and terrible torments; it was for them that he rose again. He gave himself up for us, the Gospel tells us.

You young men, in order to be happy, study, receive the Eucharist. You are searching for love? But it is not really to be found in an inconstant affection—it is in the heart of the Crucified, opened by the soldier's lance, a wound still gaping wide at all times, the source of love and happiness. . . . Do you wish to be happy? Listen to Francis of Assisi: "My God is all, my Jesus," he cried out in a blazing out of love for Jesus Christ. . . . Look at that fool who left home, land and family in order to preach Jesus Christ to the world. He founded a famous order. He amazed and astounded his century by his virtues. Look at another person—Francis Xavier, alive with love, with trials, with insults, with fatigue and he cries out, "It's enough, O my God, enlarge my heart which tends to fail." Come, saintly and heroic Daughters of Charity of St. Vincent de Paul, who have you drawn or who will be drawn to that fervor, that zeal which you display in the noble mission of ministry to the poor? In the poor you show love of another Eucharist. Thanks to you for having brought me, a poor person of Jesus Christ, from afar to lend a hand in asking for bread for them, begging for the love of Jesus Christ, who said, everything you give in my name, it is to myself that you give it. Come you, come you who hunger and thirst for happiness and love, come all of you after Jesus Christ. He will give you the whole of his heart. Love him, identify with him, he is all, all the rest is nothing but emptiness and play-acting, compared with the tenderness of his greatness. Let us love Jesus, never let me cease from turning people to his love. Let us love Jesus. There is only one happiness—to love Jesus Christ and to be loved by him.

Sermon at St. Sulpice[1]

The fairest among the children of men. (Ps 45)

My dear People,

$\mathcal{M}$y first thought as I appear in this Christian pulpit is to make amends for the bad example which I unhappily gave in this city in the past. You might well ask me, "What right have you to

---

[1] Beaurin, pp. 224-227. (Ps 110:3). This remarkable sermon by Cohen is probably too allegorical in style for modern tastes. It was his first public appearance there since his conversion, and a large crowd turned up to hear him. Cohen was recovering from a severe bout of illness at this time. The archbishop presided, and one of his attendants, Henri Perreyve, himself an artist and musician and a professor at the Sorbonne, has left us this record of Cohen's sermon. It was his first public appearance there since his conversion and a large crowd turned up to hear him. The Archbishop presided and one of his attendants, Henri Perreyre, himself an artist and musician and a professor at the Sorbonne, has left us a record of Hermann's words. About Cohen's appearance in the pulpit he has this to say: "He is handsome with finely chiseled features as pale as his smile. He is young - thirty two -, and he resembles the figures in the frescoes at Fiesole or Assisi. He has a clear voice, he does not use a lot of gestures but it is very moving to see him turn to the blessed sacrament." Perreyve remarked that the impression made on his hearers was this: 'It is something to have listened to a saint.' When he had finished his sermon Cohen went to the great organ of St. Sulpice and played beautifully while the Archbishop gave benediction.

preach to me, to exhort me to virtue and goodness, to teach me the truths of the faith, to speak to us of Jesus and Mary whom we love? You have so often dishonored them in our sight, you who have kept bad company and behaved in an outrageous way, you whom we know to have swallowed every false theory and so often insulted us with your conduct." Yes, my brethren, I confess that I have sinned against heaven and against you. I admit that I have deserved to be unpopular with you and that I have forfeited your good will. I come to you, brethren, clothed in a robe of penance and committed to a strict order, barefooted and wearing a tonsure. Mary obtained for me from the God of the Eucharist a cure infinitely more important to me than that of my bodily eyes, that is, freedom from my blindness. It was the month of Mary and they were singing hymns. Mary, the mother of Jesus revealed the Eucharist to me. I knew Jesus, I knew God. Soon I became a Christian. I asked for baptism and before long the holy water was flowing over me. At that moment all the many sins of my twenty five years were wiped out. Brethren, God pardoned me, Mary pardoned me, will you not pardon me too?

I have travelled throughout the world. I have loved the world. I have learnt one thing about the world—you don't find happiness there. And you too: have you found it, for can you say you are happy, do you not want for anything? Ah, it seems to me that as a response I can hear a sad chorus of sighs all around. I seem to hear the unanimous cry of suffering humanity: "Happiness, where can I find you? Tell me where you are hidden and I will search for you, hold you and possess you." I have looked for happiness. I have searched in cities and crossed the seas to find it. I have searched for happiness among the beauties of nature; I have sought it in the elegant life of salons, in the giddy pleasures of balls and banquets. I have sought it through the accumulation of money, in the excitement of gambling, in the hazards of adventure and in trying to satisfy my burning ambitions. I have looked for it in the renown of the artist, in the friendships of famous people and in all the pleasures of sense and spirit. Finally I looked for it in the fidelity of a friend, that incessant dream of every heart. Dear God, was there anywhere I failed to seek it this happiness? How can one explain this mystery to oneself? For human beings are made for happiness. The mystery is that most people don't know in what happiness consists. They look for it where it doesn't exist.

Well then, listen. I have found happiness, I possess it, I enjoy it so fully that I am able to say with the great apostle, "I am overflowing with joy." My heart brims over with happiness, and I cannot contain it within me. I wanted to leave my solitude in order to come and find you and tell you, I am overflowing with joy. Yes, I am so happy that I come to offer it to you, I come to entreat you to share with me this overflowing happiness. But, you object, I don't believe in Jesus Christ. I too, I did not believe, and that is precisely why I was unhappy. So much has God loved the world. It was for humankind alone that he led a life of privation and suffering and that he died in agony and finally rose again. He gave himself up for us—can you be surprised after that that there is a hell? But there is more!

One stormy night I found myself lost in a range of steep mountains surrounded on all sides by frightful precipices. The thunder rolled and the wind raged uprooting ancient trees. I was thrown down with great violence. My great loss appeared certain to me. Suddenly in the side of a neighboring mountain, a flash of lightning revealed to me a little golden door in a granite hollow. My courage revived in the hope of finding a resting place and a helping hand. I dragged myself breathlessly through the brambles and through water all disheveled, until I reached the little door on which I began to knock asking for help. As soon as I knocked the door opened and a young man, clothed in majesty and with graciousness on his lips, appeared on the threshold and introduced me to his mysterious abode. Immediately the sound of the storm abated and I was restored to peace. An unseen hand removed my mud-splattered cloak and plunged me in a refreshing bath where I found strength and health. This bath not only removed every stain of the journey but also healed my wounds, filling my veins with new life. He renewed the joy of my youth. The perfume he emitted was so exquisite that I wished to know where it came from.

Think of my amazement to see beside me the handsome young man who had opened the door to me. He held out his hands and in each there was a deep wound from which the blood was flowing. I looked at him and looked at myself and I saw that I was bathed in this young man's blood. This blood filled me with such inner strength that I felt ready to face a thousand storms even worse than the one I have just described. And I was even more surprised when his blood, far from making me turn red, made me strikingly white instead, whiter indeed than snow. . . . Gratitude and love began to stir in my heart. I was hungry, I was thirsty—the fatigue and struggles of my journey had drained me, but he made me sit down to a banquet, in a brightly lit festive hall—though I could see no lamps there. The young man himself was the lamp there and rays of light shone from his face. (Cfr. Rv 21:23.) I was hungry, I was thirsty. He gave me bread and said to me, "eat this." He offered me a cup saying to me, "drink this." He blessed the bread, then held the cup to the wound in his side and it was at once filled with a marvelous wine. When I had eaten and drunk I understood that this was no ordinary food, but nourishment which transformed me and gave me a deep joy. I looked at the handsome young man and saw him dwelling in me and being adored by angels. . . . Then the young man spoke to me. His words were like heavenly music, delighting me and causing me to shed tears of love and joy. And then he drew me to himself, embraced me and held me to his heart, caressing me and soothing me gently with the melody which fell from his lips. I lay my head on his breast and my happiness was so great that my spirit fainted. (Cfr. Jn 13 and Song of Songs 5.) I slept on the heart of my loving friend. It was no ordinary sleep, but one filled with an immense sense of peace which the young man induced in me after the storm. The psalmist sings: "In peace in him I sleep and take my rest."

I slept a long time and I had a dream of heaven during my sleep. O dream of love, I wish I were able to express it. Then he touched my eyes and I awoke at once filled with inexpressible love. Bowing down I thanked him for his welcome and he said to me, "If you wish you can stay here every day. Each day I will bathe you in my blood. I will warm you in my heart, I will enfold you with my light and I will make you sit down to my table. . . . If you leave me, watch out, for the storm will quickly begin again." "Let others," I said, "fight the storm and wade through the mud on the road, but for me, since you will keep me here, I wish to live here, here I wish to die." . . . Yes, every day I will drink from the torrent of life which flows from your open side. But tell me your name so that I can bless you with the angels. (Cfr. Gen 32:30.) He replied, "My name is love, my name is Eucharist." "O Jesus, forgive me for having got to know you so late in the day. Nowhere else have I found the joy, the happiness that I possess in you. Let us then love Jesus Christ, for there is only one happiness to love Jesus Christ and to be loved by him."

The Gambler[1]

$\mathcal{T}$he passion for gold is not alone in being the bearer of corruption for the heart; it also enkindles a state of delirium and frenzy.[2] Look at the gambler: he will sell his soul for a few pieces of metal! Emotions of greed urge him to hope for a lucky strike, rather than engage in some honest toil. He allows his field to be filled with nettles, his vines covered with thorns, and what his field and his vines cannot offer him, he wishes to procure by a game of chance. He conjures up a destiny, he embraces a thousand superstitions to attract an outcome, and if his resources are exhausted, if he has

---

[1] Flamme Ardente, pp. 305-306.

[2] Cohen's description of the compulsive gambler here has been compared to Dostoyevsky, who himself was addicted to gambling. On his way to Paris, the Russian novelist won 11,000 francs at his first go in Wiesbaden. Dostoyevsky would have known Cohen's former friend fellow Russian Mikhail Bakunin, and he certainly knew the revolutionary Herzen. Herzen, Bakunin, Cohen, and Karl Marx all lived for a period in London in the early 1860s. In his novel *The Gambler*, Dostoyevsky describes this addiction in similar terms to Cohen. In it, the city of "Rouletteberg" features as a gambling hell. Writing to his wife in 1871, the year Cohen died, he states, "Something great has taken place in me. That vile fantasy which has tormented me for almost ten years has disappeared. For ten years I have done nothing but dream of winning. I have dreamed seriously and passionately. Now it is over and done with. This was absolutely the last time." He also deals with the addiction in *The Devils* and other writings.

lost his family's patrimony, he will resort to borrowing; then when no one will lend him any more, he will risk his word, his honor, his future. He will forfeit his very family and the widow's mite as well as the orphan's morsel of bread. He will allow all ties to die because of his gambling. Then when all is no longer enough he will resort to fraud or theft, if you will, and he will come again and sit down on the green sod with the proceeds of his crime. O, the feeling of rage—he loses again. Again with red and angry face he will spew up blasphemies; it's a ferocious beast that needs to be bound and muzzled.

Such fury leads, not only reason astray, not only alters the features, not only shows itself in convulsive gestures, but adopts the sinister growl of the tiger. He blasphemes, he curses, he launches a torrent of abuse and invective. At length depleted by its fury, he locks himself away and cannot join in with his friends pals, he tires of gambling and risks everything against himself, in order to give himself up again to cruel emotions, the painful tortures of hope deceived. He has become a slave to an implacable tyrant. Passion holds him in an iron grip and prevents him sleeping by day or night. And if he does enjoy a moment's respite and a fitful sleep on his weary couch, he is tormented by horrible dreams that summon up a fevered hope of gain and a frightful deceit of loss. He wakes with a start and memory unfolds before him a desolate tableau of a desperate situation. During his prolonged insomnia, he reflects on suicide, but before carrying out his desire he has one more go at gaining a fortune.

Who can possibly narrate here the kind of dreadful catastrophes to which unbridled passion leads? O my God, what delirium, what frenzy! How do you escape from this slavery, this hell? A German Protestant officer, who witnessed his friend one day gambling like this, tapped him on the shoulder and said: "My friend, as I see it people like you are obsessed. You are so possessed by this demon that you will end up in prison." Notice this officer . . . spoke the truth. He did not know, my God, your mercy and your power.

He could not understand how it only takes a breathing of your grace to regain the strongest fortresses from the demon. But is it not a dream to be released from errors, to be set free from chains, to have the bonds of slavery broken, to be withdrawn alive from this hell.

Human Reason Left to
Its Own Devices.[1]

*T*hose who flagrantly revolt against divine Providence or the goodness and justice of God do so, not just because reason denies or fails to recognize that which it says about itself; I mean in its own proper independence and proper sovereignty—it is the fact that pride rises up and causes reason to fall into the greatest errors. *Evanuerent in cogitationibus suis.* ("They became vain in their thoughts." Rom 1:21.)

Indeed when our reason fancies itself wise with its own proper wisdom, it becomes not simply unjust but even absurd. *Dicentes enim se sapientes esse, stulti facti sunt.* ("Saying they were wise they became foolish." Ibid.) Check the course of human history. No sooner have the children of Adam cut themselves off from Revelation by a strange blindness of spirit, they degenerate into idolatry, and for four thousand years, with the exception of one people living in a small corner of the earth, all nations were steeped in complete ignorance regarding the most important questions of their existence. Yes, reason, which passes itself off as a supernatural light doesn't know where it is coming from or where it is going. Just ask those innumerable people who lived on earth up to the time of the preaching of the Gospel, what they knew about their future

---

[1] Flamme Ardente, pp. 307-309

destiny! History will answer that question for them with the greatest absurdities![1]

Then, examine, if you will, one after the other, the theories of our modern philosophers and the so-called Catholic rebels against their mother the Church, and you will also find ignorance, errors and inexplicable contradictions. Among them you will hardly find one person who, on the most important questions that interest humanity, can give you as satisfactory an answer as the first child you meet in this parish approaching with a catechism in his hand. Now I wish to talk about the devisers of systems, the makers of doctrines, the practitioners of religious novelties. Yes, I have known them, known them only too well, these gentlemen, these prophets of the future. I have myself, to my shame, dogmatized with them, I have used the same zeal and ardor in propagating their new gospels, that I almost got myself imprisoned at Spielberg. Yes, I've seen them stand beside the college principals, I have attended these prophets of the nineteenth century, eager for my brain to drink at the fountain of their famous wisdom! Lamennais, Louis Blanc, Saint-Simon, Considerant, Gueroult! I knew them, I followed them.[2] And I can say truly I tried hard to adapt myself to their positions, but they explained nothing to me, proved nothing, absolutely nothing. And after I had devoured their books, I still found myself agitated by

---

[1] Cohen here seems to dismiss natural religion, though in another place he seems to accept it. He is not a theologian but a preacher, and he is commenting on Romans, which takes a similar line. The great Cardinal John Henry Newman writing also in the nineteenth would insist on the absolute need for revelation. Newman had a deep distrust of where the "wild" and proud human mind would lead you if it refused to be taught by God. He would repeatedly insist on the need we have for that "impression" or "idea" of revelation that we can find principally in the Scriptures. He set his face against the liberalism of his time that refused to be tied down by revelation or dogma, a position, which he insisted, would destroy all religion. In this history has proved him right.

[2] All of these people were either writers or politicians (or both) in nineteenth century France.

the same doubts, the same anguish. But then one day thanks to God's mercy, I opened the Bible and on the first page of that revered book, I found more light, more peace than in all their ramblings put together. Some verses alone of that divine book scattered my doubts and caused an unexpected and indefectible light to fall on my eyes, sufficient to clarify my understanding. The moral law is simply the holiness of God reflected in our hearts by revelation, something which the wise ones of our century, because they ignore revealed religion, cannot know moral truth. That is how every philosopher invents a morality of his own by simply using his own insights, and dreams up a certain ideal of the Beautiful which varies with individual genius and according to current taste. This is also why it is the case that those elite people who have taken pure reason to the uttermost limits have abandoned the truly human itself and have ended up with the most abject theories of morality. Yes, Plato and Aristotle, those two outstanding intellects who have developed purely human reason to its highest degree, precisely in their works in which they propose to direct humankind to the highest perfection, have preached in some maxims things to which I hesitate to allude to for fear of offending the ears of Christian mothers who listen to me.[1] There you have the ideal perfection of pure reason unenlightened by divine manifestation. And this ought not surprise us; because reason left to itself becomes immoral. Because reason left to itself cannot resist the seduction of passion. It becomes venal, it becomes open to bribery, easily caught by a bait of flattery. People easily believe what flatters them. *Quidquid placet sanctum est*, Augustine tells us, and their hearts are won over by the adulation of their thoughts. As well as that, because our understanding loses sight of the heavenly light

---

[1] It is difficult to know what Cohen has in mind here. Certainly in the context where he quotes Paul to the Romans it may indicate homosexuality. Though this had gained wide acceptance in Greek culture, it was not officially endorsed by either Plato or Aristotle. It is true that Plato has been thought to have been homosexual, but he would not have approved of it for society in general.

of justice, it is not difficult to lead its integrity astray; and because it does not have the supernatural help of grace to offer resistance, because it is deprived of that divine source, it only takes a flimsy deceit to surrender the sovereignty of the firstborn for a mess of pottage, as with Esau—a moment's satisfaction for an appetizing mouthful. Indeed reason, like the prodigal son, after he had lost his heritage, engages in feeding the most unclean animals—*Ut pasceret porcos.* (Luke 15:15.) And how is this? Passion says to reason, very well, you have the insight of genius, enter into our service and you will have the glory you aspire to; plead in our favor and you will be recompensed with celebrity and fame. Invent new sophistries to legitimize our desires and you will have the credit of inventing spiritual subtleties—*Ad excusandas excusationes in peccatis.* ("To offer excuses for sins." Ps. 141:4.)

Our Lady of Peragude.[1]

A mother and her son walked along the road of life. Their complexion was burnt by the heat of the sun, their knees were trembling and their legs refused to carry them much further. They were walking in sadness and their gaze turned uneasily and often towards the forest which they were traversing, and some highwaymen attacked, stealing their treasure and almost all their clothes. To crown it all they lost their way as they proceeded in the adventure. Then giving in to fatigue they sat down to rest by the side of a ravine and soon sleep took hold of them. The son was suddenly awakened by the sound of music. "Mother," he cried, "do you not hear those heavenly voices?" "I hear nothing," said the mother, "sleep has closed my eyes, let me rest my child." Then she fell asleep again. But the son did not close his eyelids. The voice from heaven had caused to vibrate in his heart an unknown chord, and he felt a most urgent desire to hear those divine harmonies once again. He raises himself then falls on his knees and in a low voice, so as not to disturb his mother's sleep, he says: "O melodious voice, consoling and friendly voice, let me hear you again. You have wounded my soul with an ineffable sensation, do take notice again of the misfortune that befell me." He spoke, he wept and scanned the far horizon for the source

---

[1] Flamme Ardente, pp 310-315. This was preached during a visit to a shrine of Mary near Agen in the south of France.

of such sweet sounds. Again he lifts his eyes to heaven. And marvel, a brilliant light came towards him and gradually drawing near he could make out a living being; he saw a woman bright as the daystar, radiant with splendor and full of majesty. There was something divine, not human about her features. Yes, something divine was reflected in her face, bearing the stamp of goodness, of tenderness and a sweetness beyond the angelic. Her forehead shone like an arc of stars and her long dark hair fell in waves about her. Her eyes were fixed on the young traveler in maternal concern. Her whole being inspired respect, veneration, approaching adoration, "Who are you?" asked the lost child of Israel, he whom the heavenly melodies and the beautiful voice were rescuing from the sleep of death. "Are you the enchantress Rachel who captured the heart of my ancestor Jacob? Or are you Judith whose winning ways were the ruin of Holofernes? Are you that Esther who knew how to obtain the salvation of her people through her charm and love?" "I am all those," she said, "and more. I am of your nation, a daughter of Abraham, of Isaac and Jacob, a daughter of the tribe of Levi, of the priestly race."[1] "But what is that?"

"I am the daughter of the Lord, the mother of the messiah, the spouse of the Holy Spirit, who hovered over the waters on the day of creation and made them fertile by the fire of his love. I am the woman promised to the world, greeted by the prophets, whose foot would crush the serpent's head. I am the virgin foretold by Isaiah, the virgin who would conceive and bear a child, whose name would be wonderful, God of strength. (Is 9:5.) I am that wisdom of which Solomon speaks. It is through me that kings reign; I rule the world and all created things. The Lord possessed me from the beginning of his ways and has preserved me from the serpent's sting. The true Assuerus said to me in the person of Esther that the law of death affecting my people would not touch me. I am the dove of the Song

---

[1] This was significant for Cohen as he believed himself descended from the 'Cohennim' or priests of the Old Testament.

of Songs, forever beautiful, forever pure, without spot or stain. I am lifted up like a cedar of Lebanon or a cypress of Sion and I resemble the palm trees of Kadesh or the rose bushes of Jericho. I extend my branches like the vine and my flowers give out sweet fragrance and abundant fruit. . . . I am that sister, that spouse of the Beloved. And do you know what I am, what I shall be for you if you wish it? I will be your mother of fair love, of saving fear and of holy hope. In me you will find the grace of all truth and of all virtue. I am full of grace and the Lord is with me. Come then, my child, follow me and I will lead you on the way to eternal happiness.

"I will follow you, beauty of the angels, I very much wish to do so, but I dare not. See that overburdened woman you have given me today, how can I abandon her, she who since my birth has showered me with goodness? She gave birth to me in pain, nourished me with her milk, kept constant vigils over me, generous with her love; she sacrificed everything for me—how can I abandon her? O beautiful morning star overhanging my head, you possess the same goodness and I am drawn to you; but see, this poor mother sleeps and I do not have the courage to leave her by herself on the road."

And yet, my child, listen, and hear what I have to say. "You must forget your people and your father's house." (Ps 44:11) Come my son, give me your heart and your whole self and "I will lead you into solitude and there I will speak to your heart" and I will fill you with delights. You hunger for the bliss of immortality, see how I have built a palace of seven columns on this mount of Carmel, flowing with milk and honey, the abode of justice and peace. Here you will experience a spring which will allow you to taste by anticipation the joys of heaven. There I have laid a table loaded with the most exquisite fruits. There I will nourish you with a mysterious bread which is the delight of paradise. There I will nourish you with the wine and honey that gives rise to virgins. There in solitude, I will enable you to draw the bow to defend yourself from all that can despoil you. There I will immolate the victim whose pleasant odor will rise to the throne of God. So come and eat this bread which I have made with the virginal milk from my virginal bosom, and drink the wine taken from my most pure blood. . . . If you prefer to follow the mother you know, look at the fruit and the nourishment she gives. Take heed of your weakness—it is the fruit of your mother here below. And now look at the fruit of my womb —and immediately she showed me in the monstrance, the Spouse destined for me: here is my fruit and this fruit is the Eucharist.

O dear God, the Eucharist, Mary, you are the mother of the Eucharist, you give the Eucharist to me! You will nourish me each day with this manna from heaven! You will cover my lips with the precious chalice overflowing with the blood of my God! O Mary, if you give me the Eucharist that is enough. Farewell, my mother here below, you are no longer my mother: my mother is she who unites me with God who gives God to me, it is she whom I ought to follow from now on.[1] And because you do not wish to awake, because you persist in sleeping, because you always close your ears to that voice which has awakened me from a sleep more dangerous than yours, farewell then, poor mother, farewell. I depart for the land of Carmel and there I will pray for you to my mother of fair love! Farewell, I have no other mother now but the mother of the Eucharist; and do not say that I have a disloyal heart. I keep my heart to love Jesus in the Eucharist, to love Mary who has given him to me. Yes, Mary, since I have known you and loved you, I have found the way, and such a way dear God! A heavenly way, a way of love and happiness! Since I have frequented the thresholds of your temples, since I have

---

[1] Cohen's references to his mother seem harsh in the extreme to us looking back to a different era. Yet in reality he was a dutiful son and would have tried to lessen the blow his conversion caused her. One of his most impressive letters was the one to his Jewish family trying to explain how he had become a Christian and a Carmelite. In fact what he says above is softened by the final paragraph here. We need to remember that the accepted theology of the time which Cohen took seriously, held that there was no salvation outside the (Catholic) Church. That set up a painful tension in the lives of people such as Cohen.

taken from your hands the book sealed with seven seals for the godless, and which you have the right to open because you have conquered like the lion of Judah. (Cfr Rev 5. Here it is the lamb that breaks the seals, not Mary.) Since I have read the only truth which you alone teach and which replaces all others, I feel I have gained a new understanding. *Intellectum tibi dabo.* ("I will give you understanding." Ps 32:8.) My eye has discovered such insight that I believe that another sees through me. My soul is raised up above merely human truth, and placed in a region that no longer vacillates like floating clouds of opinions that ceaselessly chase each other; and now it focuses on the steady light, always glowing with your clarity, in which my heart finds repose, peace and energy and journeys gladly towards the homeland to which you guide me.

But, my heavenly mother, why have I deserted for love of you those who have been so dear to me here below, O, please have pity on them. Do not forget that I have left a mother for you also. She is, like you, a daughter of Jacob, she is then one of your own family. O, you will give her back to me, you will have pity, you will not abandon her. Already her head is leaning towards the grave, poor mother! O, Mary, I entreat you, just let her touch the hem of your shining garment, and she will raise herself to follow you also; she will love Jesus and finally will come to heaven with you also; she will love Jesus and finally will come to heaven with us.

At the Church (now Basilica) of St. Clothilde, Paris[1]

On the Theme of Thanksgiving.

$\mathcal{S}$ ome months ago I found myself by the side of a venerable priest, the perfume of whose sanctity has spread across the catholic world. I wish to talk about the virtues of the admirable Curé d'Ars. In spite of the constant crowd of penitents and pilgrims who gather there I had the pleasure of being able to speak to him for a short while. I said, "Father, have you not said that it is good to ask the Lord for those graces with which he will reward those who receive them?" "Yes," he told me, "it's very true: we are like the lepers who are cured but

---

[1] Flamme Ardente, pp.313-323. This church is now the Basilica of St. Clothilde. This sermon is less personal and less autobiographical than the St. Sulpice one. Cohen had shortly before met the Curé d'Ars and consulted him about founding a movement for Thanksgiving. This twin-spired church has a famous Cavaillé-Coll organ and Caesar César Franck was organist here for thirty-one years. It had only recently been completed, having been begun in 1847 shortly before Cohen's conversion. It was dedicated to St. Clothilde, mother of Clovis, and co-dedicated to St. Valère because it was built on the site of the demolished church of St. Valère. It was on the site of an ancient Carmelite foundation on the Rue de Grenelle. It was while playing the organ for Benediction in this church, while standing in for a friend, that Cohen had his initial conversion experience.

don't say thanks." "But, Father, would it not be possible to found a work which will have for its aim to return unceasing thanks to God for the torrent of favors which he pours out on the world?" "Yes," he said, "you are right. Do that, God will bless you. It is a lack in works of devotion, a lack that ought to be filled."

My brothers, this is the first time for me to speak in public about this thought which has not yet progressed from the state of being a simple project. Many people in close contact with God in prayer have confided to me the complaints communicated to them by the Lord about the ingratitude of the world to the gifts he has given. St. Bernard, in a sermon which was entitled, "Against the Malice of Ingratitude," asks why it is that God who is so good, so generous, who has showered us with so many gifts, and who without us asking or even desiring, gives us much more that we ask him, now that we plead for them and crave them unceasingly. Has his power become enfeebled then? Have his riches been depleted? Has his goodness in our regard changed? Unfortunately that is not the point, but the true reason is that no one thanks God for his gifts. *Heu, Heu, non invenitur qui agat gratias Deo.* (Luke 17:18. "Unhappily no one is found to return thank to God.") We don't recognize the need to return thanks, as we ought for the gifts we have received. Isn't it because Adam neglected to thank God for the gift of his glorious creation and the many riches of body and mind with which he was endowed, that God withdrew his hand from him and allowed him to fall into sin? Let us study then this important duty of the Christian, a duty so neglected and let us ask Mary who, by her fidelity to the graces she received was continually graced with new gifts. St. Thomas tells us there are three degrees of charity:

First Degree.

The first degree is that of the heart. We must stamp on our heart the memory of the great mercies the Lord has shown us, a remembrance which will monitor our feelings and removes from us any temptation to ingratitude.

Second Degree

The second degree leads us to praise and glorify God for the good things we have received. In the royal prophet we find an abundance of canticles and songs of praise and jubilation. "*Benedic, anima mea, Domino.*" Ps. 103:1 (Bless the Lord, my soul.) And he goes on to invite the whole creation to join him in his song of praise—earth and sky, all living creatures, mountains, valleys—even the very elements themselves—in a word, he invites all that is in us and around us to praise and bless the Lord, "*et omnia quae intra me sunt.*" Ibid.:v 2 ("And all that is within me.")

The Church in her liturgy places on our lips the most sublime prayers of thanksgiving: the *Te Deum* is the highest religious expression of the human race. And in her *Magnificat*, Mary provides us with a model of praise. The canticle of the angels in the Mass and the preface are other such examples. Certainly the Holy Spirit in the Scriptures has abundantly furnished us with sacred texts which can melt the heart and cause the tongue to chant in fullness of joy which answers our need to recount the graces of the Lord. "*Venite, audite et narrabo, omnes qui timetis deum, quanta fecit anima mea.*" "Come listen and I will tell, all who fear the Lord, what he has done for me." (Ps.66:16.)

We ought to thank God not only for all the good things, but also for all the trials we meet, because all these other things proceed from the same principle of love. "*Benedicam Dominum in omni tempore,*" the prophet says, "*semper laus eius in ore meo.*" "I will bless the Lord at all times . . . his praise always on my lips." (Ps. 34:1.) St. Augustine has these lovely words: "You are happy? Recognize your father who caresses you. You are in strife? Recognize your Father who corrects you. So whether he caresses you or corrects you, it is He who instructs those to whom he will give an inheritance."

God is equally worthy of praise, St. Chrysostom says, when he either punishes or pardons; for the punishment and the pardon are the results of his goodness and the proof of his benevolence. We should show gratitude not solely that he has created heaven but also that he has created hell—for isn't this the point, that it was not created for us in order to send us there but to awaken fear in us and inspire in us a hatred for sin which alone can do so. The holy man Job is an admirable example of this evenhanded gratitude—he blesses God in prosperity and in adversity, and consumed with affliction and pain, he says, "We have blest the Lord for his gifts, why do we not accept affliction at his hand?" Then he prostrates himself on the earth as he adores and says, "The Lord has given us all, and he has taken all: blessed be the name of the Lord." (Cfr. Job 1:21.) In the New Testament we find St. Lawrence giving thanks to God on his gridiron and St. Cyprian who, when he heard he was condemned to death said, "Thanks be to God." And he gave twenty-five gold pieces to the executioner who beheaded him. The courageous virgin martyr Thecla kept saying, "Let us give thanks to God," while they were burning her sides with irons. We also find that Tobit does not murmur against God when he becomes blind, but remains faithful in the fear of God to him, giving him thanks all the days of his life: *Agens gratias Deo, omnibus diebus vitae suae.* (Giving thanks to God all the days of his life.)

Third Degree

And yet our praise is not the highest form of thanks. It is through the divine Eucharist and through it alone, that you can rightly pay your debt of gratitude to God. This is the third, the highest degree of thanksgiving which consists in adding to the gratitude of heart and tongue that of hand and arm, giving back something more than one has received. To give back merely what one has received is to give nothing. It is in the holy Eucharist that we find a surplus, something freely given, of which St. Thomas speaks.

Here there appears at first sight to be a difficulty. We have nothing that is not infinitely inferior to God, and all that we have, we possess solely by his mercy. The thanksgiving we express for his gifts is itself only an outpouring of his goodness. We can say to God with even more reason than the Roman nobleman who said to Augustus who had spared his father's life—a man who had been a sworn enemy of the emperor, "Look Caesar, the only harm I have received from you, by the magnitude of the benefit you have bestowed on me, is that you condemn me to live and die an ungrateful person, without the means of recognizing sufficiently the debt I owe you."

And then, my dear brothers it seems to me that our holy faith places in our hands the possibility of fulfilling the precept of St. Thomas, who wishes that we give back to God more than we owe him. Here, it should strike us how important thanksgiving is. And first off, our faith teaches us that the demands of justice require us under God to fulfill the precepts and commandments of the Church; every time then, we do something in addition to this, something that is not strictly required for our salvation, in some manner we give to the Lord something more that he has wished us to give. Then in his immense goodness, for a great number at least he is content with them simply keeping the commandments.

Every time then you do a good work, over and above what is absolutely required, you can in some manner acquit yourself of what you do owe God; every alms you give, beyond what you owe in justice, will be an alms offered in thanksgiving. Every work of mercy, every sacrifice, every denial you impose on yourself, beyond the penance imposed by the Church, will be an act of thanksgiving infinitely pleasing to God. Every gift you give, every flower you offer to decorate and brighten up the worship we render him, every Communion you make in addition to your Easter duty, every Mass you attend in addition to your Sunday obligation—in a word, all the works of devotion and love are like a donation with which you recompense God like a surplus added on to the sacred duty of worship.

And now I come at last to a point I want to put forward in this talk—in fact I hate to be harping it so often—on the occasions of

Communions, and of thanksgiving Masses that I talk about. It is by the divine Eucharist and by it alone that we can worthily return thanks to God. Yes, by it alone in a worthy manner; for it is in the divine Eucharist that you find this *surplus* this *"gratis"* about which St. Thomas speaks. This is the point I want to emphasize to you. I say that the Eucharist is the only means of thanksgiving worthy of God that it is within our power to offer, and I can show this in the first instance from the words of the Holy Spirit himself who cries out in a holy outburst on the lips of the royal prophet: *"Quid retribuam Domino pro omnibus quae retribuit mihi?"* "What shall I render to the Lord for all he has given me?" (Ps 116:12,13.) And he joyfully replies, *"Calicem salutaris accipiam."* "I will take the chalice of salvation," he gladly sings. This chalice of salvation, this chalice of the Lord is nothing other than the Eucharist.

Secondly, I can show it from the words of Jesus Christ, when he instituted the testament of his love in the cenacle, at the moment he gave his body and blood to the apostles and to us, he said, *"Hoc facite in meam commemorationem,"* "Do this in remembrance of me," (Lk 22:19) and the thing that proves that it is in memory of his gifts is that which is written, *"Memoriam fecit mirabilium suorum, escam dedit timentibus se."* (He has remembered his wonderful works, has given food to those who fear him.) In other words, in memory of all I have done for you. The Lord in his mercy instituted a memorial of his gifts, giving himself as food to those who fear him. The sacrament of the altar has always been called the memorial, the resume of God's gifts to us.

God knows the human heart, how soon it forgets and becomes ungrateful. Just as ingratitude has its source in forgetfulness of God, so gratitude is based on the memory of God's goodness. God ordered the Israelites to keep a container filled with manna in the tabernacle, in memory of the gifts he showered on them when he fed them in the desert. Manna has always been regarded as an image of the holy Eucharist. But the name of the true manna, the lovely name "Eucharist" expresses in one word all the treasures of

God's goodness. Literally in Greek it means "thanksgiving." But since human thanksgiving is not enough, this treasure is called "the divine Eucharist"—the divine act of thanksgiving, infinite and inexhaustible, suitable for the greatness and goodness of God. O yes, I know it, O my God, when I offer you this host of praise and love, I hear again your Father's voice from heaven as Jesus entered the waters of the Jordan and you said, *"Hic est filius meus dilectus in quo mihi bene complacui."* "This is my beloved son in whom I am well pleased."

If then we offer him his well-beloved son who became our heritage in the divine Eucharist, we render to the eternal Father a thanksgiving which is infinite, agreeable, one which is worthy of him and thus supreme liturgical praise. This is what the Church sums up and professes in that truly sublime hymn in the Mass called the Preface, the thanksgiving song of creation. . . . The priest at the point of offering to God Jesus Christ himself who comes to immolate himself in order to cancel all the debt owed to the divine Majesty— debts of adoration, of acknowledgement, of reparation, of supplication—first raises his voice in order to raise our hearts to heaven and says, *"sursum corda,"* "lift up your hearts," and when we have replied that our hearts are in unison, *"habemus ad Dominum,"* "we have lifted them up to the Lord," implying that we, like him, are ready to praise and thank God for his goodness, *"dignum et justum est,"* he responds intoning the song of praise, it is truly right and just, equitable and salutary that we give thanks always and everywhere, O holy Lord, All powerful Father, eternal God, *"per Christum Dominum nostrum,"* through Jesus Christ our Lord, by whom, the Angels praise your majesty, the Dominations adore you, the Powers fear and revere you, the heavens and the powers of the Heavens, all celebrate your glory together, leaping in transports of joy. Through Jesus Christ we ask that our voices be heard, and that we join in singing with them, bowed down before you, *Sanctus, Sanctus, Sanctus!*

In this way, my dear people, we can give thanks to God for our divine mediator, Jesus in the Eucharist, the sacrifice of the altar, through Jesus Christ, without whom we cannot pay back to God either glory or praise or blessing, corresponding to the unlimited greatness of his gifts. This is what sets our faith apart compared with other religious and philosophical systems current in the world. They don't have the power or even the very concept of mediating between the finite and the infinite, between the world and its author, which unites the two in a supreme way without any confusion. Think of Blessed Henry Suso, who when singing the Preface one day appeared to be rapt in ecstasy in the presence of the congregation. Some people asked him afterwards what had happened to him and he said,

I contemplate in spirit my whole being, soul and body, my energies and faculties and around me all the creatures with which the Almighty has populated heaven earth and the elements, the angels of heaven, animals, the forest, creatures of the seas, plants of the earth and the sand of the sea, atoms whirling through the air like rays of the sun, snowflakes, drops of rain and pearls on the rose. I consider that, to the very ends of the earth all creatures obey God and make their own contribution in so far as they are able, to this mysterious harmony which rises without ceasing to praise and bless the Creator. I think of myself then in the middle of a concert like the conductor of a choir, applying all my energy to observing the rhythm. I invite myself and stir myself up by really lively movements of my heart and the most intimate movements of my soul, directing the song of all creation and joyfully singing with me, *Sursum corda, Gratias agamus Domino Deo nostro*. "Lift up your hearts, let us give thanks to the Lord our God."

What a holy person! He used his heartbeat as the rhythm of a great concert of thanksgiving and he himself the conductor of this sublime concert. It is the conductor who guides the instrumental parts. But it seems to me that it was not he who was conducting the concert—the true conductor was the Sacred Heart of Jesus Christ in the holy Eucharist. It is from him that we must take the pitch—from his divine heart which beats the measure of our gratitude, who's enkindled adoration directs and leads our voices and our hearts in the songs of praise which we owe the Most High, *per Christum Dominum nostrum.* "Through Christ our Lord." Yes through him alone the Angels themselves praise God's majesty and glorify him.[1]

Here then are my thoughts. In such-and-such a parish in Paris you can find devotion to the Immaculate Heart of Mary in place; in another, devotion to the poor souls in purgatory; further afield there is the confraternity of the holy rosary; in other places special devotion to the holy Cross for the crown of thorns of our Savior. So, in the same way I wish to see St. Clothilde's distinguished by a special ardent spirit on fire with love for the holy Eucharist. But, you will say to me, devotion to the august Sacrament of our altars is widespread, it's well established, it's alive in all the churches of the diocese. I agree, I'm glad of that and I praise God: but still here is my response:

The holy sacrifice of the Mass, the sublime summing up of all our religious acts, was instituted by Jesus Christ for four principal ends:

1. To offer God the supreme cult of adoration, acknowledging his supreme reign over all that exists;
2. To return thanks to God for all God's gifts;
3. To make reparation to God for all the offenses committed against God's majesty;
4. To obtain from God fresh grace in the temporal and spiritual order.

Now, my people, we already have three forms of perpetual adoration, which correspond to three of these principal ends; but for the fourth there remains a vacuum to be filled. In effect, perpetual adoration day and night of the Forty Hours corresponds to the first need for a supreme and unceasing cult, which is known as the cult of *latria.*

---

[1] Here is another example of the musician and the preacher blending his material.

Reparatory adoration also exists, and we admire those generous victims who spend day and night with Jesus at the foot of the tabernacle. Supplicatory adoration and intercession is found also more frequently than the others, consisting of a number of people who constantly come and pray to the divine Eucharist, whether for the conversion of the sinner, or the healing of the sick or for protection from danger. But nowhere have I seen one Eucharistic practice, having for principal and special aim to offer God uninterrupted thanksgiving for all the gifts received by means of all these other devotions which I have instanced.

The practice which I have thought through and which I will recommend to your devoted reflection, parallel to those that already exist, is a totally gratuitous and generous seal over all; for, while others ask for forgiveness or pray for grace, here by contrast we always and everywhere return thanks to God.[1] I don't of course intend to exclude those other good works—God forbid! Recommendations to prayer need no apology, for we are so poor, such great sinners, that always and everywhere we ought to strike our breasts . . . but I would like to say that these last two acts of religion are supplementary, a necessary accompaniment by reason of our weakness. But the overall intention of adoration will be precisely the recognition and, if I may use the expression, the *reimbursement* to God for gifts for which were are indebted to him and this cancellation will work itself out by means of the treasures contained in the divine Eucharist, because, as the Council of Trent states, "the Eucharist contains, embraces and absorbs all God's goodness."

---

[1] Cohen went to Rome at the beginning of 1859 and asked Pope Pius IX for permission to found such a confraternity. This was officially launched in the Carmelite Church of Our Lady at Rodez, Lyons, on December 15, 1859, and presided over by Cardinal Louis de Bonald. Cohen was instrumental in making this foundation. Pius IX issued him a Brief with indulgences, and so forth, on February 10, 1860. The pope further agreed that the movement should be elevated to an Archconfraternity so that Cohen could found other such groups throughout France.

Furthermore, just as you go to Our Lady of Victories to obtain the conversion of the sinner, or go to St. Merri for the purpose of belonging to the Archconfraternity of the Souls in Purgatory, to pray for the deceased, you will come and approach this new Eucharistic practice to offer a Mass of thanksgiving or to recite the Te Deum to acknowledge our gratitude.

Bernard Bauer

Here again we have an example of the extraordinary individuals we come across in the course of Hermann Cohen's life. Born as Paul Bauer, like Franz Liszt he was from Budapest, capital of Hungary, a member of a rich and famous banking family. His sister married into the even more famous Rothschild banking dynasty. Bauer was a very talented individual, literary, artistic, and musical. He eventually wrote a number of books, including collections of sermons and one whose title translates "Judaism, a Proof of Christianity."

Bauer was seven years younger than Cohen, and they became friends in Paris early on and mixed in with the same revolutionary friends—Félicité Lamennais, George Sand, Pierre Leroux, Michel de Bourges, and others. He took part in the revolution in Vienna in 1848. Soon after he became a Catholic Christian and out of curiosity went to hear Cohen's famous sermon "On Happiness" at the Church of St. Sulpice. He followed him from the church and expressed the wish to imitate him. Then, as Cohen himself had done previously, he promptly joined the Carmelite Order.

This is Cohen's longest sermon and has been preserved in the Carmelite archives in Rome in an Italian version; it runs to twenty-three pages and was preached at the religious profession of Bernard Bauer as a Discalced Carmelite. For text he took a sentence from the Book of Ruth: Populus tuus, populus meus `(Your people my people. Ruth 1.16) . . . Their friendship had now deepened, and in the beginning of his sermon he compared it to that between David and Jonathan. He followed up with the longer biblical quote from Ruth, "Wherever you go, I shall go." (Ruth 1:16.)

Bauer later became a doctor of theology and an eloquent and famous preacher himself throughout France and Germany. Chaplain to Napoleon's wife Princess Eugenie, he often preached in the Tuileries in Paris, the site of the former palace of the kings of France. He accompanied the royal party to Egypt and led a service at the opening of the Suez canal in November 1869. He officiated at the second marriage of Prince Wladyslaw Czartoryski to Princess Marguerite Adelaide. Czartoryski's first wife was Cohen's friend Princess Maria Amparo, whose son Auguste was beatified by Pope St. John Paul II.

It came as a great disappointment to Cohen that Bauer applied for secularization in 1864, during the time Cohen was engaged in bringing the Carmelites to England. In the run-up to Bauer's decision, he had done everything he could to dissuade him from leaving. When Bauer cited his health as a reason for leaving, Cohen responded, "You did not make your profession until sickness, but until death."[1]

In December 22, 1864, Cohen wrote to his sister Henrietta informing her of the loss he personally suffered. "I have some sad news for you. Bernard is now ex-priest Bernard. A long drawn out illness has weakened his head; doctors have persuaded him to leave the Order; he has asked for secularization from the Holy Father and now he is simply Abbé Bauer. This is a matter of great affliction for me and the amazing thing is that if I were not already attached to Carmel, this event would have further strengthened my vocation and if I were not already a Discalced Carmelite, I would immediately proceed to join the novitiate. We must ask our good Savior to grant us the gift of perseverance, the most precious gift of all."[2]

After the fall of the Second Empire in 1871, in which he took an active part, leading eight hundred "Christian brothers" in an ambulance corps,

---

[1]   Flamme Ardente, p. 243.
[2]   Sylvain, pp. 243-244.

Bauer married Marie Elizabeth Levy. Ironically he worked on Reynaldo Hahn's opera, The Carmelite, in 1902, the year before his death. He received the high French decoration "Legion d'Honneur" in 1871.

Hermann Cohen suffered a repeat experience of this loss of an esteemed colleague some years later when the famous Hyacinthe Loyson left the Carmelite Order and the church. Reading this impassioned sermon preached for a once-close friend is particularly poignant with hindsight.

❧

Sermon Preached by Hermann Cohen at the profession of Marie-Bernard Bauer, at Le Broussey, Bordeaux, June 29, 1855, Feast of Saint Peter and Saint Paul.[1]

My dearest Brother,

When Sacred Scripture wishes to depict a more ardent kind of friendship, it puts before us the example of Jonathan and David, saying: the soul of Jonathan was joined to the soul of David, he loved David like his own self, and even divested himself of his garments to give them to the one he loved so tenderly.

And so my dear David! Scarcely fourteen months have passed since that day in Paris when you realized that happiness is sought in vain in the world, that in vain one pins one's hopes on the fidelity of a friend! And then you suddenly turned to me, my friend, and said as one day Ruth said to Naomi, *Populus tuus, populous meus!* (Your people, my people, Ruth 1:16.). . . "Do not press me to leave you, or to turn back from following you. Wherever you go, I will go, where you lodge, I will lodge; your people shall be my people and your

---

[1] Discorso tenuto al novizato dei carmelitani scalzi di Broussey dal R.P. Agostino del SS. Sacramento, Carmelitano Scalzo. Treviso, 1858. (Carmelite Library, General House, Rome.) Translated from Italian by T. Tierney, with permission.)

God, my God. Where you die, I will die—and there will I be buried. May the Lord do thus and thus to me and more as well, if even death parts me from you." And I then responded like the prophet Jeremiah, "Very well then, my brother, come! I will introduce you to the land of Carmel": *Induxi vos in terram Carmeli . . .* you will be nourished with its fruit—*ut comederetis fructus eius*; of that most precious fruit—*et optima illius*. (Jer 2:7.) And now Brother, assure me that I have kept my promise? Tell me, are the friendships of the cloister as suspect as those of the world. Have you not found a happiness a thousand times greater than you had hoped for? I don't doubt your answer because I read it in the profound peace impressed on your features, in the sweet joy which they radiate: that affirms with mute though eloquent language, that the land of Carmel has not been sterile for you.

Perverse world! Here is a new victim that has escaped your clutches. Perfidious world! Here is another heart that you have corrupted almost from infancy but which Jesus has chosen to be a vessel of election! Cursed world, for whom Jesus does not pray. . . World to me so deadly that I have vowed to wage war on it to the death. Ah, if today I defeat you, if today I have won out, you David, my dearest friend, you are the trophy of my victory! Oh with what sweetest joy, with what holy inebriation I place this trophy, so dear to me, at the feet of Mary, of my august Queen, saying to her with the Angel, Ave Maria.

Bernard, my brother, today you have resolved to die to the world, to its works and pomps, and you have asked me to pronounce the funeral Service. . . . this young man was, like me, born an Israelite, like me born into a life of luxury, into that social class that is called enlightened. Enlightened, but with what kind of light, dear God! An elevated class, but with what kind of elevation? The kind that piles up riches. The family of Bernard is united by blood to wealthy and famous bankers of Europe, those who out of their surplus and immense wealth supply nations and kings! And I, a mere youth based in Paris, like him, was proudly seated every day at their sumptuous banquets, traveled in their splendid coaches, frequented their magnificent palaces; and unfortunately, at a very early age he too, like me, held a poisoned cup to his immature lips; at just twelve years of age he had already read some notorious books which twisted his spirit and instilled in his soul an implacable hatred for the name of Christian. Here do you not see Saul who persecuted the disciples of Jesus Christ? He has not indeed extended his hands to stone the martyrs of the faith; that he leaves to others, but he stirs them up and fans the flame, breaking into houses to carry off his prey. Young Christian girls and boys, escape! Here is Saul, here is the rapacious wolf: tremble. He will not rest until he threatens death on the disciples of the Nazarene.

And as for Bernard: not content to have written a book against priests at the age of twelve, where he denigrates, reviles and calumniates them, spewing out hatred in all directions and with his burning passion calling the political arm to his aid. He storms into churches, maliciously distorting the sermons of the priests, as the Scribes and Pharisees did eighteen centuries ago against Christ, running off to Vienna while the revolution was in full swing, to appear before that terrible tribunal. He took part in all the conspiracies of that group, without examining either their principles, their methods or their aspirations, in the same way as I myself conspired around the same time in Paris with Lamennais, Pierre Leroux, Considerant, George Sand, Michel de Bourges, Emmanuel Arago and their followers. But to what purpose did we strive and what did we want? Freedom. Ah, freedom, my brothers, full freedom, good freedom. We found it, but where? Here, here in Carmel alone. We opted for equality, see here is where you find it and the experience of it here is real and sublime; we arrived at the point where no one was exempt from the humblest duty in community, not even the superior.

We aspired to fraternity. And you will clearly see before we end this moving ceremony by Bernard's happy expression, and you will be convinced that he has found the complete fulfillment and the only possible kind, of the dreams of our youth. And I can point today to the truth of our religion by a *"fait accompli,"* by dint of those things that touch the human spirit through their realization here and now. But to what purpose my rhetorical subtleties? The two of us are proof positive, a breathing and irrefutable proof of Catholic power. And in fact who can stand up before us and assert that an aging religion is fading away through decrepitude? No, she is younger and more vigorous that all of you. She was born before you, will be there when you have gone and will preside at your departure. Yes, she can overcome hearts as obdurate as ours, I must say, because her power is so great and the blood coursing through her veins is so vigorous. I was a playboy, I was a prodigal, I was greedy for praise, I thirsted for power, I ambitioned fame and honors. Then six years ago or so, she took me and placed me precisely in the place which you Bernard, now occupy. My heart like yours was beating with an impatient desire to be always united to her; the priesthood which soon followed meant I would occupy the pulpit where you find me before you today, publicly unfolding page by page—and this particular page demonstrating my past shame, containing an account of things which bring a blush to my cheeks! But this blush is a salutary one for me, listen then and let your faces also blush. But the light of true religion had not illuminated our childhood or adolescence; it was the light of reason that we embraced.[1] Why then did our conscience not rebuke us? And man, though he idolizes himself, does he not perhaps have a written law in his heart? Why then does this natural law not influence us? Because our instinctive passions snuff it out: they put in its place a tyrannical law that reigns over us. Pride, and greed for gold and pleasure: these become our law. Yes, pride, the inspirer of warped advice, renders us intolerant of the good in others: we wish like Lucifer to rise above our station and dominate; we wish to grasp what does not belong to us, to possess goods not destined for us, to aspire to unearned honors, and to a possessive love, a love which yields us nothing but what is worthy of

---

[1]   The cult of reason became a badge of revolutionary France.

contempt, because it ignores even the name of righteousness—here we find appalling deception, disillusionment and bitterness.

We longed for glory: together we sought it in the fine arts—you in painting, I in harmony, and all we succeeded in doing was to heap vanity on vanity, spite on spite, bitterness on bitterness, endeavoring to satisfy insatiable desires, while we only managed to increase them with the help of the demons that devoured us. Every pleasure was followed by depressing regret, every intrigue by remorse, every uplift by a fall, every gain by a loss, every satisfaction by ill fortune. Every memory became an executioner and our security was torture. Thanks a lively imagination I was able to throw a miserable piece of crimson or purple over our nakedness, our misery! Love of the good life, or that to which we felt entitled, helped us to proceed in the meantime with great strides on the path of evil on which we had set out; feeling the need for divinity, we set up new idols over and over again, idols of metal, of smoke and of mud. But not finding our good, our happiness, our God, with all our anxious yearning, unfortunately we did not know that we were fleeing from Him who pursued us diligently until finally a day dawned . . . but the time was not yet ripe. It was not yet time and I ought to relate that in the end you became an Atheist just as I already was. You came from Germany to Paris to fraternize with more radical heroes of French ultra-republicanism and to become a propagator of more destructive ideas than in your own country. In the same way I made my way through Italy to propagate an even more deadly doctrine of Socialism and Communism. And I put a lot of zeal into a fatal mission that ran the risk of losing freedom altogether. What then is the power that can make the light shine in such profound darkness? What can control such hard hearts and what can bring them to subjection?

My brother, there finally came a time in our lives when we began to share the same degree of integrity as in other days we shared a degree of perversity. I was a Christian but you had not yet become one; but the horrors begun during the June insurrection, which professed the same principles as we had embraced, served to open our eyes to their horrible consequences; and just as you had the noble courage to admit and make reparation for the errors, as soon as you recognized them, so you suddenly turned your back on them and hastened to enlist under the doctrine of moderation and justice. And perhaps you didn't know, brother, as I did that we would later fight under the same doctrine but now a very different one and more sacred than the former. Now we fight with another group as in the days of 1848 we fought under the same flag, both animated by lofty ideas and a bountiful equality. Strangers to Paris, we loved France, though we had wrong and confused ideas; but when false impressions collapsed like tinsel and we were given in its stead the splendor of truth, we dedicated ourselves to that ideal, fighting together to achieve it. I know of no two other destinies more like our own or more conjoined to each other! *Anima Jonathae conglutinate est animae David, et dilexit eum Jonathas quasi animam suam.* "The soul of Jonathan was joined to David, because he loved him as he loved himself." (1 Sam 20:17) But why do you believe, my brothers, that the Lord has changed us and why do we come before you to relate the faults of our lives? Do you think it is pleasant for us to reveal our past? Do you not think on the contrary that it is painful for us to cast this backward look, to reawaken memories, by God's grace almost forgotten; to recall a time blotted out by the blood of Jesus Christ, a time full of shame and blame and so remote from us as to resemble a dream ... though a sorrowful dream, a scary and bloody dream ... at the very least one shudders at the remembrance. But we can do all things in him who strengthens us, and I say to you with St. Paul: God has entrusted to me the proclamation of his gospel, and I give thanks to Jesus Christ who strengthens me. I thank him for having called me to this holy ministry, though I was unworthy, I who was often a blasphemer, persecutor and outrageous calumniator of Jesus Christ! "*Qui prius blasphemus fui, et persecutor et contumelious.*"

When we first met, Bernard and I, dear brother and friend, we were both opposed to the savior of the world, to his teaching and morals. . . . But God has had mercy on us and his grace, stronger than our resistance, has been poured out on us, filling us with the faith and love of Jesus Christ! *Super abundavit autem gratia domini nostri cum fide et dilectione quae est in Christo Jesu.* (The grace of our Lord has overflowed in me, with the faith and love that is in Christ Jesus. (1 Tim:14.) It is a certain truth and worthy of all belief, that Jesus Christ came into the world to save sinners, of whom I am the greatest. *Christus Jesus venit in hoc mundum peccatores salvos facere, quorum primus ego sum.* "Christ Jesus came into the world to save sinners. Of these I am the foremost." (1 Tm 1:15)

But if God had mercy on us, St. Paul continues, it is in order to allow his supreme patience to shine out by waiting the return of sinners, and so that we can serve as an example: *ad informationes eorum.* Yes, dear brother, if God plucks out from a guilty nation two sinners such as we, the reason is that we may serve as an example and encouragement to sinners less obdurate than we. It is to show that it is not the extent of our malice, but the measure of the persistence of his grace that has been able to rescue us before the hour of judgment has sounded. That is why we should often tell the world that we are great sinners. I know that these words almost choke me associated with the holy habit which we wear and the sacred character with which we are clothed. But, once again, this rebuke is salutary, it's necessary in order to appreciate the power of the blood of Jesus Christ poured out on the soul of the greatest sinner: *quorum primus ego sum.* Do you believe, dear brothers, that God has converted us for our own sakes? No, a thousand times no. It is for you as well as for us! It is so that you can avoid the rocks against which we have been shipwrecked. Listen well to this and never forget it! Yes, we have been stationed like signs on the wide streets of hell, in order to warn you—do not go that way!

But you might say, the conversion of the Hebrews announces the end of the world and that idea frightens us. But be assured, my brothers, that danger lies in the future. Ask this novice now what would complete his happiness, enter, I say, the depths of his heart, search and amid the joy he radiates, if there is one cloud, one thought, one sorrow—a sorrow unique, but profound and heartbreaking! Ask him if the number of the Hebrews, Hebrews who have converted, is full and complete? . . . Not so, dear David! And note another and similar sorrow. I have a mother and you also have . . . God in heaven! I do not wish to talk about it. I do not wish to wish to spoil such a lovely celebration with such a sorrowful memory! But tell me how can we not think of our mothers at such a moment? God of justice, you we implore. Where are our fathers! God of goodness, where are our mothers? Can our joy be divided? Can we enjoy our victory over hell, over the world, over ourselves? Great God, great God, no, no, the end of the world has not arrived, the Jews unfortunately have not yet converted. There are only some rare exceptions: we gain a Ratisbonne and after seventeen years of priesthood, of preaching and of prayer, the conversion of just one brother and the others are drawn from a common source in that unfortunate nation.[1]

Another Israelite convert obtained after many years the conversion of a beloved sister: she now walks with giant steps along the way of divine love, in love of the Eucharist, of Sacrifice, of charity; but what about his two brothers, what about his father, or his mother? It's a painful thought.[2] My brother, in a short while you will prostrate here and immolate body and soul, heart, spirit and will until death, to the divine Crucified. Oh Brother! In this solemn moment, in that almost superhuman moment for you, certainly think of your mother, think of your parents; but I beg this favor from you, especially do not forget me! No, and for the sake of the holy friendship that unites us: because the soul of Jonathan was but one with that of David, so too Bernard, do not forget my mother. Unite in one prayer here your mother and mine. In an earlier time, sad to say, you had your white horses, your questionable security,

---

[1] Theodore Ratisbonne first converted from Judaism to Christianity, followed by his brother Alphonse many years later.
[2] Cohen is referring to the conversion of his sister Henrietta.

your modern age, but your eyes were closed to the light! Oh falsity, can you ever forget it? No! You have received God's grace and so you pluck from my heart a deep and sharp thorn! Who knows but on this special day as you give yourself entirely to Jesus, this same Jesus may not reveal himself to their spirits? What a beautiful day that would be for you my brother. But it would be a better day by a thousand times, if one ray only from this sun, from the light that washes over all, could penetrate the darkness in which our poor parents are buried, as in the shadow of death.

Now you in a short while are about to dedicate yourself for the rest of your life to this God of love and mercy. Three nails fastened the divine savior of our souls to the cross: human pride, greed and shameful lust. Three vows will today fasten you from now on to the dear cross of Jesus our beloved, and by these vows you bind yourself to a deep struggle against these three terrible and overriding preoccupations of fallen nature. You control pride and overthrow it through obedience. By the vow of poverty you dominate the desire for riches, and by the vow of chastity you keep your body under subjection, offering it as a living sacrifice, transforming you into an angel while still on earth. What am I saying? An angel does not gain merit and does not fight. A chaste man living an angelic life in a body of clay, carries off sublime victories each day; the sight of his triumphs rejoices the heavenly court; he amasses such imperishable treasures as to make the angels jealous.

But, people will say, is this triple renunciation, this absolute denial really necessary? Can we not be saved in the world? Why all this austerity? God doesn't ask so much sacrifice; he has given us the good things of the earth to enjoy, of what use is it to spend your youth in a severe and monotonous life and imprison your body in an austere habit? To what purpose do we despoil the springtime of life in fasting and sackcloth, and grow pale before one's time through long vigils and never ending prayers? And does it not seem heartless to leave one's family forever causing them such sorrow?

My brothers, I have just one word to respond to these objections: but a word is sufficient, it says it all. Why then does Brother Bernard renounce the world and its joys? It is because my Brother Bernard loves Jesus Christ. That is why—he loves, he loves Jesus, that explains everything! He has contemplated his beloved Jesus in the cenacle, who has given himself as the food of immortality, the nourishment of his heart; he has contemplated his beloved in the garden of Olives, in his anguish, in his agony, in the sweating of blood; he as counted every drop of blood his beloved shed for him at the column in the praetorium; he has counted the steps the good shepherd took to search out his lost flock; he has counted the tears shed by the good father when his prodigal son departed for a distant land; he has counted the cruel wounds caused by the crown of thorns on his forehead; he has counted most of all the drops of blood which our beloved Jesus shed on Calvary, in his hands, in his feet, in his side pierced by the lance. . . . And then those wounds of the savior were changed to fiery darts which pierced the heart of our dear Bernard who was wounded by an incurable wound; and then my brother Bernard cried—and I too, I love you! I love you, yes! And why should I, after all that, not love you? And why should I not leave all to follow my beloved? And who can reproach me for leaving my family and wealth, position and friends, in order to follow Jesus, dead for love of me? My family, my friends, what then have they done for me, my friends, after all my Jesus has done for me.

No one can show greater love than to give his life for his friends. Jesus my love has given his life for me, has died for me. Let me die for love of him. Yes, Jesus our love, we wish, do we not dear Bernard, to live and die for you! To die every day and every moment an inner death of sacrifice, renunciation and self-denial. We want to be consumed on the altar of Carmel, night and day, body and soul, spirit, heart and will, riches and honor, titles and grandeur, fortune and wealth, absolutely everything to show you our love and gratitude. And we would willingly go on our knees to the ends of the earth to make you known, to make you loved, to gain for you just one soul.

We are blamed for not having hearts when we parted from our parents. For not having hearts my God! How could we love Jesus so much and not have hearts? When obedience enjoined on me to leave my dear cell in Carmel for some days, the place where I tasted the delights of Paradise in the divine solitude of a hidden life and leave that dear enclosure, a sad thought suddenly descends on me to agitate my heart: I traverse the city, I travel through the country, and to every place I bear this sad conviction: Jesus is not loved, no one thinks of Jesus, no one speaks of him, no one does anything for him. He who is most lovable, who more than he should occupy our thoughts and concerns? The soldier gives his own life for his country, the mother spends her days for the welfare of her son, but who does anything for Jesus? And this painful awareness that Jesus is not loved is growing more and more, flowing in like an ocean wave breaking on the shore, stirring my spirit, distressing my heart, like a bitter tide leading to deep and uninterrupted pain. *Quoniam, tristitia mihi magna est, et continuous dolor cordi meo.* (Because my sorrow is great and a constant pain in my heart. Rom.9:2) Yes, indeed! I would wish like St. Paul to be accursed for my brothers, to be torn from the profound peace one tastes on the heart of Jesus, in order to make known this tender Lord especially to all Israelites, *quorum adoptio est filiorum, et gloria et testamentum et legislatio et obsequium, et promissio.* "Those Israelites who are my flesh and blood, and to whom belongs the adoption of the children of God, to whom he bestows his glory, his covenant and his laws, his cult and his promise; those whose fathers are the patriarchs and of whom finally, according to the flesh, Jesus Christ was born, who is God above all and blessed from age to age." (Roms 9:4.) And why do I promise myself on every new journey that I intend to do better and I go out forever repeating to all I meet; love then, love Jesus! Love him and you will be happy. But, my God, my voice is impotent, my pleas as unforgiving as the vastness of the desert and it is as if no one responds to my invitation!

Just over a year ago I found myself in the Church of St. Sulpice in Paris, responding to an invitation: I appealed to my listeners to renounce altogether the world's fake joy, to renounce blind greed, the ambition to achieve an empty greatness, and instead to taste real happiness at its only source—the love of Jesus. Then it chanced that a young Christian of only two years standing was present. He was the only one who understood me fully. A friend of his stood near and touched him on the shoulder: "Well, Bernard dear, what do you think of that? What will you do about it?" "Yes," said Bernard with a serious voice and deeply moved, "What he spoke about, I want to do." And as soon as the crowd departed he came and put his arms around me saying, "Father, I want to love Jesus Christ just as you do." And so the sacrifice was in fact complete. Two months later he received the habit of the holy Mother of Carmel, and neither the tears of his mother nor the potent force and tearful artifices of his brother could shake him from his resolve. And I, as I return to this loved cloister today, you must understand how great is my joy. Here I meet people, not like those who do not love Jesus, but whose hearts are very different. Many thanks dear Brother Bernard, you have done great good to my heart my dear David! My Reverend Fathers, my dearly loved brothers of the novitiate! Here everyone approaches with the holy kiss of peace, here I can read on your face and in your heart these words: I love Jesus; see, I love Jesus. I love him in the night, interrupted by the bell calling us to sing his praises, I love him in the morning when I rise on wings of prayer to the throne of glory in order to give him my heart; I love him throughout the day in fasts, in work, in penance, in sacrifice, in the peace of my cell, and when I go to battle for the Lord and rouse people to his love; in all my words, in all my thoughts, ever and always, I love. Yes, over all, in every heart, here at Carmel, the expression can be read: I love, I love Jesus.

Here, in this place, I find again hearts which love, many hearts which beat for Jesus Christ—that fact consoles and soothes me and makes me replete with joy and gladness. . . .Let me once again, dear brothers, sing with you, *Ecce quam bonum*, how pleasant, how delightful, how consoling, how agreeable it is for brothers, who live only to love and serve Jesus Christ, who breathe only for his glory, who make but one heart and one soul in Jesus Christ. Well, dear Bernard, born of grace, you have experienced this happiness now for a year or more. During your novitiate, you have breathed in the perfume of virtue and the good odor of Jesus Christ; you have admired the fervor of your brothers. In this house you have found true children of Israel, according to the heart of God, Israelites of whom Jesus said, "Here is an Israelite indeed in whom there is no guile." For as St. Paul says, "All those descended from the race of Abraham are not for that reason his true children; they are his children according to the flesh. But the children whom the Patriarch had in virtue of the Promise, they are the children of God." (Roms 9:7-8.)

Ah, what delights we have tasted since Jesus has condescended to reveal himself to us and gather us together in this balmy solitude? Who can express the joy so pure, so heavenly that inundates the child of Carmel during prayer, during those long hours of intimate and loving exchanges between the soul and its beloved . . . with Jesus? Who can indeed, express the delight and incomparable satisfaction that descend in waves from the tabernacle, when that little door opens and our God, our love, our dear and tender Jesus comes to rest on our trembling lips and makes us forget the earth and ourselves, so as to sleep on his heart and become taken up in him? We identify with him and are carried beyond the atmosphere through the sweetest mysteries to the throne of his Father as he says, My Father, look on those who love me! I pray that, as I am one with you, they also may be one with me by this holy kiss, this sacred embrace of a loving communion.

Could you ever have thought, dear brother, before the month of May in which you received the light, that life could be so wonderful, so beautiful, so inebriating, so divine? And that on earth you could have joy approaching that of heaven? Would you ever have believed, before your conversion, that you would have a mother in heaven so loving, so powerful, so sweet, so full of grace and love for you. Would you have believed that the tears you shed in Carmel are tears of joy and ecstasy divine?

Would you have believed that a man is far happier subduing his passions than in giving way to them? Would you have believed that the life of a monk is so full of holy feelings, so full of great things? Finally, would you have believed that one day you would be called to work together with the saints for the salvation of souls, by the supreme foolishness of the cross, by preaching the gospel and by practicing the highest virtue? It is not credible?

O altitudo divitiarum sapientiae et scientia Dei! Quam incomprehensiblia sunt judicia ejus, et investigabiles viae eius. "O the depth of the wisdom and of the knowledge of God, how inscrutable are his judgments and how unsearchable his ways! Who can know the mind of God and who can enter into his counsels? All from Him, through Him, in Him! To Him alone be glory and honor for all ages. Amen." (Rom:11:33-36.)

Sermon at the shrine of Our Lady of Verdelais, near Bordeaux September 8,1856.[1]

When the traveller in the Pyrenees wishes to climb the Pic du Midi, he makes a point of arriving before daybreak so as to observe in a marvelous setting, a most extraordinary spectacle that nature has to offer. The whole range of lofty mountains is still wrapped in shadow, and the climber's steps are illuminated by a pale light emanating from eternal snows.

Suddenly however all the highest peaks are touched with golden color; dawn is breaking! The heart exults with joy and hope. Gradually the pale glow grows greater and takes in the whole landscape, like a mysterious fire which sets alight the vast horizon of snow, ice and sadness. Yes, already the great mountains are bathed in glorious light. The eye is blinded even though the sun has not yet risen. What is this light that arrives to gladden "the people who sit in the shadow of death?" What is this brilliant dawn, nourished by an unseen light, which comes to shed it luster far and wide and bring joy and happiness to the earth? "Who is she who comes like the rising dawn?"

---

[1]   Carmel, *Aux Éditions du Carmel*, Marseille,1989, p.70.

The things we see are meant to help us contemplate things unseen, St. Paul tells us. The world of matter is like a ladder by which we ascend to the world of spirit.

Dawn in the Pyrenees which I admired so much is only a pale reflection of the true dawn that precedes the eternal sun. The dawn which has just been born, whose birth has rejoiced the heart of the poor pilgrim is Mary, whose birth I have the joy of celebrating for the eighth time since I became a Christian. It is also, dear brothers, a blessed day for me, as the eighth anniversary of my First Holy Communion, which I come to celebrate among you all at the feet of Mary. You are hurrying to greet this dawn of our salvation, and I associate myself in your impatient love. Let us unite with the Archangel and join with him in our salute to Mary. Yes, Mary, we greet you, our glorious dawn. Come and bring salvation to our souls. . . .

Blessed child, who has just been born, and who one day will be the mother of grace, mother of mercy and of love. You are our hope and our dear light, Mary, Our Lady of Verdelais we greet you, we bless you.

Conversion of Cohen's nephew George Raunheim[1]

My dear children,

*S*ix years ago, a little boy of seven years of age came to visit me at the Carmelite priory near the town of Agen, accompanied by his parents, both of whom, like himself were Jews. It was at the time of the beautiful Corpus Christi processions. Now, this child had been brought up with a deep aversion to our crucified Lord; in spite of this, divine grace, streaming from the sacred monstrance where Jesus, for our happiness, actually enthrones His hidden presence, was victorious over this person who was as yet a complete stranger to the mysteries of our faith. The Lord drew this young heart so strongly and sweetly to himself that the boy believed in the presence of Jesus Christ in the Sacrament of His Love before he had learned any other details of our faith. And so, by dint of entreaties and pleadings, as an great favor, he obtained permission to dress with

---

1   Flamme Ardente, pp 164-170, Sylvain, pp 151-159. This sermon was preached in the parish church of Ainay, Lyons, in the presence of Cardinal Louis de Bonald, who presided, and many of his clergy. Cohen had been asked to give an account of a Jewish conversion. The sermon was addressed to an association of young people, which was peculiar to the archdiocese of Lyons, whereby a well-off child adopted a needy child and undertook to sponsor him or her from then on, such as finding work for them and so on.

the choir children, and join them in scattering flowers before the path of Our Lord in the Blessed Sacrament. After fulfilling this holy function with an unusual and heavenly delight, he ran to his father: "Papa," he exclaimed, "what happiness! Do you know I have been casting flowers before the Lord!" These words, in the mouth of this Jewish child were nothing less than a profession of Christian faith. The father realized this, and afraid that his only son, on whom his affections were focused, should be led to change his faith, he watched him keenly from that point, and decided to take him back to Paris. Before his departure, however, another irresistible ray of grace from the Holy Eucharist penetrated the heart of the boy's young mother and made her a Christian too. In the darkness and silence of night she received holy baptism, and then the Blessed Eucharist, from the priestly hands of her own brother. On the following morning, the bishop gave her the sacrament of confirmation. Nothing of this holy secret had come to light, and the family returned to Paris without suspecting that one of its number was a Christian.

"The little George"—for this was the boy's name—couldn't forget the holy impressions which he had received during the great feast of Corpus Christi. He talked to his mother about them and she was delighted to observe this little ray of light, sparked by grace in this young heart, begin to grow and develop; she gladly spoke to him about the God of love, the gentle Lord Jesus, who had become man and was born of a daughter of Jacob, in order to save the lost sheep of the house of Israel. From this time in fact, his young heart and mind were taken up with the thought of the sacred host from which a ray of love had so penetrated his heart. Every night, after his father had gone to sleep, he got out of bed to learn his catechism and to pray earnestly to the holy child Jesus. "O my Jesus!" he would say, "when is my fasting to be over? When shall I receive you into my heart in Holy Communion?"

One topic which often occupied his thoughts was the great change he had noticed in his mother since her return from the recent visit to the south. He noticed a change in her behavior and observed a greater strictness towards herself and more simplicity in her tastes. He suddenly said to her one day: "Mamma, tell me that you are not baptized, or I'll believe that you are!" Taken by surprise at this abrupt question, his mother didn't reply immediately. "Ah, then Mamma!" he continued, "I see plainly how it is. You are already a Christian. And as I hope the kind Jesus will let me join you soon, I forgive you for going before me. But, at least, you have waited for me for your First Communion?" His mother was very moved by this, with a mixture of joy and fear, and she admitted to her son that she received her Lord and Savior almost every morning. At this, the boy burst into tears and threw himself on his mother's neck. "But why did you not wait for me?" he said, "at least let me stay close to you when you have received Our Lord that I may reverently embrace Him. Dearest Mamma, next time, keep something of your Communion for me. A mother is glad to share even her earthly food with her child." . . . And he would kiss his mother's dress near her heart. This keen longing, my dear children, lasted for four whole years. It would be impossible to tell you about the struggles and sacrifices made by this poor child to reconcile his lively faith with loyalty to his father. The overpowering desire of his heart, the chief thought of his life, was to become a Christian; he wanted to learn, to know, to serve our Lord Jesus Christ. It was a long martyrdom of love for the Holy Eucharist.

And you, my children, have you ever thought about the great privilege of having being born from Catholic parents, of having received holy baptism almost at the first moment of your life, and in such a town as Lyons, where the light of religion shines so brightly? It is possible that you have never thanked Our Lord Jesus for having made you children of His church even before the dawn of reason, to have admitted you to the banquet of His love, without your having had any difficulties to overcome. But, on the contrary, you have been helped by holy encouragements. . . . Think, then, of this poor boy of eleven years old, present at the solemnity of First Communion in his parish church. He knows Jesus, he loves Jesus, he longs only for Jesus, his young heart is burning with a thirst for Jesus.

He sees all his young friends and companions approach the holy table freely and by right, while he, concealed in a dark corner of the church, tries to keep back his tears. And meanwhile he watches all these happy boys with a holy and inconsolable envy! . . . You my children, have never felt this envy, you were never refused this treasure of your souls, your sweetest Jesus. The longing desire for Holy Communion felt by one who is still Jewish but resolved to belong to Jesus, is beyond your understanding. No! Never have you endured this keen and loving torment! But, it would not be good, my children, if the facility with which these treasures of grace and salvation are opened to you, should make you value them the less! It would be very bad, should you be ungrateful or even indifferent for this gift which surpasses all the other gifts of God. A few months after this joyful solemnity in her parish, the mother wrote to me, saying that she could no longer resist her son's tears and that he said he would go and ask for baptism from the first priest who would listen to his difficulties and whom he could convince that he had the right dispositions for receiving it!

All the difficulties of his position were taken into consideration, especially in regard also to a dearly loved father, for whom the hour of faith had not yet come, and who called upon his parental authority in order to prevent his son from becoming a Christian. But the love of Jesus Christ was stronger than all else, and it was decided that, unknown to him, I should go to Paris. If only you could have seen this boy when he came into the chapel! His mother, who was with him, was very nervous in case his escape from his father's watchful eye would be prematurely discovered. If only you could have seen little George as he knelt down, calm, happy and strong in his resolve, his face shining with joy. If you only could have heard his fervent responses to the solemn questions I had to ask him. "What do you ask for, my child?" "Baptism."

"But do you not know that tomorrow perhaps you may be compelled to go to the synagogue, to take part in their worship?" "Uncle, don't be afraid, I renounce Judaism." "But, if it so happened, that, from hatred of our holy religion, someone should force you with threats, to trample on the crucifix?" "Never fear, uncle, I would rather die than do it." "But yet," he added, "if they were to tie me hand and foot, and in spite of my cries and struggles, place my feet upon the crucifix, if my will resisted, would there be any apostasy?" "No, my child, it is the will alone which causes sin." "Then I ask for baptism. Give it to me for the love of God!"

The ceremony continued, amid the deep emotion of those who were present. Holy Mass followed, and when, with a heart overflowing with gratitude, I had received my God, and turned to hold the object of his most fervent desires before the happy child, never perhaps did the gaze of Christian faith rest upon a more touching sight. Kneeling between his mother and godmother, he received, with the deepest joy, the divine Savior, whose presence brought with it a complete heaven of happiness. Nor did anything trouble this boy, not even the thought of being found out by his father. A few weeks afterwards, he received Communion again with the same joy for the feast of All Saints. But then the hour of trial arrived. One day his father presented him with a book and said, "Let us say some prayers." "Papa, I can't pray from this Jewish book." "And why not?" "I am a Christian, I am a Catholic." "This is only a cruel joke, my child. I can't believe you're serious. Besides you know that your baptism is not valid without your father's consent." "Pardon, dear papa, in our holy Catholic religion it is enough that one has reached the age of reason, and have faith and instruction in its doctrines, to be validly baptized." The father at first concealed his strong displeasure, but, a few days later, on the third of December, he took his son to a Protestant country, four hundred fifty miles away from the mother.

Every effort was made to find out where he had been taken, but in vain. The civil and political authorities had been alerted to look for him, but as he had been placed under a false name at a boarding school, every effort to find him was fruitless, and his mother remained alone, while her boy, like Daniel in the den of lions, was made the butt of every kind of attack, in order to force him to deny his faith.

"Let me see my mother," he would often say in tears. "You will see her," was the answer, "if you make a renunciation." "No; never! I am a Christian, and will suffer anything rather than renounce my faith." And in spite of this heroic fidelity, his mother was informed by letter that her son had returned to Judaism. But she had confidence in Jesus, Mary and Joseph, and she trusted her son, and didn't believe a word of what they told her. Being left alone at Paris, she came here as a refugee to this city of Lyons, and to this parish, where she was welcomed and received by her son's godmother. And I can't let this opportunity pass without expressing my filial gratitude to Your Eminence [Cardinal Louis de Bonald.] for the fatherly and abundant consolations lavished upon her by your compassionate heart. And you, dear friends, the clergy of this Church of Ainay, have often seen this mother crying at the foot of the altar, where, each day, she prayed for new strength in receiving the daily bread of the Christian, receiving Jesus, for whose love she had exposed herself to this cruel separation from her only son.

Three months passed and she received a letter from a distant part of Germany, in which was written, "Come, your son is here." She immediately set out, and after a difficult journey of more than five hundred miles, joined her family, crying, "My son! where is my son?" "Your son—you will see him only when you have taken an oath before God that you will bring him up in the Jewish religion, and be careful not to show any outward sign of the Catholic faith which you have embraced."[1] Do you realise my dear children the great sorrow of this situation? We left the boy in anguish in the

---

[1] The reunion of mother and son and the family discussion took place on May 11, 1856.

den of lions, but God suffered them to do him no harm. After witnessing this trial for several weeks, his father so far relented as to permit a meeting, in his presence, on condition that there should be no mention of religion. The boy threw himself into the arms of his tearful mother. Neither might mention the sweet names of Jesus and Mary, but my poor sister said to me, in a letter she wrote me, "He could say nothing to me, but I felt, I knew with certainty that he had remained faithful. I saw in his look, I felt in his tender kisses, that my son was still a Christian."

But poor George found himself again deprived of the treasure for which he had braved all this persecution. He had become a Christian that he might receive Holy Communion; and yet from All Saints day until Easter a close watch had made it impossible for him to go to church, for he had been placed—can you imagine it, my children—in a town which did not have a single Catholic priest! Can you imagine this loss? . . . He has found his mother, but when will he see his Lord Jesus again? Several more months passed. Finally one day he succeeded in eluding the vigilance of his keepers, and went to play in a wood; but it is not in search of butterflies and flowers; his eager eyes seeks out a heavenly messenger. A gentleman passes by and looks at him with special interest. Yes: it is he! Who do you think he was? It was a missionary priest whose heart George's mother had filled with compassion for her son. Disguised as an ordinary stranger, he had come, as if by chance, to walk in this wood, and there, for the first time since he was abducted ten months previously, George was able to make his confession. He made it in the wood, beneath the protecting branches of a tree. . . . But this was not all. . . . How was he to receive Communion? The priest had to return across the Elbe which separated his mission from the house of the poor convert. After much prayer, and careful study of the terrain, the priest again disguised himself a few days later and, taking with him a small silver vessel enclosing the treasure of heaven, the Sacred Host, he embarked on a steamboat among a thoughtless crowd which never dreamed that the Lord Jesus Christ, true God and true

Man, was hidden among them, on the breast of this happy priest. George contrived to escape from school to his mother's room, and there, where a small altar had been improvised for the occasion, and covered with flowers and lights, they waited on their knees together for the longed-for visit of the Savior in person, who wished to come and be their strength in their exile.

At last, the priest, passing without obstacle through all the dangers of his mission, arrived safely with his precious burden, and in this town without faith, without a priest, without the true church, and in this humble room, the boy was able at last to fulfill his Easter duties and unite himself to Jesus. Listen to what he wrote to me a few days afterwards: "Oh, my dear uncle, when awake in the night I think over all the favors the good Jesus has given me since I came here, far away from all the support of religion, especially when I think of the almost miraculous Communion I was able to make in Mamma's little room, I begin to jump for joy as I lie in bed, and bite my quilt in the eagerness of my gratitude."

Again, he wrote to me a few months later: "We are close to Christmas, and, as this solemnity draws near, I am doubly watched, so that I may not by any chance receive my God. Indeed shall I have to spend these beautiful days in a painful fast, deprived of the Bread of Life? Pray to the Holy Child Jesus, that my fast may soon come to an end. I ought to be very good, so as to make up to Mamma for her not being at Lyons while you are preaching at Ainay."

And thus, my dear children, at this very moment while I am speaking to you, this dear child is thinking of us: at more than five hundred miles away he is united in intention with us, and we will ask the Holy Child Jesus to kindly console him by granting him the favor of Holy Communion.[1]

---

[1]   George Raunheim had been kidnapped by his father and taken to Harburg in Germany in 1856. This was probably the Hamburg suburb, some miles south of the city and not the central Germany town of Harburg. Cohen's brother lived here probably with their father David. In this household considerable pressure would have been put on the boy to recant.

Homily on Repentance[1]

*Y*es, my God! Yes, my Jesus! I declare it: this life was mine, before I knew you; before I loved You. Yes, my brethren, I have experienced it; and may my bitter experience serve as a warning to you. Yes; I was born and lived in this state of original sin, unransomed by holy baptism; my life was nothing but temptation and struggle, fighting and falling. Scarcely were my eyes opened to reason, when my reason, insufficient to recognize the only true good, and my will too weak to resist the inclination to evil, too unstable to follow the secret whispers of a still upright conscience, passionately attached themselves to corruptible things. Pride already breathed into my heart its evil counsels; I wished to be preferred before my brothers, the companions of my childhood; my inclinations tended to forbidden pleasures, I desired to possess that which did not belong to me, to enjoy that which was not fit for me, to reap praises which I had not deserved; and all these passions, developing with age, devastated my soul, ravaged my heart, and filled with disorder my whole moral being. Yes, I chose to acquire learning without the aid of the true light, and did but heap error upon error, ignorance upon ignorance, chimera upon chimera! I wanted to gain glory, when I only merited contempt, and I did but accumulate disappointment upon disappointment, vexation on vexation, bitterness on bitterness.

---

[1] Sylvain, pp.218-222.

I, who deserved only to be hated, wanted to be loved; and I heaped up vanity upon vanity, mask upon mask, seduction upon seduction. Lastly, I wanted to enrich myself with deceitful riches; and did but amass flattery upon flattery, breach upon breach, loss upon loss. And in attempting to satisfy my boundless desires, I did but add fuel to a devouring fire. Each of my actions was followed by remorse; every pleasure, by a bitter recollection and a poignant pain; every success, by disappointment; every gain, by a still heavier loss; every satisfaction, by misfortune.

My memory served as my executioner; my anticipations, as my torture; my imagination only threw, here and there, a few rags of gold and purple on my misery and nakedness. Enamored of the good to which I was born, I nevertheless made rapid advances in the way of evil upon which I had entered. Feeling the need of a divinity, I forged for myself idols, now of metal, now of smoke, now of mud; and plunged into an unfathomable abyss of every kind of superstition. At last, never finding the happiness I sought, I was ever fleeing from that which pursued me, until, one day . . . I enter a church. . . . The priest at the altar raises in his hands a small white disc. . . . I gaze upon the Sacred Host, and I hear these words: *Ego sum Via, Veritas et Vita*—I am the Way, the Truth, the Life! Great God, but can it be? . . .

Yes, Saul, on his way to Damascus, whither he was hastening as a rapacious wolf to ravage the Christian flock, fell to the ground on hearing this same voice: "I am Jesus, whom you are persecuting!" [Acts 9:4.]. . . "Lord, what am I to do?" Do you not see, my brethren? Order is restored. He stretches out his hands, his arms, his heart, his soul, his will, his whole being, towards this true and only end, the *will of God*. See how he's converted! May we do likewise.[1]

---

[1]   His advice was invaluable and even bears reminiscences of St. John of the Cross.

Lecture at Malines

Catholicism in England

My Lord Cardinal, My Lords and Gentlemen.

*T*he religious movement manifested in England about the year 1829, and of which His Eminence Cardinal Wiseman has given you so excellent an account in your former Congress, does not abate thank God! It is a resurrection of Catholicism in the face of great opposition. Called upon to tell you what I have seen of this from the time that the Vine of St. Teresa took root two years ago in London, I am happy to give you, for your satisfaction, some account of the improvements on which we found our hopes; and at the same time to point out to you the dangers which imperil our successes, that you, by your interest, may help us to overcome them. . . .

The *Dublin Review* aptly remarks that the Archbishop of Westminster is "the only English Catholic who could have written on the progress of Catholicism in England, without giving a prominent place to this particular topic."[1] These successes are due, I repeat, to the vigor of his initiative, to the vastness of his views, and to the generosity (I had almost said the temerity) of his Apostolic courage, in the face of the most determined opposition. Though freed from oppressive laws by Daniel O'Connell's achievement, Catholics, made

---

[1] Cardinal Nicholas Wiseman, Archbishop of Westminister.

timorous by long persecution, dared not at once to avail themselves of their improved position, and thus gather all the fruits of their emancipation.[1] It was Cardinal Wiseman who resolutely seized upon and put in action, for the good of his flock, the practical consequences of the principle introduced by the new legislation; and that too at a time when his friends, fearing for the safety of his life, counseled him not to return to England. . . .

At that time frequent Communion was scarcely known in England; public devotion to the august Mother of God was still more rare. Without doubt Catholics loved Mary, and prayed to Mary, but they ventured not openly to speak of her. Some twenty years ago, a statue of the Blessed Virgin was hardly to be seen in the Catholic Churches of England. At that period, as a worthy Canon of Westminster has assured me, rosaries had to be procured from abroad, and, somewhat earlier Monsignor Wiseman, then but lately ordained, after preaching on the Feast of the Assumption upon that mystery of the Blessed Virgin, was warmly greeted, on quitting the pulpit by a foreign priest, thus: "At last I have heard an English address upon the Glories of Mary, but you are the only man, I think, who will have preached on that subject in England to-day."

Yes, by a tacit consent as it were, the mysteries of Mary were not preached in public; but, how different now! And what a joy it is, my Lords and Gentlemen, for a Religious of the Order of Mary to stand before you and say: there is hope for us now, for not only does the Faith grow daily in England, but the gentle sway of Mary and the subduing power of her sweet devotion spreads over "that land" well known of yore as "Mary's Dowry." I insist upon this progress as being of the highest importance; for devotion guards Faith as the advanced rampart defends the citadel: a breach once made in the outer walls, and the fortress is quickly in the hands of the enemy. We

---

[1] Irish statesman Daniel O'Connell won emancipation for Catholics in Ireland and Britain in 1829. It meant that Catholics could be elected to Parliament. There was already freedom to build churches and worship.

may date, then, the happy change we have signalized, from the time when His Eminence began to guide the Catholic movement; and now we can say, that if on the one hand, Apostolic labor in England costs the Priest much sweat of the brow; on the other it presents him with refreshing draughts of consolation.

While enumerating services rendered to the Catholic Church in England, we must not forget to mention the Society of Jesus; for, to have stood their ground in that land, when hardly a priest was left there to exterminate; to have kept alive and cherished some glowing embers of the Faith beneath the ashes to which persecution had reduced that inextinguishable fire—are not these among the glories of the Company of Jesus? Yes! Honour to those valiant soldiers of Jesus Christ! When Catholics, for two long centuries stricken by the ban of rigourous penal laws, disheartened and dispersed, could hardly count one hundred Priests in all England, nearly the half of that number were sons of St. Ignatius. The modern establishment of the Jesuits in London dates from 1845, and they at once raised a statue in their chapel in honour of the Immaculate Conception. . . . Shortly after this, out of the thirteen dioceses created on the re-establishment of the Hierarchy in England, twelve were placed under the special invocation of the Mother of God. The Month of Mary is now celebrated in all the Catholic Churches; and the piety of the faithful has blossomed into new life with confraternities of the Rosary, of the Holy Scapular, and of the Holy Heart of Mary.

There may still be some who, from deference to the naturally staid, impassive character of the English, would counsel Catholics to maintain a certain reserve in their devotion to Mary, as though, indeed, there were any other than Mary who was to crush the head of error; as though there could be danger or excess where God has so wondrously surpassed Himself: can the love of Catholics for Mary ever rise to such a height, or can they honour her with glory so sublime, as that to which God Himself has chosen to exalt her?

The Brown Scapular of Our Lady of Mt. Carmel.

As if this filial homage could be out of place in England, the birth-place of the devotion of the Holy Scapular, the favoured spot to which the Blessed Virgin came, bringing from heaven that pledge of salvation, to bestow it upon a Religious, not of Italy or of Spain, but on an English Saint, born and bred in England, English in his labors, in his mission, and in his election as General of the Carmelite Order. This preference for England as the scene of that revelation, and the choice of an Englishman, St. Simon Stock, as the receiver of the promise attached to the Scapular is, to my mind, a pledge of the future conversion of that nation. . . .A devotion yet more sublime, that towards the Adorable Sacrament of the Altar, has in England received a development about which I am happy to give you some account; for you would reproach me if I did not speak to you of the Most Blessed Sacrament. Often, unfortunately, God in the Blessed Eucharist is, as you know, even in Catholic countries, "the unknown God," a God forsaken, and there are few who come to make in the ingratitude of the immense majority of Catholics. . . . ."

Who would believe it? Seven Communities of the Perpetual Adoration already exist in full activity in England. They are, with one exception, of recent foundation; and here again the proportion is in favour of London, which possesses two. The Forty-Hours' Prayer is celebrated during the entire course of Lent. Each Church in London enjoys, for two whole days, in turn, the Station appointed for it; and the Clergy, as well as the people, vie with each other to solemnize, with the greatest splendor possible, these days and nights of adoration. The Association of the Nocturnal Adoration for men is now established in the Archdiocese; and is carried out several times each month all through the year: these nights of sublime love are celebrated with edifying fervor, and a good number of those who have been recently reconciled to the Church then pray for the conversion of their brothers and sisters. I feel bound to state, and

I do so with great satisfaction, that, in the worship of the Divine Eucharist, as well as in all other religious ceremonies in England, the Roman Liturgy is followed with such respect for the laws of the Sacred Rite as does honour to the Bishops and Priests of that country. The three Provincial Councils held in England since the re-establishment of the Hierarchy have regulated the position of the religious Orders in conformity with the Canon Law of the Church, so that thorough union exists between the secular and regular clergy, and both can work harmoniously in the extension of true Religion.

I had lately an opportunity of observing how excellent is the spirit animating the English priesthood, for, called last month to give an Ecclesiastical Retreat, I was greatly edified by the holy demeanour and pious recollection of the Priests of two dioceses united for those holy exercises; and this spirit, eminently Catholic, is diffused by the example of the Clergy among the faithful. The members of the Conferences of St. Vincent de Paul, whose President General for England is among us here, achieve on the other side of the channel wonders like to those which claim our admiration in Catholic countries. Is there not here, then, solid ground on which to build our hopes? Further than this, I venture to affirm that the attitude of English society, in the face of Catholicity, improves day by day, and this in proportion as the good outcome of emancipation introduces Catholics, more or less, into every branch of public employment. Prejudices are dying out, Protestant fanaticism had charged to our account, the most strange and hateful absurdities as worthy of credibility; but evidently Catholicism improves upon acquaintance, for many, formerly opposed to us have now learnt to regard their Catholic fellow-countrymen with esteem and friendship. This year; the first time for centuries, a Catholic has been raised to the high dignity of one of the twelve Judges of the kingdom.[1]

---

[1]   This was Mr. Justice Shee.

Flowery Land Pirates.[1]

But allow me to introduce an episode, the striking incidents of which have supplied a topic of general interest: - I was sent for, in February last, to Newgate, where eight Catholic sailors, one of whom was a Spaniard, and the rest natives of the Philippine Islands, were in prison for piracy and murder. I doubt if there exists in these days, any Catholic country in which the officers of a prison would receive a Priest with the considerate courtesy which I received from them in London. Owing to the kind thoughtfulness on the part of Mr. Jonas the Protestant governor of Newgate, we were able to spend some hours daily with the prisoners.

Fortunately our Novice Master was a Spaniard for they understood no European language except Spanish, and during nearly a month he was able zealously to devote himself to these unhappy men. Six were condemned to be hanged at the Old Bailey, with a seventh, who was a schismatic Greek. To the glory of our divine religion let us declare it: during the fortnight which intervened between the sentence and its execution, the Faith changed these wolves into lambs,- yes, into lambs, submitting without a murmur to offer up to God the sacrifice of their lives. One proof of their conversion was the earnestness with which those who were guilty pleaded against the sentence passed upon two of their comrades, who, they insisted, were innocent,

---

[1] This public execution (and another around the same time) occasioned a change in English law. 'Owing to the disturbances caused by mobs gathering on Sunday evenings to be in time for Monday morning's show, hanging day was changed to Wednesday early in 1865. But this was only a first fruit of the Pirates and Muller episodes. Abolition of public executions, which had been urged perfunctorily for several years, was now pressed for in earnest, with the result that some four years later the reform received parliamentary sanction. Private executions in London in accordance with the present system were inaugurated September 8th.' *(1868 Victorian London - Publications - Social Investigation/Journalism - London and Londoners in the Eighteen-Fifties and Sixties, by Alfred Rosling Bennett, 1924 - Chapter 34 - 1864 - Murder on Sea and Railroad.)*

and for whom, with our assistance, they succeeded in obtaining an acquittal, so that five only, four of whom were Catholics, were doomed to ascend the scaffold.

"Oh! could you have their hearts. And when we reflect that, thirty-five years ago, this would have been impossible in England! Impossible for Catholic prisoners to receive the Sacraments of their religion ...! On the day of the execution, while it was yet dark, three priests, provided with a safe-conduct, made their way through the vast crowds which, all night long, had stationed themselves in the streets near to the prison, in order to enjoy the most frightful of spectacles. Imagine - (for I am speaking to Christians of a lively faith) - imagine what were the feelings of a priest, when, through this multitude, he bore, concealed within his habit, the God of the Eucharist! . . . Jesus Christ, Who willed to take possession of these condemned before they were handed over to the executioner. Probably the jailors did not know what the mysterious Treasure was which entered with us into the prison (for in England the Sacred Viaticum is not carried openly), but, if they did not kneel as we passed, I can testify that they nevertheless received us with every mark of religious respect, and, for two hours, left us, as it were, masters of the terrible enclosure. We found the condemned kneeling before their Crucifix. They had spent the night in prayer. When they had received the Holy Viaticum, the terrors of death, the anguish of the ignominious end which was waiting them, at the distance of only a few steps off, and in the space of only a few minutes, disappeared before the brightness of the divine life which Jesus, in the Eucharistic embrace, had just bestowed upon them. Never, during the thirteen years that I had been a priest had I so strikingly experienced the power and efficacy of the Blessed Eucharist and of the Priesthood. During these two long hours, their last on earth, their hearts were raised above, to regions where there is no more sorrow, where there are no more tears; and, while my ears were horrified by the sounds which reached us, of the sinister yells of the crowd, impatient to feast upon the spectacle of their sufferings, these young convicts spoke to us only of the peace which filled their hearts, the smallness of their expiation compared with the greatness of their crimes, and of their hope of soon seeing the Good God, - and forever . . . Then I took care to exhort them to, confidence in our Blessed Lady, who's Holy Scapular they wore. 'But will they not take it from us,' they asked, 'when the moment comes for the gruesome preparation of the condemned'? 'Oh, Father', they added; 'Get leave for us each to keep upon us our Crucifix, Rosary and Scapular.' "At this moment, I was sent for by the High Sheriff, who wished to know the state of the prisoners. 'Were they very angry and violent he asked?' When I responded that I had never seen men more resigned to die, he asked if they wished for anything which it would be in his power to grant. 'They desire three things,' I answered: 'First, that they may be permitted to keep about them the signs of their Faith.' 'I willingly consent, he said.' 'They also wish for their Priest to attend them to the place of execution.' Though I had been notified the evening before that our ministry must end before the men mounted the scaffold, great was my satisfaction, therefore, when the answer was: 'Tell them that you will be with them'. Their third request was likewise granted, namely, that they might bid each other goodbye. Then followed a scene which I shall never forget, and which drew tears, not only from these men who were going to die,-not only from us who had become their fathers in Christ Jesus, but from their jailors also, and the governor, present at the interview.

Picture to yourselves these young men, the oldest of whom was not twenty-six; for the most part wild people convicted of crimes of atrocious cruelty; but now, how changed! Falling on their knees before the others, to ask their pardon, then, sobbing in one another's arms, they said, pointing to Heaven, 'goodbye, brother! *Au revoir;* for we soon shall meet again.... 'The Spaniard, who had been convicted as the instigator of the mutiny, exclaimed with enthusiasm: 'I am happy! In half an hour, I shall see the Good God!' It was he who had said, on the first visit of the Spanish Priest, 'Ah, now that I have a priest of my own nation, I no longer fear to die!'

"It was time to part. The governor asked them if they were satisfied. We only wish one thing more: to embrace our comrades who have got their pardon!' "And yet, there is scarcely time . . . any matter. The governor was visibly affected. 'Go yourself and fetch them,' he said to me. And the puzzled jailors had to let me enter seen these men, a few days before their execution, receiving Holy Communion, in the condemned cell, you would have been moved at witnessing the deep joy which filled the other cells and bring out the prisoners. When they joined the condemned, something mysterious passed between them. 'God knows it! - God knows all,' one exclaimed. These farewells were more distressing than the former.... At this moment the bell began to. toll. They knelt and received a last absolution....

"I hasten on. Francisco, the youngest, scarcely twenty years old, had already mounted the fatal ladder, and called to *me,-'Padre, Padre; me no deje usted* '- 'Father, do not leave me!' I hurried on before the rest and stood on the plank of the gibbet, in view of 30,000 spectators, several of whom, and, amongst them, ladies of high position, had paid more than forty pounds for a place at the windows! The dull murmur of the crowd rose in my ear like the roar of the ocean, and I expected that the sight of a priest (for the stole and tonsure indicated a 'papist'), would raise a storm of curses in this quarter of the city, where, formerly, the public had frequently committed fearful excesses, in their hatred against the Catholics.

"Two other Priests were with me on the scaffold. The condemned stood facing us, in a line, beneath the five gallows. The Cross, Rosary and Scapular were worn visibly by each, but not a hostile murmur arose; on the contrary, as soon: as we appeared, the words, 'Hats off!' ran through the crowd, and every head was uncovered. "Meanwhile, pressing round our penitents, we held before them the Crucifix, which they kissed, making aloud, the Acts of Faith, Hope, Love, and Contrition, and invoking the Names of Jesus and Mary. At this moment, Lopez, the Spaniard, with a strong effort, broke the cords which bound his arms. And why? That he might cross himself. In a moment he had lifted the cap with which the executioner had covered his face, and made the Sign of our Redemption in his forehead, lips and heart; then striking his breast three times he addressed the crowd, with an eloquent gesture, the only English word he knew: 'pardon; pardon; pardon.'

A shout of sympathy and approval broke from the crowd, some of the people even clapping their hands;...but at the same instant, from almost under our feet, the plank was gone, and the five men were hanging. They had no time to suffer. Strangulation instantly deprived them of consciousness. At this moment, the High Sherriff, standing on the ladder, touched us with his wand of office. We were to descend. The Spanish father withdrew the crucifix from the lips of the penitent to which it was still pressed.[1]

When we reached the ground, this good Father Joseph buried his face in his hands and burst into sobbing. 'These are my children', he said to me, 'my children whom they have snatched from me.'! For they had truly become his children in Jesus Christ. The magistrates then invited us to rest awhile in the governor's rooms, and asked in the kindest manner about the state of mind of these poor young men, in their last moments; - at the same time showing us every mark of courteous respect, and ordering two of the police officers to escort us home.

But his precaution was needless. As we passed through the crowd, we received nothing but marks of respect also. The Times newspaper, in its remarks upon this quintuple execution, observes that, when the corpses were inspected in the afternoon, it was noticed with surprise that, contrary to the effects produced by this manner of death, the faces of the four men had undergone no change, but were calm and composed, 'as if in a gently sleep,' while the fifth was hardly recognisable from the fearful contortions caused by the last agony. "The same journal gives the name of this unfortunate man. He alone was not a Catholic.

---

[1] This scene reminds us of St. Thérèse praying for the condemned criminal Pranzini.

The Blessed Eucharist had left its stamp upon the rest. This Divine Sacrament, while preserving their souls to eternal life, had also preserved their countenances, the mirrors of their souls, from distortion. And now, let us glance back forty years. Picture to yourselves this same execution taking place in London previous to Catholic Emancipation, when these unhappy men would have been doomed to suffer death without the help of a priest. Would they not, everyone of them, have died reprobates? Their good dispositions dated only from the time when the Spanish Father first began to visit, them. Forty years ago, no Priest would have been able to reach them: no man under sentence of death could have been fortified with the 'Bread of the Strong,' the 'Bread Which came down from Heaven' nor, at that time, would the London public have endured the sight of a Catholic Priest by the side of a convict on the scaffold of the Old Bailey.'[1]

Yes, Gentlemen, while in our day, on the Continent, a priest can hardly travel without meeting with gratuitous insult from men who volunteer to profess themselves *liberals*—in England public opinion is daily improving—prejudice diminishes, and the priest, or if you will, the "cleric," can appear in public without facing insult to his religion.....

Yes, you will aid us by your zeal, by your efforts in behalf of the glorious missionary work for the propagation of the Faith in

---

[1] It should be noted that part of this speech offended Archbishop Darboy of Paris. It seems that the passage that offended the Cardinal was Cohen's insinuation that, unlike the situation in England, in other Catholic countries (such as France?), there was not a good relationship between the secular clergy and the religious orders. Cohen would have had some evidence to support his view but obviously in this case the truth did not matter! Yet as Cave also points out, Cardinal Wiseman of Westminster would appoint him 'Examiner to the Synod' and 'Examiner of the Clergy' together with a Dominican priest. Wiseman also put him in charge of Eucharistic Devotion in London. Cave suggests Cohen made an apology of sorts to the Archbishop! Darboy was the third Archbishop of Paris to die a violent death, having been executed by the Communards in 1871.

England, and when we return to that land, we will tell our dear, though separated brethren, what we have witnessed here; yea, with a yearning heart, we will tell the children of that noble nation, whom so many sterling qualities mark as worthy of enjoying the true Faith like their ancestors, that the only *power* that is wanting to them is that by which we are united on earth to Jesus Christ in the unity of the *one only* Church founded by Him; that the only *liberty* wanting to them, the most precious of all liberties, is that of which St. Paul says that it delivers us from the powers of *darkness*, "with the liberty wherewith Christ has made us free." We will show them in the pages of their own history that the institutions of which the world envies them the possession, their Parliament, Trial by Jury, the Universities, the Laws for the Observance of Sunday, and many more, are not the fruit of the *modern school*, nor of the *new system*, but the work of their Catholic ancestors who matured them under the sun of the Papacy which enlightened their minds.....

"Jesus was made man for humankind (as Mgr. Pie, the great Bishop of Poitiers, remarks); for beings essentially composed of a soul and a body, and destined for social life"; it is for this reason that no one can attempt, without injustice, to exclude the authority of Jesus Christ from *anything* that may affect the welfare either of nations or individuals. The venerable President of the great National Congress of Belgium, who deservedly presides over this current Catholic Assembly, remarked very appropriately right at the beginning of this meeting, that the spirit which is now referred to as "modern," the code that is now called "new," will soon be spoken of by posterity as "old" or "obsolete"; and I may venture to add, that modern society may really end up throwing herself into the maternal arms of the Church, as did the prodigal son who made up his mind to return to his father.

Oh, Jesus! You who have so loved Thy Church, your spouse, as to wash her in your Blood, can there be among you any who would undertake the task of training and educating their Mother, and of counseling her to subscribe with her own hand her civil and political interdiction? Lord Jesus! Thou you are the only source of that authority without which there never will be true liberty, look upon these nations for whom Thou hast shed Thy Blood, these nations whom the Father has given Thee as Thine inheritance; "They have set you aside, discarded you, repulsed you, saying, *Recede a nobis*," "Depart from us." I have borrowed these words, Gentlemen, from that great and valiant soldier of the company of Jesus, Father Felix, whose much-valued presence we welcome here. Annually for twelve years his audience at Notre Dame of Paris, without doubt one of the most intelligent in the world, has hung upon his lips; and what, gentlemen, did he say? Did he seek to captivate the enthusiasm of the youth, by flattering their ardent souls, and burning idolatrous incense to the vaunted ideas of our day? Not so. During those twelve years he has not ceased to preach constantly from this one text, *Crescamus in illo per omnia qui est caput Christus!* That performing the truth in charity, "we may in all things grow up in Him who is the head, Christ!" (Ephes 4:15)....

There is no progress apart from Jesus Christ. *Without me*, declares the Savior, *you can do nothing.* The great obstacle to progress is that the Master has been excluded from all Laws, Constitutions, and Governments, Yes, the people have said 'Our Laws are only human; the divine element goes for nothing.[1] England, Gentlemen, England has been pagan twice. Converted first in the second century, under her British Christian king Lucius, she relapsed into paganism under the Saxon rule. Converted a second time by the Benedictine monk St. Augustine, she has once more forfeited the tutelage and teaching authority of Jesus Christ.[2] But why should there not happen, in favour of truth and salvation, the same success which has prevailed in the case of nationality? Why, I say, should not the Church have

---

[1] This has in fact happened in our own time in the case of the new European Constitution where there is no reference.

[2] The Pugin church Cohen had built in London later had a panel depicting Pope Pius IX sending Fr. Augustine-Mary (Cohen) to England with a similar mission. Another panel depicted him in his final mission at Spandau.

her *terza riscossa*, her third decisive shock, finally victorious for the lasting religious unity of her children?....

Yes, Gentlemen, once more I repeat that I foresee the return to better days, when *truth* shall enjoy greater privilege than *error*; when *justice* as revealed by God shall predominate in human society over *injustice* (and I call injustice that revolting indifference in religious matters)—when, in a word, the "rights of God" shall rank before the "rights of men." . . .gain, in the Church of the Oratory founded by Father Faber, where every evening the word of God is preached to a numerous audience, conversions are of almost daily occurrence. The Reverend Fathers of the Society of Jesus also receive, year by year, into the bosom of the Church, a great number of Protestants, especially from among the higher classes.

And this, Gentlemen, is the practical aim of my address; a subject worthy indeed of the attention, solicitude, and zeal, of the Committee of your Congress. . . . If on the one hand we consider the rapid increase of the Irish population in London, and on the other what an immense influence England exerts over the whole world by her navy, and her distant possessions, may we not conclude that England can become the most powerful Missionary for the church, extending by word and deed the reign of Jesus Christ to the utmost limits of the earth? Oh! that His Kingdom might come! *Adveniat!* That divine Truth might take possession of the minds of men! That the authority of Jesus Christ might rule the nations! *Adveniat regnum tuum!*

Oh! that the name of Jesus, healing the people, might be the bond of peace between citizens, and of peace between all races of peoples! That the Blessed Virgin Mary might soon number all the children of England among the offspring of her love! That there may be but one fold and one shepherd, *Unus Pastor, unum Ovile!* One heart, one soul, one only Lord—*unus Dominus!* That there may be one people, one God! and that thus, in communion with the Holy Spirit, we may be always, and altogether, united in Jesus Christ, as He is one with His Father.

❀

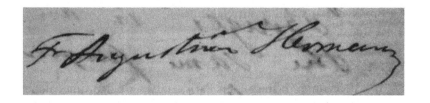

Extracts from the Letters
of Herman n Cohen

Letter from the Novitiate at Le Broussey, near Bordeaux.

To Raymond de Cuers, December 30,1849.[1]

I strongly advise you to *enjoy* an ardent devotion to the child Jesus. It brings joy and lifts the spirit above everything. During Advent each novice in turn was allowed to have in his cell for twenty-four hours at a time, a little statue representing the divine Infant, and there, each in turn, arranged in his honour, a small altar, and thus prepared for the joys of Christmas. Pray in a special way that the Infant Jesus will bring you happiness. I have composed in his honour a little carol, which is sung in the evening at the extra recreation allowed at the time of the great Feasts.

---

[1] The Carmelite Order promoted devotion to the Infant Jesus. This custom prevailed in Carmelite novitiates down to Vatican Two. The carol in question is included in Cohen's collection Flowers of Carmel. It goes: `O solitaries of Carmel, interrupt your penance, intone a joyous Noel to the Infant Jesus of Carmel`.

Au Broussey, par Cadillac sur Garonne.[1]

My dear mother, Sister, Brother, and Brother-in-law,

It is now a month since I left Paris, and I have had time, alone with God and far from the world, to reflect upon the line I ought to take, in order to lead henceforward a life in accordance with my convictions and the God's will for me.

You rightly foresaw that I was about to quit the world, as well as the dangerous profession which detained me in it; but you do not yet know to what kind of religious life I am about to devote myself. Well, then; what you so much feared is not going to happen. You will not see me at Paris in the cassock of a priest; you will not see me a missionary, although this is a beautiful thing. It is another lot which I have chosen, that of solitude, silence, retirement, a life hidden and unknown, a life of self-denial. In short, I find myself in the novitiate of a religious Order celebrated in history for its austerities, its penances and its love of God. This Order had its beginning among the Jews, 930 years before the birth of Christ, and was founded by the Prophet Elias on Mount Carmel in Palestine. It is an Order of true Israelites, of the children of the prophets who looked for the messiah, who believed in Him when He came, and who have perpetuated their Order to our own day, always living in the same manner, with the same bodily privations and the same joy of heart, as they lived on Mount Carmel 2,800 years ago. . . . There are two kinds of Carmelites: the one, finding the life led by the Prophet Elias too severe, had its rigors somewhat lessened, about 500 years since, by the Church—these are the mitigated Order of Great Carmelites:[2] the others chose to resume all the original severity of the Rule; for instance, never to eat meat, to go barefoot, winter and summer, to fast almost throughout the year, to sleep on a wooden plank, without

---

[1]   Cave, 1-- 13-15.

[2]   The old Order of Carmelites was referred to as "grande" or "great" in French.

sheets, mattress or paillasse, to be clothed in a sort of woolen serge next to the skin (linen being only allowed to the sick), to practice almost continual solitude and silence, to rise from midnight until two o'clock, every night, to sing the praises of the Lord and meditate on His holy law, day and night. These religious usually live on some elevated spot, outside a town, but still, near enough to be able to give spiritual assistance there when needful. They are distinguished in the following way from the missionary Orders such as the Marists and the Jesuits—The Discalced Carmelites remain in their solitudes, only leaving them to assist their neighbors when asked for, whether to hear confession, say Mass, preach, etc., but, as soon as the work of charity is done, they return to their solitude—their dear cell of six feet square—mine is about 7 feet long, by 4 or 5 feet wide; and, in it, I am more happy and content than if I were enthroned in the great hall of the Tuileries or the Imperial palace at St. Petersburg. It must be remembered, too, that we are never unoccupied; every moment is filled up with one duty or another, and, every hour or half-hour, the bell punctually reminds us of what we have to do. . . . In the time of the Jews in Palestine, there were already numerous societies of pious men who practiced this life—and wherefore? To draw down the mercy of the Almighty on the world, and turn away His just anger, ready to strike those who offended Him . . . to suffer in the stead of those who, shrinking from suffering, live in pleasure; and, lastly, to love God as He has loved us, and copy the life that Jesus Christ led when He came on earth to save men, by sufferings, self-denial, sacrifice, obedience, submission, humiliation, poverty and death. This is the life which I have chosen, and when you see me, one day—as I very much hope you will—you will see a face contented, happy, and serene, a heart which loves you—which asks and will *daily and nightly* ask the Lord to shed upon you His paternal blessing, to enrich you with abundant happiness, and with everything which can tend to make you happy. Should anyone among you have the misfortune sometimes to displease or offend Him, I would ask Him to make me expiate this offence, here below upon earth, in order that he who gave it should not suffer for it eternally, and that we may all be one day re-united in the bosom of our common father Abraham. . . .

You will do me a kindness by letting my father know of my new position, since he is prepared for it by my letter. He will be surprised to see his son *barefoot*—a begging monk, and very glad to be so. We live solely on the charity of our neighbors, in a word, on alms, and we glory in this. One day you will understand it all. . . I wish that you could experience the inward peace and gladness which for two years past I have enjoyed without intermission, and especially since I have given up all for God. He daily repays me a thousand-fold for all that I have sacrificed for Him, by pouring into me the treasures of His grace. Adieu!

Your most devoted and affectionate,

Hermann.

To Sister Marie-Pauline du Fougerais,. Jan 10, 1851.

Our Lord Jesus has raised me to the dignity of a deacon . . . and, I thrill with emotion when I think of it—at Benediction on the Feast of the Epiphany, He suffered Himself, in His measureless mercy, to be carried in my unworthy hands. Judge if I did not tremble, as I placed for Exposition on the Altar, the Creator of the Universe, held in my feeble hands . . . O, love of God![1]

To Sister Marie-Pauline du Fougerais, April 18th, 1851.[2]

Let us be taken up with His glory; I also had this thought, that, having caused the death of Him Whom I love; having so often killed Him by my sins, I was going to make reparation, *tomorrow*, in

---

[1]   Sylvain, p.92.

[2]   Beaurin p.166.

returning Him in some way to a new life, through my consecration by the bishop; but even if I were to say Mass every day for thousands of years, I could never give Him this new life as often as I have put Him to death afresh, by the hateful ingratitude and crimes with which I have offended him.

To Sister Marie-Pauline.
[After Cohen's ordination on April 20, 1851.]

I hope later to have time to give you more details regarding the thrilling event which has affected me so deeply in the last few days. . . . I have not yet recovered—and I hope I may never recover from that event. May the fervor of love grow within me, poor as I am, and unable to the overflowing gifts showered upon me. Pray that I may be faithful, grateful and a lover of the cross as well as thirst for God's glory.[1]

Letter from H. Cohen to Mother Marie-Thérèse Dubouché, April 1850.[2]

J.M.J.T.
Brussey par Cadillac sur Garonne (Gironde)
My very dear Sister and Reverend Mother,
May Jesus fill your heart with his holy love, Amen.

Monsieur de Cuers, whom you already know, as he was one of the first founders of the Adoration at Notre-Dame des Victoires, and

---

[1]   Sylvain, pp.92-93.
[2]   Beaurin, p.157.

of us three who have stayed with the Marist Fathers, will give you this letter. He comes from Marseilles, and was kind enough to pay me a short visit before going to Paris, where he will spend five days.

I am very anxious that you would be good enough to talk to him about the position of the Work of Adoration in Paris, especially with regard to the work for men. I have received no news for more than three months. It is said that the work has stopped, but I know nothing about this. But I have hope that M. de Cuers' stay in Paris will not be fruitless for our beloved Work. I have been wanting to write to you for a long time. Recently, our Rev. Master of Novices has given me permission to do this, and wishes me to ask you for exact details about your beloved Order. He has quite urgent reasons for wishing this information. And I would be very much obliged if you would write a few words about the establishment, the aim, the customs and Rule of your Third Order. Naturally, you may speak of it in all confidence to our Father Master through me, for he would never make any use of it which could be displeasing to you; but it is, I believe, a question of a foundation which would be put under your jurisdiction. Monsieur de Cuers, who has spent several months at sea, is much closer to our feelings about the future of the Adoration in Paris than he was during his first visit. He now understands that we will need people from society, but that it is better to be a small, stable group than those semi-devout people who might show weakness later. I urge you to encourage him as hard as you can, although he will not be staying in Paris at this time. I think God will deign to use him later to establish a Third Order of Carmel for men, with Reparation by adoration of the most Blessed Sacrament of love. My novitiate progresses with alarming speed; half of it is already gone since the 6th of this month, and I wish it could have lasted for ever after that: it is the most beautiful time of my life, and I cannot express how constantly happy I have been with a truly heavenly happiness. Since I received the (religious) habit, interior joys have hardly ever left me for a moment, and the love of Our Lord in the Most Blessed Sacrament has occupied me day and night, so that

I regret the approaching time when, after my Profession, I shall have to devote a good part of my time to study, and say farewell to those hours of adoration and intimacy with the Good Master. May his holy will be done. Help me to give him thanks for the immense favors he has bestowed upon the most wretched of his creatures. In my life as a musician in society, I had no childhood—I was "presented" in the Salons from the age of twelve. God in his great goodness has made this up to me most fully in this novitiate, where I enjoy all the delights of a spiritual childhood, floating in the milk of consolations, and wishing for nothing else in the world but to see the holy will of God accomplished in myself and in all souls. Communion is my chief preoccupation: thanksgiving, preparation—I prolong these acts to the point of being in a sort of perpetual Communion. This must be very like the happiness of Paradise, I think, since here we are almost continually, day and night, in the real presence of the Blessed Eucharist. For some time we adored from dusk to dawn, but since the departure of many of the younger Fathers for the college at Agen we have had to restrict this. The tranquil life is infinitely pleasing to me. And, since I attribute my vocation to the fervent prayers of the Carmel de la rue d'Enfer, you may imagine that, filled with gratitude, I do not forget you in my poor prayers, nor the Reverend Mother Prioress and all at the double House. Continue to pray, I beg you, all of you, for all people of your spirituality give me assurance that my interior joys are the forerunners of a life of the cross and of great ordeal. As God wills! My heart is ready; his grace will not fail me. *[This refers to Dubouche's community doubling up with the nuns in the Carmel on Rue d'Enfer.]*

I wish that the Reverend Mother Prioress would send me her news.

Since about the New Year I have heard nothing from outside this priory. I must say it is delightful to live completely away from what is happening in the world. But since the Carmel in Paris is far above terrestrial things, I am by no means distracted by hearing about them. I do not know what has become of young Fage's vocation.[1] Father Bertholon has given me no answer either.[2] Please tell him how much I respect him. Forgive me with charging you with so many messages, and for writing such a long letter. If the Reverend Mother could get some Mass stipends for our Fathers, she would be doing us a service as we are short of funds at the moment, and that is our main source of livelihood.

Finally, in closing, I pray God to make you, Reverend Mother, as great a saint as your humble servant could wish.

Brother Augustin-Marie of the Most Blessed Sacrament.

Discalced Carmelite Novice

P.S. I think it might be useful if M. de Cuers [Raymond de Cuers] were to be allowed to meet the Reverend Mother Prioress.

Pax Christi, JMJT   +   Kensington 8th September 1863.[3]

My dear daughter in Jesus Christ,

I have spoken with the fathers about Robert ; they think that in order to keep his health for the time when he will be able to go through the novitiate, and also in order to void the anger of his oncle (sic) who can injure his holy vocation, it would be wise to put your son in a college in Belgium where he can learn <u>latin.</u> And as you are providentially in Belgium now, I would advise you to speak with the superior of Trinity

---

[1]   Charles Fage was a member of Cohen's first group of Eucharistic adorers.
[2]   Bertholon was a Marist priest in Paris whom Cohen hoped to enlist in his Eucharistic projects.
[3]   This letter was addressed to Cornelia Freeman regarding her son's vocation as a Carmelite. She was a member of the Third Order at the Kensington church and Cohen wrote several letters to her.

College and ask if Robert can learn latin there, if not, you could place him in Bruges in an English college for the same purpose.

My opinion is that you ought to profit by the opportunity of being in Belgium, and to place him there for the end of the present holy days.(Sic)

I could inquire for an occasion of sending Robert to you with a secure person, when you have settled with the director of a college.

If Robert continues to abstain from meat during the time of growing it would be to expose his health for ever, whilst after some years, he will be able to keep the rule.

Please write to me, what you think of this proposition.

Sending you my blessing, I remain,

Yours in Xt,

fr Augustine Hermann.

❧

Hermann Cohen's Advice to Master of Novices, London 1869.

My Reverend and beloved Father Master,

In accordance with the wish which you have expressed to me, I want to focus on those points which appear to me to be most essential for the task, which the good God has willed to entrust to you.

At the moment your principal duty is to give the novices an uplift, and to be their model in regular observance, and the practice of virtue.

Here are three points, which ought to engage your attention in the direction of the novices.

1. Give a model of cell practices to each one, well adapted to the needs you observe in him, both as regards the inner life, as well as from the standpoint of knowledge. And have regard to inform yourself often if the novices diligently perform their cell duties.

2. Insofar as our Constitutions p. 2a, Ch. VI, recommend to the Father Master, you ought to have a great desire to instruct the novices in spiritual things, in the perfection of monastic life, in our ceremonies, our practices, our holy customs of the Novitiate, etc.—To this subject you ought to assemble the novices every day in the oratory of the novitiate in order to impart these instructions. Here is the arrangement which they can ordinarily follow for these instructions.

    On Sunday as we always have sermons here, after evening office the novices go the Father Master's cell to ask for their mortifications for the week, one after the other, and they won't need the ordinary instruction.

    On Monday Father Master asks each one of the novices which virtue they have chosen for the week; what is the reason for their choice of this virtue, what consideration, or what means will they use for best practice, etc.

    Tuesday is normally the day chosen for the chapter of the Novitiate; Fr. Master begins by a short instruction on the subject, which he deems most suitable, and then they come to the correction of faults, which will be marked by admonishments by *means of charity* [underlined)] by the *zelator* of the novitiate.[1]

    Wednesday one will explain the ceremonial or the Manual instructions, etc., in a word it is the ceremonial customs of our holy Order which should occupy one.

    On Thursday Father Master takes a lesson from the *rule*, which the novices ought to know *by heart*; then he explains a point of the rule which they have studied, and a chapter of the Constitutions relating to the point they have studied.

    On Friday they will sing Vespers of the Child Jesus in the oratory of the Novitiate but with no instruction properly

---

[1] Zelator was a weekly duty for someone in the community whose job it was to report on infringements of the Rule.

so called. Saturday, if the number of novices is great, is dedicated to instruction in our ceremonies, customs, and usages, but if there is a small number one day each week will suffice for the ceremonies, and then one would be better off to give a moral instruction that day.

3. You will have a great need of *spiritual communication*, as we call it, with the novices; it is in this intimate exchange, that you ought to appear to the novices not only as a father but also as a good mother; to inspire them with great trust, and to allow them to reveal their interior life. You will do well to begin always by asking them if their health is good; if they experience any sorrow; if they are happy in their vocation, and bit by bit to access the inner person. If during an exchange you do not manage to meet his needs it would be good to return to it later.

These spiritual communications ought to take place not less than once a month with each one and more often if someone needs it. . . .It seems to me that these three points, of which I have given you some details, will be enough to give you some idea and help you focus on the main obligations of the novitiate. I would add also that there is a great need for you also to remain constantly in the novitiate, unless you are obliged to be away on business . . . the presence of the Father Master in the Novitiate is a powerful means to preserve recollection, fervor, and the devotional life of the novices, but if he is frequently absent, the opposite results will be the inevitable consequences.

There, my good Father, is what I believe to be useful and sufficient for the moment. If you wish to ask additional explanations, I am always at your disposal in whatever way I can be of service and as regards what is agreeable to you.

Pray for me, please.

Fr. Augustine of the Most Blessed Sacrament.[1]

---

[1]   Typed letter by Cohen in 1869 in the Carmelite Archives, London.

❧

Introduction to Jean-Baptiste Gergères's Selection of Letters of Hermann Cohen.

I now present a translation of the following selection of twelve letters as found in a little book written in French by a good friend of Cohen's named Jean-Baptiste Gergères. It was entitled "Conversion du pianiste Hermann" and first published while Cohen was still alive. It ran to several editions. The author described himself as an "ancien magistrat," or former magistrate. Eight of the twelve letters are addressed to A.M., and this indicates that these were personal letters of Gergères. The letters are intimate in tone, which further suggests that Gergères was the recipient. If further pointers are needed, Gergères mentions in his book how helpful Cohen was to him at the time of his sister's death. Letter 11 was written on the first anniversary of Gergères's sister's death. A long extract from Gergères's book was published in The Rambler, an English Catholic magazine that for a short time was edited by Cardinal Newman. Hermann Cohen's former concerts were remembered in England and the news of his conversion would have aroused interest in English readers. This was some years before he in fact restored the Carmelite Order to England.

The First Letter was addressed to Father Castels, Chaplain of St. Andrew's Hospital in Bordeaux. He gave a talk on the occasion of Cohen's first profession at Le Broussey.[1]

---

[1] Jean-Baptiste Gergères, *Conversion du pianiste Hermann (Père Augustin-Marie du Très-Saint-Sacrement)*, 5th ed. (Paris: Ambroise Bray, 1861), chap. 9.

Letter 1

J.M.J.
Pax Christi. Hermitage of Agen, February 9, '51

My dear Monsieur l'abbé,
May Jesus reward you for your goodness to me, in making your beautiful peace abound in my heart, quam *mundus dare non potest*! (Jn 14:27. "Which the world cannot give.")

Our Reverend Father Provincial came to Carcassonne today, where he comes to arrange a foundation; and so I would like to have a moment to express to you my recognition of you and deep respect for you. His reverence is unable to write to you, being weighed down overrun with correspondence; he's entrusted me with this task in his name. What should you say about my poor insignificant person? That I am happier each day, during my exile here on earth, near the tabernacle of love! All my aspirations are for Jesus in the Eucharist.

But all this doesn't begin to express the marvels which our beloved Jesus wishes to work in his unworthy creature. . . . O, Father, in giving thanks with me to the Lord, help me support the overwhelming weight of favors that I receive. When you hold in your hands the adorable Victim, tell him that I wish to love him with all my heart and to stop being ungrateful. Ask him to give me the humility of the cross; for I really need to suffer something for love of him. I suffocate in this furnace of happiness and it seems to me that the cross will give me some relief.

We are about to begin vespers; Jesus calls me, allow me to leave Jesus for Jesus and pardon this scribble,

Your unworthy servant in Jesus and Mary,
Brother Augustin=Mary of the
Most Blessed Sacrament, Discalced Carmelite.
Vive Jesus! Vive Mary! Vive the folly of the Cross.

Letter 2.

A.M. [A.M stands for Ancien Magistrat, or former magistrate...]
J.M.J.
P.C. All for Jesus.[1]
Carmel of Carcassonne, November 6, '52

My dear Monsieur and beloved brother in Jesus, may our hearts be so united and so merged in Him who has so loved humanity. . . . I would be so well comforted to have your welcome news and that of M . . . and our mutual friends in Bordeaux. You have and will always have a place apart in the *Memento* of holy Mass and also in my poor heart which is so indebted to you!

To be given a friend like you is not one of the least graces that Jesus has given me! But do me this favor—tell me home truths about myself and don't spare my weakness by those tender words which I don't deserve. O, dear friend of Jesus, let us love this dear Master truly! Let us be all his; let us burn, yes burn with love for Jesus! O, if you could have heard dear Father Marie-Louis last Sunday, you would have felt an electric shock from the volcano of love that burns him up.

I envy you and I'm almost jealous that you are going to leave us for Advent. I ask you, in order to console me, that I may embrace you tenderly and tell you how much I love you in Jesus, our Savior, and in Mary, our dear Mother.

Your unworthy servant.

Fr. A-M. du T.-S,-S.[2]

---

[1] A phrase he always used in his letters. This would be the title of a book by Frederick William Faber of the London Oratory who would later become a friend of Cohen's. It was translated into French.

[2] He will use these initials from now on.

Letter 3.

A.M.
J.M.J.
P.C. All for Jesus.
Carmel of Carcassonne, 25 December, '52. (Christmas)
My beloved brother and friend in Jesus,

Vive the Child Jesus!

I wish you an altogether special graced visit of love of this divine Infant who comes to comfort the earth during these blessed days. . . . If I have not written to you, it is because the good Jesus has not put us on this earth to do what pleases us most, but to go against and test out our own inclinations, so as to leave some traces of this good Master, who never for an instant did his own will during the time he spent here below! I have to prepare numerous instructions, the theology of St. Thomas and the divine offices, so solemn at this time, absorb all my time and energy; then there's class, the Order, the study of the Holy Scriptures and the holy Fathers—all add up to the thought that I will write to you *tomorrow.* Thank God, as you see, that tomorrow has not become *never.*

Thanks for that good news that you give of our Fathers on mission. Jesus does as he wills! He wishes then to convert and to embrace all and make them glow with his delicate love. We are wholly penetrated with the magnificent Christmas night; we have sung and *rejoiced* until we were breathless for almost six consecutive hours, so as to welcome our Savior with the limited means at our disposal. . . .

Pray for me, that I will change, for I am always your very poor and very unworthy servant.

Letter 4.

In Jesus and Mary.
Fr. A-M. du T.-S-S.
P.C. All for Jesus.

Carmel of Carcassonne. 2 January '52.

My dear Monsieur and friend and beloved brother in Jesus.

May the Child Jesus fill you with his most generous gifts!

Father Charles is constantly telling us from the pulpit that instead of following the worldly custom of only wishing you a good year, we should wish one another *a good eternity!* Let me then offer you this heartfelt wish on the occasion of these great festivals which we are celebrating. I can hardly say how fervent, joyous and holy they are this particular year! Our Reverend Father Provincial assures us that he has never known them to be so solemn since he joined the Order: so we can repeat with the verse of the Christmas canticle:

Never was the night more beautiful,
Never the day so bright.

I leave you at the foot of the crib and I'm going there to leave your heart also.

Holy obedience obliges me to postpone everything I wish to say to you. "Let us love Jesus! That says it *all.*

All for you in his heart and in that of Mary,
Your unworthy servant,
Fr. A-M. du T.-S.-S.

"Our Reverend Father and all the community wish you a good *eternity.*"

Letter 5.

P.C. All for Jesus.
Carcassonne, Palm Sunday
20 March '53.[1]

My dear friend in Jesus Crucified,

If I have been so long in replying to you, it is because I have been to Lyon, to Avignon, Montpelier, Pamiers, etc., to preach the word of the good Jesus. So don't be surprised. Our Reverend Father didn't wish me to undertake any ministry for three years, but I have been suffering continually from a severe nervous affliction, so a famous professor from the faculty of Montpelier has advised me to travel, to engage in the active life and do some ministry; in fact it would be impossible for me to give you any idea of the way Jesus has willed to *bless my* first forays in the apostolate. I returned from Lyon energized with such *consolations* as you would find it hard to believe.

I am due to spend the month of Mary in Geneva, a Protestant enclave, and one of the main venues of my scandalous past life![2] Pray for this important undertaking!I gladly and thankfully take up

---

[1] On March 8, Cohen spoke at the profession of a young woman in the Carmelite convent in Pamiers. The chapel was full to capacity. The occasion was given great coverage by the local paper *Gazette du Langue doc*, which quoted the end of Cohen's talk. On March 12, Cohen gave a sermon at the church of St. Bonaventure in Lyons to raise funds for the St. Vincent de Paul Society, which raised the enormous sum of six thousand francs—although the congregation numbered three thousand. The archbishop requested the Provincial to ask Cohen to found a group dedicated to Perpetual Adoration, and to preach in all the parishes on the Eucharist. Soon after he founded similar groups in the towns of Beziers, Montpellier, and Avignon.

[2] As it happened, due to the state of his health this undertaking was not carried out.

the project of the good woman—this project can perfectly accord with nocturnal Adoration. This is what I mean: The nocturnal adorers are so numerous in your dear town as to make their holy vigils once a week.

Then every Wednesday evening of each month they can spend delightful nights at the feet of Jesus; at 6 am Adoration for women can begin and be combined with High Mass and solemn vespers. If that nocturnal Adoration cannot move from Wednesday to Wednesday, from church to church, still that new foundation will be united, *spiritually* and by intention, to our Work; [oeuvre] we will deal later with the question of how to make these diverse elements as a whole as complete as possible.

I should have the satisfaction of going to Bordeaux next Summer with our Reverend Father, during his provincial visit. Then I will have the joy of seeing you and embracing you and see for myself these great works for the glory of the divine Eucharist! I'm sorry to have to leave you now; a number of tasks call for my attention, but I wish to reside in the suffering heart of our Jesus during these days of his sorrowful Passion.

Adieu! Let us ask Jesus to grant us some tears this week, at least tears of the heart.

All for you, at the foot of the cross, in the pierced heart of Mary.

Your very unworthy servant,
Fr. A-M. du T.-S,-S.

Letter 6.

A. M. Joseph Schad, famous pianist in Bordeaux.[1]
P.C. All for Jesus.

My dear friend,

"The grace of Our Lord Jesus Christ be with you!"
    Many thanks for remembering your sinful friend.
    Many are the transformations worked by the mercy of the good Jesus; but the one that surpasses them all is the fact that I am going to preach the month of Mary near *Geneva!!!* How our old friends will be taken aback!
    After all Jesus can do everything! I hope that you will help me with your prayers in this difficult work. On my part, I will pray for your wife and yourself.
    Tomorrow I leave for Marseilles (57, rue Saint-Savournin), and during the month of May my address will be with M. le Curé of Geneva. I hope to receive your news.
    Always count on my sincere affection in Jesus and Mary,

Your unworthy servant,
Your very unworthy servant,
Fr. A-M. du T.-S,-S.

---

[1]   Schad had been a professor of music with Cohen at the academy of music set up by Liszt in Geneva. His waltz music was a forerunner of Strauss and has distinct overtones of the same. (Cf. Philip Sears, "Fleur des Alpes" *Flowers of the Alps*, YouTube.)

Letter 7.

A.M.
P.C. All for Jesus!
My dear Sir and beloved brother in Jesus,
Let us love Jesus!

Suffering and travel slows me down. Today especially I have been suffering intensely. But I wish to comfort myself with you in discussing projects for the glory of our Jesus with you.

I was not able to go to Geneva—the doctor and my brain would not allow it.

Our good Master allows me almost uninterrupted suffering, and I bless him, because I believe that it is one of the greatest proofs of love.

I have preached at Beziers, Montpelier, Avignon, Toulon, Marseille; Jesus has blest it all as at Lyon. Tomorrow I will baptize a 36 year old Jewish person at Toulon; two other very distinguished people from Marseille are reflecting hard, as well as a non-Catholic lady ; I return on Monday. After the sermon the bishop of Marseille embraced me at the foot of the altar in front of everyone in the church.

Let us bless Jesus for *everything*.

Adieu, believe me always, at the feet of Jesus and Mary.

Your unworthy servant.
Fr. A-M. du T.-S,-S.

Letter 8

A.M.
P.C. All for Jesus.
Carcassonne, 23 May '53.

My dear Monsieur and beloved brother in Jesus our Love.

Your excellent letter has filled me with consolation. After a long journey I arrive at Lyon, Grenoble, Marseille, Avignon, Montpelier, etc. At Lyon three young Israelites have decided to become Catholics; one of them I hope will be baptized in a few days. I think I told you that I had the happiness to administer solemn baptism to a 36 year old Jewish person at the cathedral of Toulon and he made his First Communion with admirable faith. Also the lady at Marseille made her profession of faith to me the day before.[1]

I am filled with consolation and in fact, seeing all the immense mercies of our good Jesus, *superabundo gaudio*! (I abound with joy.) At the same time I suffered greatly from my brain and my nerves; and these trials are not the least of *my joys*! I hope to suffer for Jesus until my last breath. I have been sent to Hyeres during the month of June to follow up some treatment during which I will apply myself to musical compositions if my head can relax a bit. Our Reverend Father Provincial will have the joy of seeing you *many times*. I envy him.

His Reverence will rejoin me at Marseille, returning from Rome with great outcomes for Carmel in France. . . .

Pray to Jesus and Mary
for your very poor servant.
Fr. A-M. du T.-S,-S.

---

[1] This woman had formerly been a neighbor of the Cohen family in Hamburg. He baptized her children also. Cohen's influence in speaking to her in her native German swayed her in favour of Catholicism. After First Communion, he invested her with the brown scapular of Our Lady of Mt. Carmel as he always did. The ceremony took place in the church of the Oblates of Mary Immaculate.

Letter 9.

Castebelle near Hyères. (Var) 6 June '53.

May the divine Eucharist be our love and our happiness!

I would have already let you know before now what you have been often asking of me, only I'm so weak and suffering a lot. . . . Yes, I am suffering but I love to suffer! How good it is to suffer for Jesus! To suffer for love of Jesus—I can tell you in confidence that my happiness has increased a lot over the last two years.

Until now I have always lived on Thabor, filled with consolation. But something was missing. I had not held to my lips the cup of suffering of Our Lord Jesus. I thirsted, thirsted to suffer for the love of my Jesus! Now for the past two years, I have not had a day without tasting this divine vinegar, which I love so passionately.

May I reside on Calvary with my Savior until my last breath. I ask for nothing else. I can say that I take more joy in suffering than in my former divine consolation.

M. de C [Raymond de Cuers] has written to you at length: you will soon receive his letter. So allow me to be brief because the miserable state of my health rebels at the least fatigue and often prevents me from writing—not even a line.

Here we have the great favor of having the Blessed Sacrament in the house. I wish I could remain with him day and night![1]

Let us love Jesus! That's the great secret of being happy.

I ask you to believe that in Jesus and Mary,
I am your unworthy servant.
Fr. A-M. du T.-S,-S.

❧

---

[1] This favour was granted by the bishop of Frejus.

Letter 10.

P.C. All for Jesus.
Castebelle par Hyères (Var), 23 June '53.

My dear Monsieur and friend in Jesus!
Long live the cross of the good Jesus!

I can assure you I am *really* on the cross and I could not be more satisfied. Yes, my happiness has increased, and grows every day, on which I have lifted the cup of suffering to my lips. To suffer for Jesus, in union with Jesus, is that really anything? But it is delightful! . . .

I have been sent to the Pyrenees until 10 August: but will I be restored to health? I am lying here, stretched out on a mattress with a bad leg infection, from the foot to the knee, covered with open wounds. I will be obliged to spend a few days in Bagnères-de-Bigorre, where I hope to arrive on 9th July; my address will be at the house of the good Carmelites. I'm pleased that M. [Charles] Desgenettes remembers me as well as M. Walsh and M. [Charles] Asnarez.

Unfortunately for five days now I have been unable to write a line—and that prevents me from writing to so many people who have been so good to such a miserable person as I. I'm happy that you know Father Moreau whom I greatly esteem and who I love very much; he is a loyal Christian. My sister regrets she did not see you in Paris. She has just written me a marvelous letter. I am here in an enchanted countryside. Just imagine the climate of Hyères, a garden on the edge of the sea, a beautiful valley, sheltered from the northern winds by a semi-circular range of mountains covered with olives, orange trees, umbrella pines and charming almond trees. Two magnificent palm trees extend over the isolated house where I am staying. You might think you were in the Orient. The sea lies at the bottom of the valley, bluer even than the sky. And there out to sea lie the charming *golden isles*, so often celebrated by the poets. A chorus of tireless nightingales lulls us to sleep with their music. And here among these beautiful surroundings, quite near me and close to the camp-bed on which I rest, there is a little tabernacle, and in that tabernacle there He is, Jesus our love who is there expressly for me during my stay in this balmy solitude. . . . O, what thanksgiving I give to this dear Jesus. And then I think of the great care lavished on me unceasingly and with great love. You must admit that if Jesus wishes to cure me he has all he needs here without the need to work a miracle in order to restore a dying person to health. In fact however my health has not improved and I am drawing to the end of my stay here. . . . I must leave on 1 July. Forgive me for writing at such length and that in fact tires me a lot. I have been unable to write a single line of music—complete incapacity. The will of Jesus is my paradise.

> All for you in Jesus and Mary,
> your unworthy servant
> Fr. A-M. du T.-S,-S., Discalced Carmelite.

Pray for me!

Letter 11.

A.M.
P.C. All for Jesus.
Bagnères-de-Bigorre, 15 August '53.

"Requiem aeternam dona eis Domine."

My dear friend in Jesus.

I have returned from Tarbes quite exhausted and my health is no better than it was before I was sent to Montpelier. May Jesus draw glory for himself from it; let us wait upon and welcome his will.

I pray especially today for a person who is so dear to you; but I can assure you that during the month of August last year your tears have fallen on my heart, and I haven't missed a single day without placing that dear person in the *Memento* of the mass, so much so that we can hope that she is in no further need. But what does this imply? She will do good for us from heaven and that a hundredfold.

Recently we have visited the ancient Benedictine Abbey of Escala-Dieu, which is now owned by M. Nerac. This gentleman, a Protestant, was a most gracious host. We had many conversations about you for I know that you have just come from Escala-Dieu;[1] I have set foot on the ground there with much joy because of your dear remembrance.

My regards to Sister Marie of Jesus.

In Jesus and Mary.
your very unworthy servant
Fr. A-M. du T.-S,-S.

---

[1] Literally, *Stairs of God*. This beautiful former Cistercian abbey dating from the twelfth century is now a tourist attraction, open to the public. The walls are covered in creeper, and Since 1997 it has belonged to the Council of the High Pyrenees.

Letter 12.

P.C. All for Jesus.
Carcassonne, 28 January '54.

I am calling back to respond to your valued souvenir. It seems indeed that winter, which is so hard on the poor, is holding up the work on the church at Bordeaux. The will of Jesus be done!

I think that you have received my letters about my interesting neophytes; I believe they will be baptized during Eastertide, and I will be present at . . . . I should also be making the journey to Paris on April 24 to preach Lent in Pamiers. I will be in Broussey at the beginning of May.

Recommend me to the good prayers of your friends and don't forget me in your prayers. I am indeed poor.

All for you in Jesus and Mary.

Your very unworthy servant.
Fr. A-M. du T.-S,-S., Discalced Carmelite.

Letter to Lemann Brothers.[1]

My beloved friends in Jesus,

Oh, how slowly the time is going for me to see you perfect Christians at last. I can already see you throwing yourselves into

---

[1]   These were twin brothers, Joseph and Augustine Lemann, the "neophytes" referred to in the above letter. They later became canons of the cathedral of Dijon and domestic prelates of St. Pius X. Their family strongly and violently resisted their conversion from Judaism. Their parents were deceased. At one point the guardian of one of the twins tried to strangle

the arena of combat, like valiant soldiers of Jesus Christ, fighting for souls which have cost him dearly, cost him his blood! May we have the consolations of bringing back many of our Israelite brothers to Him, to the true faith—you may count on my friendship.

Fr. Augustine-Mary.

Letter of Hermann Cohen to his brother Albert, August 17,1862.[1]

I have to admit that to me it's a real sacrifice to leave France, where my role as priest and religious gave me so much consolation. Here, I cannot even leave the house without changing out of my Carmelite habit and dressing in a black coat, stiff white collar, and a black scarf; and this wretched collar imprisoned my neck, my head, my thoughts and my heart – I'm only half-alive; but no matter, since religious life is one of sacrifice, why not take a few more steps forward when it's a question of helping so many Catholics of all nations who are scattered throughout this huge city of London, and, as far as any religious assistance is concerned, abandoned almost entirely to themselves.

(Unsigned)

---

him and was only saved when his brother called the police. Joseph later became a prolific writer with many books to his name, mainly on Our Lady, especially La Dame de Nations (The Lady of the Nations) in two volumes. Both were theological advisers at the First Vatican Council. They provided St. Peter Julian Eymard with furniture for his first house in Paris.

[1] Albert and his brother Louis were successful businessmen in Harburg, near Hamburg at this time; the rubber factory they founded is now the multinational Phoenix AG. Albert would have given a substantial donation to the building of the church in London.

Letter of Hermann Cohen to the Prior of Kensington from Berlin.
April 11,1868.
Alleluia! Surrexit Dominus vere, Alleluia![1]

I have received a letter from our very Rev. Father General informing me that from now on I belong to the Province of Aquitaine. In ceasing to form a member of your community, it is my duty to offer my grateful thanks for all the love you have shown me, and to ask pardon for all the faults I have committed. I also express my regret that I should have so often disedified and hurt them by my conduct. I hope that you, Rev. Father, and the community will ask the Lord Jesus to forgive me and change me.

The retreat now ended has been helpful to the people who attended. My health is good. Again I wish you a happy Feast. I leave tomorrow for Posen.[2] Give me your Blessing!

Cohen's Letter to Hyacinthe Loyson.

J.M.J.
Pax Christi [Peace of Christ – sometimes shortened to P.C.]
Desert of our Father St. Elijah at Tarsteix,
September 27th, 1869

My dear Father Hyacinthe,

Give ear to a friendly voice pleading with you from this solitude to return to yourself, to your brothers who love you, and to holy mother the Church of God which you must serve as a faithful minister, not as judge of final appeal.

---

[1] Though Cohen left London in 1866, he was still officially a member of the community in Kensington which he had founded.

[2] Posen was then part of Prussia but originally was part of Poland. It is again the important Polish city of Poznan.

Please reconsider your decision and come back. Will you not again sing with us of "*how good and how joyful it is for brothers to live in harmony.*" Think of those you have left sorrowing behind you, and remember the joys of the Carmelite life. I will never accept that you will find peace of conscience in your present position. No, you will never regain this peace unless you return to your spiritual family, saying, '*I will arise and go to my father and say to him, Father I have sinned against heaven and against you.*"

You cannot imagine how dear to my heart you are. Come, make haste, you are still in time. We shall welcome you most tenderly; we shall cure your wounds with the oil and wine of the good Samaritan. I beg you for the love of Mary, Mother of God, whom you taught us to love so tenderly; yes, in the name of the most clement Virgin Mary, Queen of Carmel, I beg you to return to this dear home where you were so happy and where you have vowed to live and die.

I couldn't resist the urge to send you these lines. You may disregard my solicitude for you. But don't reject the appeal of your friend and I beg this on my knees. Comfort the hearts of the good people who are so disappointed at what you have done! Everything can be renewed in this life provided only we don't shut out the light of grace. You can have my full permission to treat my intervention with contempt, if among your new friends of the world, you find an affection as pure, disinterested, and firm as mine.

In Jesus and Mary
Your very unworthy brother,
Augustine of the Most Blessed Sacrament
Discalced Carmelite.[1]

❦

---

[1] Sylvain, pp. 235-236.

Cohen's letter to his sister Henrietta.

Montreux
November 21ˢᵗ 1870.

Dear sister in Jesus,

(Today I'm not free.)

I shall say holy mass for George on November 24ᵗʰ, the feast of our father Saint John of the Cross. That day I am leaving to bring help to the unfortunate prisoners interned in Germany.

The French priest who wanted to go could not get permits. I felt I could not refuse this holy mission; since Jesus says to those he rejects, "I was in prison and you did not visit me."

People think I shall probably be successful in the work because of my having relations in Germany...so, I set out on my way under the protection of Jesus, Mary and Joseph. How I am longing to comfort these poor prisoners, who are in such dire need!

(Unsigned)

Letter to his sister Henrietta.

December 6ᵗʰ 1870.

I am at Spandau where you made your First Communion in the sacristy. In this sacristy I vest every day to say mass and to preach to the French prisoners.

I have been named Chaplain to the five thousand three hundred French prisoners of war who are here. 500 are sick with typhus and dysentery, so that I am fully occupied. Every morning, about 400 of these soldiers are conducted here with their company to my Mass, in such a way that they are all obliged to come and see me in turn. Then I go to the hospital to minister to the sick, and in the afternoon I go to the barracks to visit those who are well. Pray hard for their conversion. Those who are well have not all been to confession yet.

(Unsigned)

Letter to his brother Albert's wife.

The prisoners besiege me from eight o'clock in the morning until evening. I have given myself to them, they make good use of me. They have permission to come to the presbytery; when not a spiritual matter, they come to share their physical sufferings because of the cold. I must admit they fully repay the love I show them. We have on average fifty soldiers coming to confession and Holy Communion.[1]

(Unsigned)

---

[1] Sylvain, p. 86. Cohen acquired sweaters and blankets of the prisoners.

Various Spiritual Counsels.[1]

*Y*ou cannot be mistaken when you obey in faith him whom Jesus has inspired to help you and to save your soul as well as his own. So do what I say and you will have peace of soul. Obedience is without sin."[2] He was quite demanding with those he directed, wishing to lead them along the way of holiness; he showed them how prayer was the way to achieve this and a life of prayer was essential. "The way of prayer infallibly leads to perfection, and it is in prayer that we learn to detach ourselves from the world, and to live here below as exiles longing for our homeland."[3]

+++++

The important thing is not to encourage in ourselves a desire for worldly-living. That is what prayer day by day does—it kindles in the heart a desire for Jesus alone. An excessive taste for material things is not compatible with possessing the God of love. The God of love is a jealous God who wishes to dwell alone in the heart so as to be loved, experienced and desired for himself. . .We ourselves are too poor and worthless to merit much attention from others. Our

---

[1] Again drawn from various Carmelite sources, especially Flamme Ardente.
[2] Tierney, p. 84.
[3] Ibid., p.84.

Lord is so noble and attractive that it is foolish not to be always taken up with him. Think of Jesus and not of yourself and Jesus will think of you. Try hard to preserve the deep peace of Jesus within you. . . . When someone entrusts himself or herself to Jesus, and to reflecting on his attractiveness and divine qualities, Our Lord takes particular care of that person, keeping him or her in peace—as he did on the sea of Tiberias when he came to Peter walking on the water."[1]

+++++

The reason why our master does not always allow us to hear his voice is because he wishes to be sought after. There is nothing he wants more than someone who has been attracted like the Magdalen and questions the whole of creation saying, 'Where is my God.' We must long for Jesus as the thirsty deer longs for living water.

A second reason is that we are kept humble. If we always enjoyed consolation, we would surely swell with pride—we who are nothing and worse—sinners. How good of the Lord not to throw us off but rather to support us in spite of all our faults.[2]

+++++

As for death, it will come to you at a time God wishes. That will mark our deliverance, and an end to our faults. That will be the moment we see Jesus, the moment in which we lose ourselves in his divine heart—are you afraid of that? You must look on death as the day of your true espousals with Jesus for all eternity.[3]

In another letter, (not specified) he portrays death in the context of the peace that Jesus alone can give. "You must try to maintain a deep peace within you. Do not allow yourself to be troubled, the world

---

[1]   Ibid., p.241
[2]   Flamme Ardente...p. 326.
[3]   Tierney, p. 85.

cannot give peace. Jesus the lamb of God has come so that we can have it abundantly. However we shall only have perfect peace in heaven. Here below we are only passing by, but we must keep on aspiring for that perfect peace which awaits us in the arms of God."[1]

Again he writes,

I would like you to live totally by the Eucharist. May he be the source of your thoughts, feelings, words and deeds. May he be the light that guides you, your inspiration, your model and your constant preoccupation. As Magdalen shed tears and poured perfume over the feet of Jesus, may you never tire of offering your prayers, aspirations and gifts before the tabernacle. I wish the Eucharist to be for you a fire of love, a burning fire, into which you can throw yourself so as to emerge as a flame with love and generosity. May the altar where Jesus sacrifices himself, also receive your sacrifices, so that with him you may become a victim of love, whose odor of sweetness rises before the throne of the eternal.[2]

+++++

Peace is a gift of God which is obtained by being faithful to prayer and to a long thanksgiving after Holy Communion. Dedicate a quarter of an hour to your thanksgiving after Holy Communion, and keep yourself in peace united to our dear Lord. There is no need for much activity—one word says it all, 'love.'"[3]

+++++

Do you know that between me and St. Paul there is some resemblance. First he was a Jew like me. Also as he confessed

[1] Ibid., p. 85.
[2] Ibid., p. 85.
[3] Ibid. p. 85

himself, that his youth was not beyond reproach, nor was mine. Perhaps here I might add, in spite of my shortcomings, that from the time the Lord called me to his service I have not willingly turned back or given in to selfish motives. "I plant, another waters"—this is where I also see a special resemblance between his vocation and mine. The same thing happened to me on a smaller scale. I had a certain gift for initiating things and for facing up to obstacles—in a way the qualities that are needed, together with God's help, in order to begin new projects. Hardly are they well established when the Lord takes me away from them.[1]

From Letters of spiritual direction to various people.[2]

Be attentive to the need to mortify self-love and often too your own will, that you must oppose a lot if you wish to approach divine union.

+++++

Peace is a gift of the Holy Spirit which one obtains by fidelity to prayer and through prolonged thanksgiving after Holy Communion.

+++++

Dedicate a quarter of an hour to thanksgiving after Holy Communion and maintain yourself in peace, united to our dear Jesus, without trying to say a great number of prayers. One word suffices: Love.

+++++

[1] Sylvain, p 275.
[2] Flamme Ardente. pp. 323- 327

Always in your conversations, you ought to direct people to God and to God's love and service.

+++++

Let us serve Jesus for himself; let us affirm it is good for us to be deprived of joy here below, to be humbled, to be tried, and realize that Jesus will always give us much more than we deserve. We ought to love Jesus crucified, *the cross of Jesus*. We will taste Thabor in heaven.

+++++

Responding to the wish of your husband to attend places of secular amusement, I repeat that when you go somewhat unwillingly and against your inclination, you don't risk any danger. I further advise you that when you can do so *prudently*, resort to some excuse or some legitimate pretext which will put an obstacle in the way. I believe that will be something pleasing to Our Lord if you can wisely combine some plan to avoid being party to pleasure of that kind.

+++++

On all occasions that present themselves, practice a great love of doing God's will, especially in matters which crucify your own will. Nothing is more apt to lead us to divine union than to triumph over your own will and your natural attractions. This indeed is more than just resignation, it is a *joy* when God's will takes us captive. That way we will make a lot of progress, and it will provide us with something to sacrifice each day; the sacrifice should be ourselves. In these sacrifices we are at the same time, like Jesus Christ, priest, altar and sacrifice! That is something beautiful, great, sublime and glorious! . . . This cannot be achieved without unremitting struggle. It is up to Our Lord himself and never we who should choose the arms and the arena for the struggle. Those unforeseen providential happenings of every day are what challenges and proves our love for God.

+++++

Don't be alarmed at the strength of your affections for members of your own family, provided that you lift them by intention, to the dignity of supernatural feelings, and that you remain tenaciously bound to God's holy will in their regard. The love of Jesus makes all affections holy which are not contrary to God's law; not only should religion *not render the heart cold*, but it should give us a *warmer heart* for those we love in God's designs.

+++++

Spare no effort in maintaining that delicate peace of Jesus; a good way, is to think less of yourself and more of Jesus; when one gives oneself up to the contemplation of the charms of Jesus and his perfections, then Our Lord takes charge of one's guidance in a special way, and it produces that peaceful calm which prevailed over the sea of Tiberias, when Jesus came to Peter walking on the water.

+++++

Especially during Lent try to have periods of solitude, silence and recollection alone with Jesus in the desert. Minister to him with the angels, work for him after the example of St. Joseph in the home of Nazareth, and live in the world as if not living there: when you have to mix with people, try to be *unnoticed, unknown and accounted as nothing*.

When you tend to greatly resent seeing evil around you, correct that movement by a *supernatural* act of mercy for the sinner. Sin merits our hatred, but the sinner is worthy of our *mercy:* mercy then should put the brake on indignation.

+++++

One of the most frequent movements of our miserable nature, which shows our lack of humility, is the wish to complain every time we suffer something. The saints made sure to hide their sorrows from others, so that Jesus alone would witness it as an agreeable offering to him.

I specially recommend to you, each time you are aware of some imperfection in yourself or some natural weakness, that you humble yourself, sincerely, expressly before our dear Lord.

+++++

In order to become humble, you ought not compare yourself with a human but with the divine model which God has given us in Jesus. Jesus is God and man: we ought to become another Jesus in the eyes of his Father, if we wish to please Him. Compare your humility with that of Jesus, Mary or St. Joseph, and you will be attending a school where you learn to science of humility.

+++++

The reason why the good Master does not always allow us to hear his sweet voice, is that he desires us to seek him. Nothing is more pleasing to him than the efforts made by a person drawn by his love as was the Magdalen, who addresses herself to the creatures of heaven and earth saying, "Where is my God?" We must desire Jesus as the thirsting deer longs to drink from the fountain. A second reason is in order to keep us humble. If we were always enjoying the consolation of intimate exchanges with Jesus, we would end up thinking we were something special, whereas in fact we are dust and ashes, and what's more sinners! How good and merciful Jesus is not to cast us off, but to undertake to support us in spite of our cowardice and inconstancy in his service.

+++++

You must try to maintain a deep peace in yourself and not allow yourself to become troubled. Ask Jesus to command the winds and the storms and bring about calm and tranquility in inner life. The world cannot give peace. Jesus the Lamb of God has come so that we may have it abundantly. But of course we shall only have perfect peace in heaven. Here below where we are only in transit, we must keep aspiring to that peace which awaits us in the arms of God. One day we shall fall asleep and rest, as the Psalmist says, in Him who *Himself* is eternal peace.

+++++

Material worries ought never turn your attention from God, because it is precisely to God that we ought to turn to smooth over difficulties, and in all things, you ought always to keep God before you with the greatest purity of intention for God's good pleasure.

I commend your discretion when you believe that you ought to interrupt your regular timetable in order to carry out some act of fraternal charity. Still, I advise you that at times you should give *priority* to your rule of life. Sometimes people in the world need to realize that God has his rights. Too often the very people who are most devout are often inclined to relegate their religious duties to something extra, and which according to themselves, they ought always to accommodate to their arrangements for recreating themselves. So while your rule of life ought sometimes to yield to the needs of neighbor, you can also ask your neighbor to leave you in peace, so that God can have the first place, that which is God's due.

+++++

Don't be afraid of people passing remarks or criticism. . . . If you always try to please people, giving in to their whims, you will still not please, says St. Paul, a servant of God. Show a certain firmness and do not be drawn aside by the fashions of the day; this means that in a certain way you place the good God at your side. Be assured that my interest in your wellbeing is always the same.

+++++

It is very important to recall what I have said to you previously about the *first movements* of the heart. First movements occur, simply natural inclinations, followed by a temptation of the devil or by a divine impulse of grace. In either case they are neither blameworthy nor meritorious, until the will reflects on them and either gives consent or offers resistance.

+++++

Our Lord says in the Scripture . . . "I am a worm and not a man"; [Ps.22:6] he wished to be humbled, says St. Paul, to be reduced to nothingness, to be treated like the very least. We can have no part with him unless we share in his humility or better, his humiliation, because this is the bond by which we enter into an exchange with him, and by which we become his brothers (and sisters). Also when we cease working at humbling ourselves, we cease to share with Jesus Christ, for in that case Our Savior will be infinitely removed from us. You cannot then make progress except in this way: denial of self, self-deprecation and a constant fear lest some secret complacency creeps in to damage your soul; nothing could be more prejudicial to you than that. May you be blest—love in all things.

Eucharistic Reflections
and Dedications

*I*n order to contemplate you as fully as we desire, daylight hours fly by too quickly. I called together some like-minded Christians and we went along to spend the nights in your churches . . . a priest directed us . . . and the dawn found us still kneeling before you.

These first nights of nocturnal adoration made a great impression on Cohen, and he would recall them later in the "dedication" of his hymns to the Eucharist. He addressed fervent prayers to God, expressing his Eucharistic devotion in typical sentimental tones that have grated so much on the ears of his critics.

Oh Jesus my love, I should like to kindle in the hearts of my former friends the fire which burns in me. I should like to show them the happiness you give to me. . . . If you no longer see me trying my utmost for applause and empty respect, it is because I have found my renown in the Eucharist. . . . If you no longer see me wasting my resources in casinos or chasing riches, it is because I have found wealth and inexhaustible treasure in the cup of love sealed in the Eucharist. If I no longer come and drown my worries in noisy parties, it is because I am nourished at the wedding feast with the angels of heaven. It is because I have found true joy. Yes I have found it, what I really love, it is mine and no one can take it from me.

Unhappy riches, cloying pleasures, honors that only debase—those are the things I looked for in your company. But now that my eyes have seen, and my hands have touched and my heart has beaten on the heart of God, I can only be sorry for your blindness in pursuing pleasures that are unable to satisfy your hearts. So come to this heavenly feast which has been prepared by eternal wisdom. Come, draw near. Abandon your baubles and empty dreams, cast off the rags that cover you. Ask Jesus for the shining robe of pardon, then with a new heart, with a pure heart quench your thirst at the limpid fountain of his love. Cast yourselves down at his feet.

Give your heart to him and he will bless you, and you will taste joys so great that I cannot describe them for you—unless you come and try them.

"Taste and see how sweet is the Lord."

If King David danced before the ark which prefigured you, O my true covenant, then with what songs of triumphs ought I break out?

And again Cohen prayed:

Having loosened worldly bonds, I can now penetrate the dark cloud that surrounds the tabernacle and open myself to the piercing rays from the sun of your grace, and plunge into this sea of light so as to be burnt in the flame of this blazing furnace. Then, taking shelter in the shade of this tree of life I can taste its fruits. For me those days and nights pass joyfully in intimate converse with your adored presence, between the memory of today's communion and the hope of tomorrow's, God united with the least of his children.[1]

+++++

[1] Carmel, *Aux Éditions du Carmel*, Marseille, 1989, p.11, Tierney p.110.

Dedication of the Canticles, *For the Love of Jesus Christ*, (1851) composed by Hermann Cohen.

Adorable sacrament, blessed spring from which my dry lips can drink the first fruits of eternal life, my heart is filled with joy. I need to bless you and sing your praises in songs of joy and thanksgiving. Indeed I have learnt that my brothers in Paris can now adore you each day in the practice of perpetual adoration. The church bells in the city are ringing, and processional banners go before you. The Archbishop is promoting this devotion, calling Christians together to arrange the altars and asking the children to come and sing. He himself is taking part in this uninterrupted adoration from church to church, making it a kind of image of the eternal praise given by the blessed to God. . . . O adorable Jesus, adorable for me whom you have led into the solitude that you may speak to my heart . . . for me whose days and nights pass sweetly away in heavenly exchange with Your adorable presence; between the remembrance of today's Communion and the hope of the Communion of tomorrow . . . in the loving union of God with the poorest of His creatures; I fervently embrace the walls of my beloved cell, where nothing disturbs me from my only thought, where I breathe but to love your divine sacrament; where, freed from the burden of "perishable" possessions, stripped of all that holds to earth, and breaking through the snares which take the senses captive, I can, like the dove, fly upwards to the heavenly region of the Sanctuary, pierce the clouds of mystery enveloping Your Tabernacle, bask in the searching, rays of this bright Sun of Grace, plunged in an ocean of light, and consumed as in the flames of a glowing furnace. . . .

Then, taking shelter in the refreshing shade of this Tree of Life, I inhale the fragrance of the flowers, I enjoy the sweetness of the fruits. . . . I am soothed by the melody of your loving words, and, overcome with happiness and love, I fall asleep at the feet of my Beloved. .... Let those come who knew me formerly, those who despise the God Who died for love of them. . . . . Let them come, O my Jesus! and they will learn if You can change the heart. Yes, worldly people, I say to you, prostrate before this Love so misunderstood—if you see me no more upon your soft carpets, straining to win applause, and courting empty honors, it is because I have found glory in the lowly a Tabernacle of Jesus in the Blessed Sacrament—Jesus our God. If you no more see me stake on playing cards the inheritance of a whole family, or rush eagerly after money, it is because I have found riches and treasures inexhaustible in the ciborium wherein is Jesus in the Sacred Host!

If I no longer take my place at your sumptuous tables or give myself up to your frivolous festivities, it is because I have found a feast of delights, in which I am nourished for immortality, and rejoice with the Angels of Heaven; it is because I have found the highest happiness; yes, I have found it; that great good which I love is my own, I possess It, and no man can take It from me! Poor riches, pitiful pleasures, humiliating honors were those which I so eagerly ran after with you. . . . But now that my eyes have seen, my hands have touched, my heart has beaten beneath the Heart of God! Oh! how I pity you who, in your blindness, pursue those pleasures which are powerless to satisfy the heart!

Come, then, to this *Heavenly Banquet prepared for you by Eternal Wisdom.* Come, draw near. Leave behind you your baubles and fantasies, cast away these mocking rags which cover you; ask of Jesus the white robe of pardon, and, with a new heart—with a pure heart, drink of the limpid fountain of His love. Believe me, now that your Divine Savior, to give you audience, daily ascends His throne within your churches, He will hear you with still greater clemency. Throw yourselves at His Feet; give Him your heart, and He will bless you, and you will taste joys—joys so immense that, if you do not taste them for yourselves, I cannot describe them to you. Taste then and see how gracious the Lord is!

O Jesus, Beloved, would that I could show to them the happiness You give to me! No, I can venture to affirm that if faith did not teach me that to contemplate You in Heaven is a still greater joy, I could not believe greater happiness possible than that which I experience from loving You in the Eucharist, and receiving You into my poor heart—so rich through You! . . . What peace! what blessedness— what holy gladness!

You have given me o God of love, the language of harmony. Am I to remain dumb and not use it? If your friends do their best to adore you o divine sacrament, have I not also a hosanna to sing to your glory and a palm branch to place beneath your feet? Adored Lord, I must unite my songs with the hymns of Paris! For it was in that great city, hidden in the Eucharist that you revealed the truth to me, and the first mystery you revealed was that of your real presence in the blessed sacrament. Even then, although I was still a Jew, I wished to present myself at the holy table and receive you.

I was anxious for baptism in order to be united to you. But I did indeed receive untold consolation from you. What you did to console me during this time of painful waiting, I cannot tell here; it's a secret I keep to myself. And when at last I could receive the heavenly banquet I found there the strength I needed, and I was changed. It became my protection against worldly temptations. This treasure detached me from all that held me captive. I longed to drink that living water and I hungered for the bread of angels. I am now obliged to sing joyful hymns to you, because it was your sacrament that did all this, that turned me away from what was harmful to a frugal life, and from an extravagant life to one of a humbler kind – from seeking glory to an obscure religious house. Not only have I made solemn vows which consecrate me to you in Mary's order and makes me your beloved for ever, but, out of your jealous love, you ask me to make a further vow appropriate to your divine sacrament, a vow that will bind me with indissoluble bonds to the love of love itself. [The vow referred to was Cohen's resolution never to preach without mentioning the Eucharist.]

O Jesus my love, how I want to enkindle my former friends with the love with which you have enkindled me. How I want to witness to the happiness that you give me. But unfortunately I stop short, not able to say any more, for my songs don't have the fire of love I wished them to have and I can do no more. It is to you O God that I come for help. Give me the hidden strength with which you alone know how to attract me. Then like a torch thrown on a heap of wood, it will light a fire of love for the Eucharist. Amen. *(Agen, house (priory) of Discalced Carmelites, March 1851.*[1]

---

[1]   Various sources. Carmel, *Aux Editions du Carmel*, Marseille, 1989, Beaurin, Tierney, pp. 110-113.

Canticle from Cohen`s Collection final collection "Thabor".[1]

The Divine Prisoner`s Little Flower.

Between two cold bars there grew a little plant
Which brightened the tedium of the prisoner.
This was the sole joy of his suffering spirit
His only pastime in his lowly abode!
Beneath the gloomy walls of his sombre retreat,
His hand had planted it…his tears had watered it!
And in exchange for his care
He saw the humble plant
Emit the fragrance of its flowers
With all its energy.

Ah, my divine master, inside the tabernacle
A prisoner of love, for eighteen hundred years
In spite of our coldness, by recurring miracle
You have made your dwelling within us,
And there more neglected, more lonely still

---

[1] French text, Francophonia.net. Translation – Timothy Tierney. Accessed May 19, 2017. Cave states that the "Jesus part" was composed by Cohen. (Cave, p.11-28) Author of first part unknown. The whole canticle is a dialogue between the soul and Jesus.

Than the poor captive whose loneliness I lament
Your tenderness implores from your faithless children
The hearts which they refuse to give you.

Sadly, as they shun you, O God of my heart
Look down out of pity, on my lowliness,
I will be for you my Jesus, your humble little flower…
Listen to my soul's repeated prayer,
It's you who inspires it, Lord, so hear me.
And tell me how to please you as a little flower,
Within your hands may I forget myself forever.

Jesus[1]

Indeed it is in faith, in naked faith
That my hand has planted this little flower
That lives only for me…unknown to most,
It needs no other sun except but the light of my heart.

In place of Root for this frail flower
I wish to see hope in me which never fails,
Infinite hope in my divine goodness
The trust of a child who knows that it is loved….

For Stem it must be without desire or fear,
A tranquil, joyous, ready acquiesance
In the faintest call of my holy will.
No hesitation, no deliberation.

And then I would be pleased if its Foliage
Consisted of contempt for human esteem,
Enabling it to hide from prying eyes
Welcome Gifts from my own hands.

---

[1] Cave, French text pp.11-28-12-29, translated T. Tierney.

For Blossom I wish her daily joy,
Which no trouble could undo...or any sorrow...
Who even when suffering or to bitterness a prey,
Could still rejoice in my happiness.

For Fruit my will be a quality so pure
That looks only to God, on earth as in heaven
Which has eyes for no one else
To carry out its wishes.

And so my plans being realized,
It will have deserved the richest gifts I have:
On my sacred heart I will graft this lowly plant
And uniting it to myself, I will be its happiness.

Prayer for the Beatification of Hermann Cohen

(Known in religion as Father Augustine-Mary of the Most Blessed Sacrament, O.C.D.)

Mary, Immaculate Virgin Mother, at the grotto of Lourdes you restored to health Father Augustine-Mary of the Most Blessed Sacrament that he might serve you faithfully in your Order of Carmel. Obtain from the Blessed Trinity, I ask you, the grace [here insert your intention] through the intercession and merits of your devoted servant. His joy was to suffer for Jesus. In answer to his heartfelt prayer, he received the grace to consecrate his life in its entirety to God's will, service and glory.

Mary, Mother of the Eucharist, we ask you to glorify your servant. Through the redeeming power of Christ present in the Holy Eucharist, he was brought to the knowledge of the truth. We ask you to make known this apostle who was fired with devotion to the Sacrament of your Son's love. May he bestow upon all God's people his burning zeal. Through his intercession may the divine presence in the Eucharist be adored, may the Mass be celebrated with reverence and sincerity, may Holy Communion be received frequently and with devotion.

Grant that soon throughout the world the Eucharistic Kingship of Jesus, the Living Bread who came down from heaven, may be established. Amen.

(With approval of Peter Theas, Bishop of Tarbes and Lourdes).

Principal Dates in the life
of Hermann Cohen

Birth	10 November, 1821
1831	Tours as a Concert Pianist
5 July, 1834	Arrival in Paris
April 1835	First Concert in Paris
1835 (age 15)	Professor of Music at the Conservatoire in Geneva
Friday in May 184	First step in conversion at church of St. Valère
8 August 1848	Second stage of conversion in a church at Ems Germany
28 August, 1847	Baptism
6 December, 1848	Founds Nocturnal Adoration at Notre Dame de Victoires
16 July, 1849	Novice at Le Broussey, Feast of Our Lady of Mount Carmel
7 October, 1850	First Profession as a Carmelite
19 April, 1851	Ordained Priest

21 September, 1858   Meets Bernadette Soubirous in Lourdes

June 1862   Audience with Pope Pius IX who sends Hermann Cohen to England to restore the Carmelite Order there.

October 16, 1862   Carmelite Foundation in London on Feast of St Teresa of Avila

April 1868   Retreat at the Holy Desert of Tarasteix, a hermitage founded Hermann near Lourdes at the time of the apparitions to Bernadette.

Circa October 1869   Cohen takes up residence in the Desert House of Tarasteix

May, 1870   Hermann Cohen elected Vicar-Provincial of the Province of Aquitaine and Novice Master in Le Broussey.

Franco-Prussian war 1870,   Departs for Berlin as chaplain to the French POW`s.

20 January, 1871   Dies in Spandau, Berlin. Buried in St. Hedwig`s Cathedral

December 2, 2008   Hermann Cohen`s remains disinterred from Berlin cemetery and returned to Bordeaux to rest near the tomb of his mentor Dominic Arbizu y Munarriz.

Bibliography

A Call to a Deeper Love, *Blessed Zélie & Louis Martin*, Translated by Anne Connors Hess, St. Pauls, New York, 2010.

Annales de N. D. de Lourdes, November,1868.

Bacon, Pamela, *The Flowering of Carmel*, The Story of St. Joseph`s Parish, Gerrards Cross, 1990.

Bartrez, Benedict-Marie, *Carmel, La Pére Hermann*, Éditions du Carmel, Avignon, 1989, N.54, p. 23.

Benoit-Marie De La Croix, *Les saints Déserts de Carmes déchasses*, Londres, 1914. Blanc, Henri, *Un Grand Religieux*, Chez les Soeurs Carmelites, Carpentras, 1922.

Bouchaud, Jean-Baptiste OCD, *Miłość za Miłość*, Wydawnuctwo Karmelitow Bosych, Krakow, 2006.

Beaurin OSB, Dom Jean-Marie. *Flèche du Feu*, Edition France-Empire 1982

Collected Poems of St. Thérèse of Lisieux, *The Atom of Jesus-the-Host*, translated by Bancroft, Alan Gracewing 2001

Carmel, *Le Père Hermann, Aux Éditions du Carmel*, Marseille, 1989.

Cash, Damien Cash, *The Road to Emmaus*. (Kew East, Australia: Congregation of the Blessed Sacrament Fathers and David Lovell Publishing.

Craven, Augustus, *La Soeur Natalie Narischkin, fille de charité de Saint Vincent de Paul* (Paris: Didier et Cie, 1877)

Cave, Donald SSS, *L'Oeuvre eucharistique pour les Hommes*, Religieux de Saint-Sacrament, Rome. 1985.

Cave, Donald, *The Years 1845-1851*, Rome 1969.

Davies, Norman *Europe: A History*. Pimplico, London, 1997

de Foucauld, Charles, *Voyageur dans le Nuit* – Ecrits Spirituels, Edit. Nouvelle Cité, 1987.

De Mendiola, Domingo A. Fdez., *El Carmelo Teresiano en la Historia*

Ephemerides Carmeliticae, Philip Boyce, OCD, 1979.

Foucauld, Charles de, *Voyageur dans la nuit,* Paris: Nouvelle Cité, 1979.

Gergères, Jean-Baptiste, *Conversion du Pianiste Hermann*, 5th ed. (Paris: Ambroise Bray, 1861).

Guitton, André, Peter Julian Eymard, Centro Eucharistico – Ponteranica, 1996.

General Archives of Discalced Carmelites, Rome, Italy.

Hales, E.E.Y, *Pio Nono*, Image Books, New York, 1962.

Haton, René, *Hermann au Saint-Desert De Tarasteix*, Paris, Editeur, 1877.

Hazan, Eric, *The Invention of Paris*, Verso, London and New York, 2011(Translation David Fernbach)

Honey from the Rock, compiled by Roy Schoeman, Ignatius Press, San Francisco,

Hussey, Andrew, *The Secret History*, Penguin Books`06.

Journal of the American Liszt Society, Puzzi` Revisited, Richard E. Cross 1994.

Kung, Hans, *The Beginning of All Things: Science and Religion*, trans. John Bowden (Grand Rapids, MI: William B. Eerdmans, 2007

Sheppard, Lancelot C, *Lacordaire*, The catholic Book Club, London, 1964.

Laurentin, René, *Bernadette Speaks*, Pauline Books, 1997.

Letters of St Thérèse of Lisieux, Volume 11, translated by John Clarke OCD, ICS Publications, Washington D.C.

Mongin, Hélène, *Louis et Zélie Martin*, Editions de L'Emmanuel, Paris, 2008.

Mogador, Celeste, *Memoirs of a Courtesan,* Translated by Monique Fleury Nagem, University of Nebraska Press, Lincoln and London, 2001.

Mount Carmel, Vol. 40, No. 4, Boars Hill, Oxford, 1992.

Mémoires de Céleste Mogador, Paris Nouvelle, 1858.

Moreau, *Hermann au Saint-Désert De Tarasteix*, Paris, 1875

Peltier, Henri, *Histoire du Carmel*, Editions du Seuil, Paris 1958

P. Jean-Baptiste, *Joseph Kalinowski*, Liège, 1923.

P Silverio de Santa Teresa, *Historia del Carmen Descalzo*, Burgos 1946. 1979.

P. André De Sainte-Marie, *L'Ordre De Notre-Dame De Mont-Carmel*, CD, Bruges,1910.

Praskiewicz, OCD. Szczepan T. *Saint Raphael Kalinowski*, ICS Publications. Washington D.C 1998.

Rohrbach, Peter-Thomas OCD, *Journey to Carith*, Doubleday and Company Inc,1966.

Sainte-Beuve, Charles Augustin, *Poésies complètes*, Charpentier et Cie, Paris, 1845.

St. John of the Cross, Poems. Translated by Roy Campbell, Penguin Books 1968.

Story of a Soul, John Clarke OCD, ICS Publications, Washington D.C, 1996.

Story of my Life, (George Sand), edited by Thelma Gurgrau, State University of New York, 1991.

St. John, Bernard, *The Blessed Virgin in the Nineteenth Century*, Burns, Oates and Washbourne Ltd. 1903.

Sylvain, Abbé Charles, *The Life of the Reverend Father Hermann*, Translated by Mrs. Raymond-Barker, New York, P J. Kennedy and Sons, 1925.

The Collected Works of St. John of the Cross. ICS Publications, Washington. D.C 1979

The Ten books on the Way of Life and the Great Deeds of the Carmelites, *Edited and translated by Richard Copsey, O. Carm,* St. Albert's Press, Kent, 2005.

Tierney, Tadgh, *The Story of Hermann Cohen*, Teresian Press, Oxford, 1991.

Tierney, Tadgh, *The Carmelite Church of St. Luke and St Teresa,* Service Publications, Wincanton, 1970.

Tierney, Timothy (Tadgh) *Saint Raphael Kalinowski,*(Apprenticed to Sainthood in Siberia,) Balboa Press, Bloomington, USA, 2016.

Victor, Walther, *Puzzi*, Verbano-Verlag 1936.

Walker, Alan. *Franz Liszt*: The Virtuoso Years, 1811-1847, Vol.1. 1988.

Watson, Derek, *Liszt,* Oxford University Press, 2001.

Zimmermann OCD, Benedict, *Carmel in England*, Burns Oates,1899.

Index

Pope Pius V11
Pope Gregory XV1
Pope St. Pius X
Poitiers
Posen (Poznan)
Prayer
Prussia
Radziwill, Duchess Marcellina
Ratisbonne, Alphonse and
    Theodore
Ranise OCD, Luke
Raunheim, George,
Rauzan, Duke, Duchess
Religion, religious
Revolution
Romanticism
Rothchilds,
Rossini,
Rousseau,J.J
Repentance
Reparation
Rodez
Revelation
Rome
Rozies, Abbé
Rue de Bac,
Rue d'Enfer
Rule of St. Albert
Sand, George (See Dupin)
Schubert, Franz
Saracens
Sayn-Wittgenstein, Caroline
Saint-Exupéry, (Mother de)
Schad, Joseph
Second Empire
Sisters of Charity
Sisters of Sion
Sibour , Marie-Dominic
    (Archbishop)

Stock (Saint Simon)
Solitude
Soubirous, St Bernadette
Saint-Beuve
St. Clothilde
St. John Mary Vianney, (Cure
    D'Ars)
St. Joseph
Sergent, Lise
St. Simon Stock
St. Sulpice
St. Mary Magdalene
Saint-Simon
Spandau
St-Valère
Sylvain, Charles
Tardhivail, Antoinette
Teresa St. of Avila
Teresa, Mother (Aragones d'Orcet)
Tarasteix
Thanksgiving
Thérèse St. of Lisieux
Davila, Thomas of Jesus
Vatican 1 and 11
Vernet, Horace
Veuillot, Louis
Victor, Walther
Victories, Our Lady of
Vizcarra, Joseph-Louis
Virgin Mary
Wagner, Richard
Walmesley, Thomas
Waterford, Ireland
Wiseman, Cardinal Nicholas
Wincanton, UK
Xavier, (Princess Mary de
    Grocholska-Czartoryska)
    Mother

Printed in the United States
By Bookmasters